D0375091

TRIP OF THE TONGUE

TRIP OF THE TONGUE

*Cross-Country Travels in Search of
America's Languages*

ELIZABETH LITTLE

BLOOMSBURY

New York   Berlin   London   Sydney

Published by Bloomsbury USA, New York

All papers used by Bloomsbury USA are natural, recyclable products made from wood grown in well-managed forests. The manufacturing processes conform to the environmental regulations of the country of origin.

LIBRARY OF CONGRESS CATALOGING-IN-PUBLICATION DATA

Little, Elizabeth.
Trip of the tongue : cross-country travels in search of America's languages / Elizabeth Little.—1st U.S. ed.
p. cm.
ISBN 978-1-59691-656-2 (alk. paper)
1. Language and culture—United States.   2. Multilingualism—United States.   3. Sociolinguistics—United States.   4. Americanisms.   I. Title.
P35.5.U6L57 2011
306.44'60973—dc23
2011039005

First U.S. Edition 2012

1 3 5 7 9 10 8 6 4 2

Typeset by Westchester Book Group
Printed in the U.S.A. by Quad/Graphics, Fairfield, Pennsylvania

For my father

Use what language you will, you can never say anything
but what you are.
—RALPH WALDO EMERSON

For words, like Nature, half reveal
And half conceal the Soul within.
—ALFRED, LORD TENNYSON

Q: What do you call someone who speaks three languages?
A: Trilingual.
Q: What do you call someone who speaks two languages?
A: Bilingual.
Q: What do you call someone who speaks one language?
A: American.
—TRADITIONAL

CONTENTS

New York City: American

Although I didn't know it at the time, this story began some five years ago, when I hired a decrepit U-Haul and drove a ragtag collection of books, clothes, and particleboard furniture from a cramped two-bedroom in Brooklyn to a bright and spacious one-bedroom in Queens. Much later, looking back, I realized that at just under eight miles this was by far the shortest leg of my journey. Remarkably, it took me two years to make it.

When I first moved to New York, Queens seemed to me a vast and forbidding land, home to airports, big-box retailers, and *The Nanny*. I'd come to New York to experience the quicksilver tempo of big-city life, and Queens seemed run-of-the-mill. It had neither Manhattan's consequence nor Brooklyn's self-conscious cachet. I didn't know anyone who lived there. I didn't even know anyone who went there. The *New York Times* seemed to admit its existence only begrudgingly. Worst of all, it was home to the Mets. So for the most part I stayed away.

I'd like to say I eventually found my way to Queens because I had some sort of grand epiphany, but the truth is I met a guy, and that guy's apartment happened to be just fifteen minutes from my office. Obviously, I moved in with him.

I made my new home in Sunnyside, a relatively small neighborhood nestled between Long Island City and Woodside, six stops from Grand Central on the 7 train. Sunnyside is unpretentious and friendly, and even its most affluent pockets are unmistakably urban. Its sidewalks are bustling if not crowded, and the muted rattle of the subway is underscored by the ever-present commercial hum of Queens Boulevard. If you look down 43rd Avenue, you can see the Chrysler Building. If you look down Greenpoint, you can see the Empire State Building.

It's also a remarkably diverse neighborhood. My first apartment in Sunnyside was located on a street that boasted a Turkish grocery, a Korean acupuncturist, a Chinese dry cleaner, an Ecuadorian bakery, and a Romanian nightclub (which featured, delightfully, occasional appearances by a DJ named Vlad). I frequently supplemented my meager kitchen skills by taking a short walk to the Lebanese sandwich counter, the Colombian pupuseria, or the Bangladeshi-owned French bistro. After a particularly bad day in front of the computer, I had my pick of half a dozen legitimately Irish bars.

For a language-lover like me, living here was heaven. Each day I'd hear at least six different languages as residents switched between their native tongues and what was far more often than not a very fluent form of English. At the time of the 2000 Census, out of 8,142 respondents in my ZIP code, 29 percent reported speaking English as a first language. The rest were native speakers of more than thirty other languages, including Spanish, Korean, Chinese, Romanian, Arabic, and South Asian languages such as Hindi, Gujarati, and Bengali. There are apparently so many Irish-speakers in Sunnyside that there was at one point a push to convince Chase to include Irish on its ATM menu. I was even given an opportunity to dust off my French when a mentally unhinged downstairs neighbor began sending me handwritten notes complaining about the noise from a nonexistent air conditioner.

Although New York City is unquestionably an enormously diverse city, a little-discussed truth is that it is shockingly easy to avoid that diversity, linguistic and otherwise. For some it can be a conscious decision—a lease in a tony neighborhood, the sort of job that considers a Dartmouth grad a diversity hire—but for many it's an unexpected consequence of institutionalized segregation and technological isolation. I lived in New York for three years before taking much notice of the languages around me. My neighborhood in Brooklyn was largely white and lower-middle class, and my industry was largely white and upper-middle class. In between, I listened to my iPod.

But my move to Sunnyside naturally piqued my curiosity, and so, finally, I started to pay attention. And then I started to explore. I began in small ways, by staying on the train an extra stop or two or maybe even occasionally taking the bus. I quizzed my friends, my husband, the nice Turkish brothers at the grocery store, anyone who knew more about Queens than I did—which, at that point, was basically everybody. Before long, I began to get a sense of the borough beyond my quiet little neighborhood.

With only 110 square miles and a population of almost 2.3 million—roughly half of whom are foreign-born—Queens is one of the most densely populated areas in the United States and one of the most ethnically diverse areas in the world. Each of its individual neighborhoods offers a glimpse into the world's language and cultures. Take Astoria, for instance, a sprawling neighborhood along the East River that's known for its large Greek population. In 1927, when sixteen Greek families settled in Astoria, they wanted to construct a Greek Orthodox Church, but they were able to raise only enough money to build the basement. So that's where they worshiped—for thirteen years. Despite such humble beginnings, by the mid-1990s nearly half of Astoria's population was Greek, making it the largest Greek city outside Greece.

Today Astoria is home to an even wider range of nationalities, from Brazilians to Bulgarians. There is in particular a strong Arab presence, and if you walk up Steinway Street toward Astoria Boulevard and the Brooklyn-Queens Expressway you'll find yourself, as I did, surrounded by cafés, hookahs, and Arabic script. This part of Astoria, with at least ten mosques and several thousand Arabic-speakers, is known as Little Egypt. Here I found a tiny Egyptian restaurant—hard to miss thanks to the conspicuous Wedjat eye over the entrance—and dined on clay-pot stew while the owner talked my ear off about his homeland.

Northwest of Little Egypt, on 24th Street just past Astoria Boulevard, is the Bohemian Citizens' Benevolent Society (known more familiarly as the Bohemian Beer Garden), the one place I'd visited before moving to Queens. The Bohemian Citizens' Benevolent Society was first formed when large numbers of Czech and Slovak immigrants began arriving in Astoria in the late nineteenth century. Though the society completed construction on the beer garden in 1919, Prohibition went into effect in early 1920, and so it took a few years for the beer garden to properly come into its own. But it is today kept in booming business on balmy days by throngs of twentysomething city-dwellers.

Astoria is just one corner of the borough. Back to the east, past Sunny-side and Woodside, is Jackson Heights, a neighborhood with one of the largest percentages of foreign-born residents anywhere in New York City. Here you will find not only Latin American immigrants—Colombians and Uruguayans and more Argentineans than anywhere else in the city—but also New York's largest South Asian shopping district. With more than one hundred nationalities living in Jackson Heights, it's hard to imagine that Queensboro Realty, the company that originally devel-oped much of the housing stock in the area, initially did its best to keep Jews, Catholics, and blacks from moving in.

Farther east still is Flushing, once hometown of Fran Drescher, Mar-vin Hamlisch, and the Weinstein brothers and now a part of the city that looks more like Chinatown than Chinatown itself. Here you'll find 50 percent of the borough's Chinese population and, if hypercompetitive foodies are to be believed, 100 percent of the city's "authentic" Chinese food. You'll also find the busiest branch of the busiest library in the country. The Flushing community library, which includes materials in Bengali, Chinese, English, French, Gujarati, Hindi, Italian, Korean, Por-tuguese, Punjabi, Russian, Spanish, and Urdu, holds more than 50,000 books in 76,000 square feet. In this bustling neighborhood, new arriv-als use the library not only as a resource for language learning and job training, but also as a community center. According to library statistics, more than 5,000 people use the library each day, with circulation hovering around 200,000 items a month, a testament to the vitality and initiative of immigrant life.

Then there's Rego Park, a Jewish neighborhood probably unlike any you've ever seen. Located south of Elmhurst and Corona in eastern Queens, Rego Park is, along with nearby Forest Hills and Kew Gardens, home to tens of thousands of Bukharian Jews. The Bukharians are de-scendants of an isolated group of Central Asian Jews who, incredibly, managed to survive centuries of oppression before eventually finding their way to more hospitable lands such as Israel and Queens. Along 108th Street—known as "Bukharian Broadway"—a variety of Bukharian shops and synagogues stand alongside Uzbek and Tajik restaurants. It was here that I first learned about Bukharic (or Bukhori), a language that shares a number of similarities with Tajiki and Farsi but has over the years absorbed a large number of Hebrew words and is traditionally even written with the Hebrew alphabet.

You could spend a lifetime in Queens and still find ways to be amazed each day by all the little pieces of the world it contains. Before I moved to Sunnyside I had the idea that ethnic neighborhoods tended to be concentrated and homogenous, that there were Chinatowns and Little Italys, but that they were always separated by some kind of Canal Street. In Queens, however, the realities of size and population preclude hard-and-fast geographical divisions. Sometimes within a single block you can circumnavigate the globe.

At this point I did something uncharacteristic. If you've read my first book, you know I'm kind of a serial dater when it comes to learning languages. I take great pleasure in idly flipping through the grammars, dictionaries, and phrasebooks for dozens of languages. Japanese, Tibetan, Arabic, Portuguese, Hungarian, Norwegian, Sanskrit, Old Norse—you name it, I've leisurely investigated it. Over the years I've spent thousands of dollars on tapes and CDs, on group classes and private instruction, on adding ever more volumes to my sprawling, eclectic, and deeply impractical library. I typically need only the flimsiest of pretexts to embark upon a casual affair with a foreign language. It is both my virtue and my vice.

Much to my surprise, however, I didn't start a course in Korean or Punjabi or even Irish when I moved to Queens. Instead, I found myself thinking more and more about English, the language I knew best and that had heretofore interested me least. See, I've always liked to think of language as the box of baking soda in the back of the refrigerator of humanity. In its words, sounds, and structure, language keeps track of our history and our culture, our troubles and our triumphs, and so forth. But, fairly or not, I had also decided English was the largely humdrum result of a bunch of old white dudes hanging out with another bunch of old white dudes. I'd never considered the implications of linguistic contact in the New World—it hadn't occurred to me that English had something to teach me about my own country.

That's when I read about syphilis.

A chronic systemic infection by the bacteria *Treponema pallidum*, syphilis is a primarily sexually transmitted disease that has afflicted such varied and prominent figures as Franz Schubert, Leo Tolstoy, Paul Gauguin, and George on *Grey's Anatomy*. The disease first became widely known throughout Europe in the late fifteenth century when Charles VIII, then king of France, laid siege to Naples as part of the First Italian War. Although epidemiologists are not entirely agreed on the origins of the disease, what is certain is that in 1495 soldiers and camp followers on both sides of the dispute began to suffer from a particularly gruesome illness that was, depending on which country you asked, known variously as the French disease, the English disease, the Spanish disease, or the Italian disease. From Naples, it spread throughout Europe and then around the world.

Physicians and patients alike were eager for therapies and potential cures, and one treatment that particularly caught the fancy of the public relied on the use of a New World ingredient. In 1519 the poet, scholar, and syphilitic Ulrich von Hutten published an account in which he claimed to have been cured by a decoction prepared with the gum of a tree found in tropical and subtropical regions of the Americas. This treatment was soon the therapy of choice throughout the continent, its popularity bolstered by the marketing efforts of the family that held the monopoly on the importation of the tree in question.

Given its purported medical value, the tree was frequently referred to as *lignum sanctum* or *lignum vitae*—Latin for "holy wood" or "wood of life." But its everyday name is guaiacum, a word borrowed from the Taíno language of the Bahamian island where the tree was first found. And just as the names of popular pharmaceuticals such as Prozac, Valium, and Viagra have become part of vernacular English, so too did guaiacum insert itself into the languages of Europe. By 1553 guaiacum had made its way into the written English record, by way of a translation of Sebastian Münster's *A Treatyse of the Newe India*.

Of course, von Hutten was wrong about guaiacum. He succumbed to syphilis in 1523, only four years after the publication of his "cure." Had he been right, we might still use the word *guaiacum* in our everyday speech—not to mention in our everyday health care. But with the advent of new treatments, the vogue for guaiacum faded away, and so too did the pressing need to know its name.

English may be an Old World language, but for the past four hundred years it has made the New World its home, and its words reflect that history. In the word *guaiacum* alone there is the story of the spread of a horrible disease, the scientific naïveté of those who longed for a cure, and the ruthlessness of a merchant family that controlled Atlantic trade. There is also the story of contact between Taíno, the indigenous language of an island in the Bahamas; Spanish, the language of those who would rule that island; and English, the language of those who wanted to buy pieces of that island.

In English and the other languages of the New World there are so many stories like this to be found, linguistic keepsakes of years and peoples past. Just look at the languages of New York City. Before the arrival of European fishermen, traders, and explorers, the area in and around Manhattan was inhabited by a people who called themselves Lenape.* The Lenape primarily spoke a language known as Munsee, an Eastern Algonquin language related to Mohegan, Powhatan, and Mi'kmaq. Although I would hazard that few Americans would know the names Lenape or Munsee off the tops of their heads, they might be surprised to discover that Munsee has given American English two extremely common words.

The Lenape's most lasting contribution to the English language is undoubtedly the name of the island they sold to the Dutch for sixty guilders. Although there is no firm consensus on the meaning of the name *Manhattan*—or *manna-hata*, as it was first recorded by Henry Hudson's crew—the widely accepted translation is "hilly island." This translation assumes the name is a combination of *mannah*, a Munsee word for "island," and an Algonquin suffix indicating hills or mountains. "Hilly island" is only one of many suggested translations, however. Other

---

* The Lenape are also frequently referred to as the Delaware Indians.

suggestions range from the similar if slightly more poetic "place of many hills" to the entirely dissimilar "good place to collect bow wood."

The second-most-common translation of *Manhattan* may have less linguistic support, but it is undoubtedly my sentimental favorite. In the course of his study of the customs of the Lenape, a Moravian missionary named John Heckewelder was told an interesting story about the origin of *Manhattan*, which Edwin Burrows and Mike Wallace relate in a footnote of *Gotham*, their great first volume of New York City history:

> The Lenape gave a Pennsylvania missionary their version of what happened when the first white men landed on Manhattan: they sighted a "large canoe or house" moving across the water and decided that it belonged to the Supreme Being, "the great Manitto," who then appeared before them dressed entirely in red. After a preliminary exchange of courtesies, he offered them a toast and they all got happily drunk—whence the site came to be known as Mannahattanink, "the island or place of general intoxication."

When Heckewelder passed this information along, he remarked, "Facts are all I aim at, and, from my knowledge of the Indians, I do not believe every one's story. The enclosed account is, I believe, as authentic as any thing of the kind can be obtained." I would love to be able to take his word for it.

The other Munsee word we all know a version of came to English less directly. In 1886 a coffee broker named James Potter was invited to an estate of the Prince of Wales. When Potter inquired about appropriate attire, he was directed to His Royal Highness's Savile Row tailor, where he was fitted with a tailless dinner jacket. That fall Potter wore this same jacket to a ball at his club back in the United States. The jacket was widely remarked upon, and the style was later named for Tuxedo Park, the town where it had first been seen. The word *tuxedo* itself, meanwhile, most probably came from the Munsee word *p'tuck-sepo*, or "crooked river."

Then there are the European languages of New York. The first European we know of to visit New York City stayed just long enough to merit having his name, centuries later, assigned to a bridge between Brooklyn and Staten Island.* It wasn't until Henry Hudson sailed the *Halve Maen* into Lower New York Bay in 1609 that a new language gained a foothold in the area.

By the time the British took over New Amsterdam and the rest of the colony in 1664, Dutch was a language of considerable influence in the area. In fact, Dutch remained the official school language in New York until nearly the nineteenth century, and as of 1756 there was still a sizable enough Dutch-speaking population to cause bureaucratic complications. William Smith, a local historian, observed at the time that "English is the most prevailing Language amongst us, but not a little corrupted by the Dutch Dialect, which is still so much used in some Counties, that the Sheriffs find it difficult to obtain Persons sufficiently acquainted with the English Tongue, to serve as Jurors in the Courts of Law."

Though many of the words Dutch loaned to English have fallen out of use, plenty remain to bear witness to the important—if brief—role the Dutch played in early American history. Some of these words are New York City–specific. *Stoop*, for instance, is an anglicization of *stoep*, "a small porch with seats or benches." The Dutch also contributed place names such as Brooklyn, Harlem, and the Bronx, as well as topographical terms such as *kill* (creek) and *hook* (angle). *Bowery*—which in modern New York is for reasons I have been unable to uncover always preceded with a definite article—originated from a Dutch word for "farm." Dutch words used outside the five boroughs include *cole slaw*, *waffle*, *caboose*, *snoop*, and *spook*. Some of these words, such as *cookie* (from *koekje*, "little cake"), *cruller* (from *krulle*, "crooked piece of pastry"), and *Santa Claus* (from *Sinterklaas*, a shortening of *Sint Nikolaas*), are particular favorites of many Americans.

One lingering trace of Dutch in the English language serves as a reminder that no matter how red-white-and-blue American something

---

* Eagle-eyed New Yorkers may have wondered why the official spelling of the Verrazano-Narrows Bridge has one fewer *z* than its namesake. This is not exactly a misspelling, but a choice: Giovanni da Verrazzano was born, lived, and died in France, and accordingly he adopted and used in public the French version of his name, Jean de Verrazano.

might seem, in a nation of immigrants just about everything we have has at some point been influenced by a foreign language or culture. To wit: although there have been a wide range of etymologies suggested, it seems likely that we have the Dutch to thank for the word *Yankee*. In his book *American English*, the linguist Albert H. Marckwardt writes, "The most credible [etymology] seems to be Dutch *Jan Kees*, 'John Cheese,' a term applied to the New Englanders somewhat contemptuously, or at least patronizingly. This was mistaken for a plural by the English-speaking colonists and a new singular, *Yaenkee*, was derived through the process of back-formation." Though the word's modern-day connotations are rather more complicated, it will surely please southerners and Red Sox fans alike to know it was derogatory from the start.

To me, however, the most interesting story English has to tell about language in New York is the fact that English is spoken at all. Though Dutch was the first colonial language of New York and remained for many years an important second language, even in the very early days of the colony it was only one of several languages spoken in the area. New Netherland was home to French, Norwegians, Danes, Germans, Scots, and Irish, and by 1644 there were reportedly already eighteen languages spoken in Manhattan. Just over a century later, the city's cosmopolitan community was large enough to require separate houses of worship. In 1748, Manhattan boasted two Dutch churches, three English churches, two German churches, one French church, and a Jewish synagogue.

Soon enough, the floodgates opened. Between 1815 and 1915, nearly 33 million immigrants came to the United States from all over the world. Three quarters of them arrived via New York, and they brought their languages with them. Today the city is home to nearly 350 daily, weekly, and bimonthly publications representing more than 50 languages. City services are required by law to provide support for speakers of the city's six most widely spoken languages, which are currently Spanish, Chinese, Russian, Korean, Italian, and Haitian Creole. If you call 311, the city's non-emergency service line, you can request assistance in any of 192 languages. More than 150 languages are spoken in its public schools, 138 were listed on its Census forms, and as many as 800 are heard on its streets.

And yet, despite this multiplicity of languages and dialects and cultures and homelands, if there is one thing New Yorkers have in common, it's English. We are all, with varying degrees of necessity and success, trying to understand English or trying to make English understood. When languages other than English are spoken at home, they are spoken, overwhelmingly, by first- and second-generation immigrants. Although some new arrivals may never have the chance to learn English at all, much less fluently, the acquisition of English by later generations is inevitable, even in the relatively insular communities so casually maligned as "language ghettos." At the end of the day, English—and English alone—is the de facto official language of New York City.

This, ultimately, was the lesson I learned in Queens, a lesson I couldn't have learned until I found myself in a borough where every day I encountered and interacted with Korean, Turkish, Romanian, Spanish, and Japanese. Until then I had been so consumed by my efforts to learn everybody else's languages that I failed to notice everybody else was learning mine.

The fact of the matter is this: outside of grammar class, we don't often think about the whys and wherefores of our native languages. If you grow up in an English-speaking family and in an English-speaking community, it is easy to underestimate the number of men, women, and children throughout the country who are busy supplementing their native or traditional languages with English. It is even easier to overlook the fact that this has been the case since the very earliest days of United States history.

Whenever I find myself forgetting this, I try to think of the 1910 Census. If you look at the reports from Schenectady, New York, you will find, in a long list of handwritten names with suspect spellings, the names Martin and Franziska Lupka. A laborer and a housewife, respectively, they came to the United States in 1889 with their son Franz and settled in New York City before eventually moving up to Schenectady. According to their Census data, twenty years later they still spoke Polish. At the same time, halfway across the country in North Dakota, Edvard and Mina Knain were raising their seven children on a farm just outside Northwood. Though they had emigrated from Norway in 1884, by 1910 Mina still spoke only Norwegian.

Meanwhile, Franz and his siblings and Edvard and his children already all spoke English.

Martin and Franziska and Edvard and Mina are my great-great-grandparents, and they serve as a reminder to me that, throughout history, men and women in America have experienced language in two radically different ways. While I use English with rarely a second thought, just a hundred years ago my ancestors were struggling—sometimes successfully, sometimes not—to adapt not just to a new way of living but also to a new way of speaking.

The diversity of Queens, the artifacts of language contact, the persistence of English. Individually these may seem like ordinary observations. But taken together, they led me to think seriously for the first time about what it has meant to be a minority-language-speaker in the United States. What was it like to learn a new language before Berlitz or Pimsleur, much less Rosetta Stone or Google Translate? What challenges did these men and women face from the English-speaking community? Why do some languages last while others fade away? And did speakers of languages in the former group feel less American than speakers of those in the latter? How, ultimately, has the language experience affected the American experience?

Queens may have led me to these questions, but the answers, I knew, could only be found outside its borders. So I culled through books, blogs, magazines, and Census data for information on language communities past and present, thriving and extinct. I looked for languages that had died out and been reclaimed; languages that had somehow managed to remain mostly the same, despite the entropy born of adaptation and assimilation; languages that were clinging to survival solely through the efforts of communities determined not to lose touch with the past. I looked for European languages, American languages, African languages, Asian languages. I looked for languages that had been here for centuries and languages that had been here for months.

But most of all, I looked for languages that would be able to tell me something about why language communities in the United States have, again and again and again, eventually yielded to the seemingly implacable preeminence of English. I didn't just want to better understand language in America; I wanted to better understand the language experience in America.

Then I printed out some maps, packed up my Subaru, and hit the road.

Over the course of the next two years, I drove more than 25,000 miles, traveling through every continental state save Vermont and Rhode Island. I stayed in hotels and motels, in cabins and on couches. A few of my trips were quick jaunts down the coast or up to New England. A few were cross-country marathons. Along the way, I lost four tires, three windshields, and my favorite pair of pants. But I found Norwegian in North Dakota, Spanish in the Southwest, and creoles in Louisiana and Georgia. I learned about Crow, Navajo, and Makah. I picked up my first words of Haitian Creole on the streets of Miami, and I struggled with Basque spelling in a dusty corner of Nevada.

This book is not a comprehensive outline of the history of language in America or an exhaustive catalog of the country's heritage-language communities. It isn't even an unabridged record of my travels. The fact is, despite my preparation and enthusiasm, my expeditions weren't always successful. Sometimes I'd visit a city or a town and find only the vaguest hint of the language in question. Sometimes there wasn't anything to see or do. Sometimes no one would talk to me. On one occasion my plans were foiled by severe winter weather and on another by my friend Damian, who kept finding ways to convince me to go out drinking. But, in the end, I learned far more than I'd anticipated.

What follows are my accounts of the people, places, and languages that were the most interesting, the most revealing, and the most surprising. Together they tell a story of conflict and kinship, marginalization and assimilation, and, ultimately, one part of what it means to be American.

CHAPTER ONE

Montana: Crow

T HE FIRST PLACE I'm going to tell you about is Montana. This might seem a strange place to start, particularly given that I didn't make my way there until midway through my travels. But it was in Montana that I began to get to know the diverse group of languages and cultures that have been in America the longest. And, therefore, it was in Montana that I began to lay the groundwork for my understanding of everything that came after.

Going into my research, this first group of languages—the languages of Native America—was without a doubt the group of American languages I was least familiar with. I like to think I had a fairly liberal education, but as a child I was exposed to only the barest minimum about the people and cultures of the Americas before the arrival of European explorers, colonists, and conquerors. Much like millions of other American schoolchildren, I learned about the first Thanksgiving, the construction of tipis, and, of course, the way that the Indian appreciated the earth and therefore honored each and every last piece of the buffalo. The only notable difference in my experience was, perhaps, my proximity to and therefore slight familiarity with the Cahokia Mounds.

Not that I could tell you very much about the Cahokia Mounds, apart from the fact that they are, indeed, quite moundy.

The languages of Native America were also the languages I found most intimidating. I'd read a few pages here and there about Algonquin noun class or the Cherokee syllabary, but only as part of my general fetish for linguistic novelty. I had never stopped to consider the broader scope of Native languages, either in terms of linguistic complexity or in terms of their role in American history and culture.

So five years ago languages such as Crow or Navajo—much less Lushootseed, Quileute, or Makah—would have primarily inspired in me an intellectual trepidation. I was, you see, afraid to discover just how much I didn't know. As Douglas Adams once wrote, "In an infinite universe, the one thing sentient life cannot afford to have is a sense of proportion." Once I opened my eyes to the vast landscape of indigenous American languages, I feared I would have to acknowledge just how microscopic the dot was that said "You are here."

I wasn't wrong. To call the time I've spent with Native languages eye-opening would be a gross understatement. But they provided me with a crucial framework for understanding the mechanics and ramifications of language loss. And, even more critical, they awakened in me an unexpected zeal. The languages that I once approached so cautiously—so reluctantly—are now the languages I would defend most ardently.

I came to Montana from South Dakota, driving west along Interstate 90 through the Badlands and into northeast Wyoming. In a city called Buffalo the highway jogs north some 120 miles before heading west again at Hardin toward Bozeman Pass. Along this stretch you'll find two great landmarks of the American West: the inn in Sheridan, Wyoming, where Buffalo Bill Cody auditioned for his Wild West Show, and the Little Bighorn Battlefield, where George Armstrong Custer had his last stand. You'll also find my eventual destination, the great, grassy expanse of Crow Nation.

The Crow Indian Reservation is the largest reservation in Montana and the sixth-largest reservation in the United States, comprising some 2.3 million acres. It is home to more than 8,000 Crow—about 70 percent of the tribe's total enrollment—the majority of whom work for the tribe or for federal programs. The bulk of the tribe's businesses and administrative offices are located in Crow Agency, an unassuming town just north of the Little Bighorn Battlefield on I-90. I stayed in Billings, some sixty miles to the west, hoping my research might benefit from the city's relatively more expansive tourist infrastructure. But as I picked through the conspicuously flimsy collection of maps and brochures in my hotel's lobby, I realized I wasn't sure what I was going to find here—if, indeed, I was going to find anything.

When I was a kid, I'd thought Montana impossibly uninteresting. Every few summers we would drive out to visit my father's family, and Montana felt like an endless in-between. It was past Mount Rushmore but still days from the Pacific Ocean, north of Yellowstone but south of my grandmother's house. There were so few other cars to spot that my license plate tally invariably leveled off, and despite being promised otherwise, I never saw a single grizzly bear. It was the kind of state that made me want to catch up on my reading—or my sleep. The only thing I remember clearly from those trips is how the roads seemed to have an improbably gradual slope, as if I were seeing the Earth itself curving away into space.

By the time I drove onto the reservation for the first time I was re-thinking things. I decided instead that the landscape in Montana is like a Rorschach inkblot. Before long you start to see in the grass and trees and ground all the things that happen to be swirling in your subconscious. And that day I was clearly fixating on my own inadequacies.

The view from the highway through the reservation is the same as it is anywhere in eastern Montana, a panorama of compact, grassy hills and wide, grassy plains. But tucked out of sight are the valleys fed by the glittering, meandering tributaries of the Bighorn and Little Bighorn rivers. To the south the hills give way to the Bighorn, Pryor, and Wolf mountains and the part of the reservation that is open only to members of the tribe. As a child I'd thought there was nothing to see in Montana, but as an adult I began to wonder if maybe I just didn't know what I was looking for. I was perpetually aware of some great presence looming in the distance; I worried I would never get close enough to know its shape.

I didn't pick the Crow language out of a hat. I picked it because Crow is one of the more vital Native languages in the country, and I wanted to visit a Native community that still spoke its traditional language on a regular basis. But I was also interested in exploring the relationship between Natives and outsiders, between the preconceptions of a non-Native and the discoveries of a fully engaged visitor. And each June, this patch of Montana provides an opportunity to do exactly that, as members of Crow Nation, residents of nearby Hardin, and tourists from across the country gather to celebrate the anniversary of one of the most famous armed conflicts in American history, the Battle of the Little Bighorn.

The seeds of the Battle of the Little Bighorn were sown in the early 1870s, when gold was discovered in the Black Hills of the Dakota Territory. Previously, this area had been set aside by the U.S. government for the exclusive use of the Lakota Sioux, but the illegal intrusion of white prospectors led to escalating tensions between the Lakota and their allies and the government. In 1875 U.S. leaders decided to stop enforcing mining restrictions in the Black Hills, and in the first sally of what would later become known as the Great Sioux War, the commissioner of Indian Affairs ordered all Lakota and Cheyenne to report to their agencies or face the threat of military force. Hostilities commenced soon after the January 31, 1876, deadline.

By June 1876, several thousand Lakota, Cheyenne, and Arapaho—including the men known as Sitting Bull and Crazy Horse—were encamped along the Little Bighorn River. In an effort to drive the Indians back to their reservations, General Philip Sheridan sent three columns of soldiers to the area. George Armstrong Custer got there first. And despite warnings from his scouts about the size of the encampment, which some estimate held between ten thousand and fifteen thousand people, Custer chose not to wait for reinforcements.

And so, on the afternoon of June 25, 1876, a cavalry force led by Major Marcus Reno crossed the Little Bighorn River and began the battle that would take its name. Very quickly, Reno recognized that he was seriously outnumbered and retreated, inadvertently allowing the Lakota, Cheyenne, and Arapaho forces to concentrate their efforts on Custer and his men. There are conflicting reports about what happened next, but one thing is certain: every U.S. solider who attacked with Custer died that day. It was the greatest defeat the U.S. military has ever suffered at the hands of American Indians.

The Little Bighorn battlefield has been catnip for curiosity seekers ever since. The first gathering at the battlefield took place just a year after the battle itself, and the first reenactments were held at the tenth anniversary. In 1964 Crow Nation and the Hardin Chamber of Commerce agreed to produce an annual reenactment, but mounting political tension and criticism from the American Indian Movement led to the show's cancellation in 1976. Hardin revived the reenactment in 1990, and today it is a part of the town's Little Bighorn Days Festival, which includes a fancy-dress ball, a parade, and a variety of local events.

When I arrived in Hardin, I went first to the County Historical Museum and visitor center to pick up a schedule and tickets for the reenactment. The two teenage girls working the desk pulled out a pair of pamphlets as soon as I approached the counter. Hardin, just fifty miles east of Billings, is otherwise the kind of town that typically merits only a cursory sort of acknowledgment in a travel guide: *By the way, you can probably get gas and a sandwich here.* Little Bighorn Days is, as you can imagine, the most popular tourist attraction in town, and there was something refreshing about the fact that no one expected me to be here for any other reason. It's not like New York, where locals can't seem to help but roll their eyes at the tourists who come to see a show and eat at Sardi's.

I took the pamphlets gratefully and asked how much the tickets cost. "Which one do you want tickets for?" they asked.

"What do you mean, which one?"

"Which reenactment. There's the one here in Hardin, then there's the one the Crow do."

"Competing reenactments?" I asked, a bit dumbly.

"Something like that."

"Which one do you recommend?" I had visions of cold war–style one-upmanship, possibly involving horses, definitely involving pyrotechnics, but ideally involving both.

They shared a smug look. "Oh, ours, for sure—it's way better."

Not wanting to seem rude, I smiled and bought tickets for the Hardin reenactment. But, of course, I also took down the information for the

Crow reenactment. After all, I hadn't driven two thousand miles just to get one side of the story.

The Hardin show takes place a few miles west of the town center, in a field between Old U.S. 87 and the railroad. The set for the reenactment was larger than I expected, about the size of a football field. To the left was the façade of a wooden fort; to the right was a cluster of tipis. Behind the bleachers was a sort of souvenir shantytown, tables and booths that sold an unexpectedly eccentric array of items, from gyros to quesadillas to crossbows. Just a stone's throw away, a Burlington Northern Santa Fe train rumbled past.

I found a space on the metal risers and settled in. Quickly I discovered that the show was less a strict reenactment than a historical pageant. The early minutes of the production were dedicated to the story of contact between Natives and European explorers, traders, and settlers. We met Lewis, Clark, and Sacagawea.* We were introduced to mountain men and covered wagons and war cries. We were shown how to erect a tipi. Eventually Sitting Bull, Crazy Horse, and Custer and his wife made their appearances. Then, finally, we eased into the events of June 1876.

I don't exactly have a strong background in military history, but as far as I could tell, the battle was true to life in at least one respect: it was messy and fast. I watched in some dismay as a chaotic tangle of men on horseback resolved almost immediately into two groups: victors and corpses. If you're looking to understand with any precision how exactly Custer's forces were defeated in the battle, a reenactment like Hardin's will likely be of little help.

Nor did it manage to convey a sense of how horrific the battle must have been, despite the grave tone affected by the show's narrator. Rather, the Hardin reenactment had the sweet self-consciousness of any

---

* This is the most common spelling as well as the spelling used by federal agencies. If you ever travel to North Dakota, however, you will much more frequently encounter the spelling *Sakakawea*. Born a Shoshone, Sacagawea was kidnapped as a young girl by the Hidatsa, who gave her a name from their own language: *Tsakáka wía*, "bird woman." *Sakakawea* is the Hidatsa's preferred anglicization.

amateur production. The participants weren't quite able to summon the
ferocity of battle, and any hard edges were rapidly smoothed by the pat-
ent delight on the faces of the younger actors. Many wore costumes that
wouldn't have looked out of place on a middle school stage. Some wore
denim shorts under breechcloths; others simply donned khaki shorts
they decorated with leather fringe. After the show, audience members
climbed down from the bleachers to take pictures with and beg autographs from the actors—many of whom, I got the impression, they already knew.

There were moments of solemnity and there were moments of revelry, but the Hardin reenactment felt overwhelmingly like old-fashioned
family fun, with all the historical accuracy that implies. Although the
narration and program emphasized that the reenactment was based
on the notes of a Crow tribal historian and was from the "Indian perspective," it was clear that a number of choices were made to privilege
pageantry over pedagogy. One of the more blatantly sentimental scenes,
for instance, depicted Custer taking leave of his wife, Libbie. Even if
you're relatively uninformed about the history of the American Indian
it's quite clear that Custer wouldn't be considered a romantic hero from
the "Indian perspective."

The Crow reenactment is a more intimate affair. One of its main
selling points is that it takes place in sight of the Little Bighorn River, a
few miles south of Crow Agency on Real Bird Ranch, on land that was
actually part of the original battlefield. This fact is, as I understand it,
enough to coax dedicated and experienced historical reenactors to participate for free. The other feature that distinguishes the Crow reenactment
from the Hardin show is that it purports to show the "Native American
perspective."

I sensed from the start a vague hint of controversy surrounding this
assertion, but at first I couldn't figure out why. Frankly, the two shows
are not substantially different. The reenactments may take place on two
different plots of land and they may employ two different George Arm-
strong Custers, but they tell largely the same story. As it turns out, both
scripts were written by members of Crow Nation. (The Crow script
was, in fact, written by the grandsons of the author of the Hardin
script.) To be sure, the show I saw on Real Bird Ranch had a slightly

greater focus on Native traditions and cultures than the version I saw in Hardin. Though it, too, included set pieces about Lewis and Clark and the arrival of Montana's mountain men, it also, for instance, took the time to emphasize the cultural importance of the horse in Crow culture. Participants wore traditional breechcloths and rode bareback, the latter choice adding immeasurably to the suspense of the battle sequences. And at various points during the show, a circle of tribe members sang and played traditional instruments while the show's stage manager, a stout man in a yellow plaid shirt and a cowboy hat, rode back and forth on his horse issuing curt instructions in Crow into a walkie-talkie. Custer was referred to pointedly as "Custer Yellow Hair, the one who killed babies and old people."

But though their dramatic accoutrements felt outwardly more authentic, the Crow reenactment was, in the end, still a twenty-first-century show starring enthusiastic but amateur performers. The children in the Real Bird production had the same braces, sneakers, and eager expressions as those in the Hardin production.

It wasn't until much later that I recognized why the Crow reenactment—or any Crow reenactment, for that matter—was potentially problematic. In laying claim to the so-called Native American perspective, the Crow had glossed over an important fact of history: the Crow actually fought on Custer's side.

I feel the need to emphasize that an alliance between Natives and the U.S. military was not standard practice. The Crow, like so many other Native groups, suffered the brutal one-two punch of disease and diplomatic trickery. The first treaty the Crow signed with the United States was an 1825 "treaty of friendship" that laid out very little in real terms save an official acknowledgment of the supremacy of the U.S. government. It wasn't until the signing of the Fort Laramie Treaty in 1851 that boundaries for Crow lands were set down. And though this treaty granted the Crow 38 million acres, their territory was reduced just seventeen years later to only 8 million acres. Over the course of the next forty years, Crow Nation was further reduced to 2.3 million acres, the reservation's current size.

Nevertheless, at the time of the Battle of the Little Bighorn, the Crow were at odds with the Lakota, Cheyenne, and Arapaho, whom they

believed to be encroaching on their territory. So the Crow, briefly, allied
with the U.S. Army. Today, I understand, there still exists some discord
between the groups both on account of the proximity of the Northern
Cheyenne and Crow reservations and the fact that territorial boundaries give the Crow the right to conduct "Native American" tours of
the area where the Lakota, Cheyenne, and Arapaho claimed their historic victory.

It would be very easy at this point to pretend I'd known this
from the start. But in the interest of making a larger point, I'll own
up not just to not knowing these things but also to the sticky bit of
prejudice that led me to assume the Crow had fought against the United
States. I had been so focused on the potential dichotomy between
Native and non-Native that I'd fallen into an old trap and let myself
forget that all Native peoples are not, in fact, part of one big, homogenous culture.

I realized then that if I was going to learn about the Crow language, I
would probably benefit from a general familiarity with the breadth of
Native American language.

As I've said, my exposure to Native history and culture was next to
nothing. But my exposure to American Indian languages was even
less—which is to say *actually* nothing. And I'm not alone in this. Fewer
than 4 percent of American high schools offer instruction in languages
other than Spanish, French, German, and Latin, much less in languages
such as Crow, Cherokee, or Algonquin. Colleges are little better. Harvard, for instance, offers courses in Old Church Slavonic, Medieval
Welsh, Akkadian, Hittite, Sumerian, and Egyptian. But the only indigenous American language you can take is Classical Nahautl, the language of the Aztecs.*

---

* Interestingly, Harvard might not still exist were it not for its admission of Native
students. Shortly after its creation, the school found itself in some financial difficulties. Luckily, the English Society for the Propagation of the Gospel in New England
was willing to give the college money if it would provide tuition and housing for
American Indian students. Accordingly, Harvard's founding 1650 charter explicitly
mentions its mission to educate the "Indian Youth of this Country."

Now, this isn't true across the board. You can, for instance, get an associate's degree in Shoshoni at Idaho State University. You can also go to the University of Alaska in Fairbanks, which offers majors in Inupiaq and Central Yup'ik, or to its affiliated Alaska Native Language center, which offers courses in Aleut and other indigenous Alaskan languages. But according to the Center for Advanced Research on Language Acquisition at the University of Minnesota, there are currently only about a hundred two- and four-year programs—that's about 2 percent of all institutions—that offer Native language instruction in the United States.

So for me and many other Americans, the history of the relationship between English and indigenous American languages began in one of two places: sometime around the fourth Thursday in November or the second verse of "Colors of the Wind." There isn't really any popular conception of Native languages that is much more sophisticated than the fictions propagated by old Hollywood westerns, where Indians played the villains or sidekicks, invariably relying on pidgin English and the word *kemosabe*. Somewhere along the line most of us are taught to hold up our hands and say "How" in a deep, booming voice, and we are often given the idea that most Native personal names are of the verb-preposition-animal variety. And that's about as nuanced as it typically gets.

Luckily, I'd put together something of a traveling language library before leaving New York, and so it took only a few minutes of digging around in the trunk of my car to pull together a crash course in indigenous American languages. Here's what I learned—what I wish I'd learned long ago.

Estimates of the pre-contact population of North America are varied and unreliable, and the same goes for the estimates of the number of pre-contact languages. Nevertheless, reputable sources have suggested that anywhere from 250 to more than 400 languages were spoken prior to the fifteenth century. Modern-day estimates are more reliable, but still less than conclusive; Michael Krauss of the Linguistic Society of America estimates that 175 indigenous languages are still spoken in the United States.

The two most well-known language families in the eastern United States are probably the Algonquin and Iroquois languages. The Algic family, which according to linguist Marianne Mithun "covers the widest territory of all North American families," includes Mi'kmaq and Malecite-Passamaquoddy in the East; Arapaho, Blackfoot and Cheyenne in the Plains; and Wiyot and Yurok in California. The Iroquoian languages, largely concentrated in the East, include Seneca, Mohawk, and Oneida.

Then there are the Caddoan languages (Pawnee, Wichita, and Caddo), which are spoken in several Plains states, and the Muskogean languages (Choctaw, Creek, Alabama, Chickasaw), which can be found in the Southeast. Kiowa-Tanoan languages (Kiowa, Oklahoma), meanwhile, are spoken on the southern Plains and in the Southwest. Also found in the Southwest is the Yuman family, which includes Mohave and Havasupai-Hualapai-Yavapai, the languages of the Grand Canyon. (Havasupai is spoken by the people who live at the bottom of the canyon, Hualapai by those on the south rim.)

The Athabaskan-Eyak-Tlingit family, which encompasses more languages and more modern-day speakers than any other North American language family, includes Navajo, Apache, and eleven Alaskan languages.* Other large families include Salishan in the Pacific Northwest (Clallam, Skagit, Snohomish, Lushootseed, Spokane, Coeur d'Alene, Quinault), Siouan in the Great Plains (Crow, Hidatsa, Mandan, Assiniboine, Dakota, Lakota, Osage, Ho-Chunk), and Uto-Aztecan in the Southwest (Hopi, Comanche, Shoshoni).

Also found in Alaska are the Eskimo-Aleut languages—languages such as Inuktitut, Inupiaq, and Yup'ik that are spoken not just in the United States and Canada but also in Russia and Greenland. And far to the west but still under the auspices of the U.S. government are the Pacific Islands of Hawai'i, Guam, Samoa, and the Northern Mariana

---

* Recent and fascinating work by the linguist Edward Vajda suggests that Athabaskan-Eyak-Tlingit languages are actually genetically related to Yeniseian, a mostly extinct family of languages in central Siberia.

Islands and the indigenous Austronesian languages Hawaiian, Chamorro, Carolinian, and Tanapag.

All in all, an impressive number of indigenous languages are spoken in the United States. Though this level of linguistic diversity isn't unheard of—more than 400 languages are spoken in India, for instance, while SIL International's Ethnologue currently lists 830 living languages in Papua New Guinea—neither is it unremarkable. Because if you compare the languages of North America to, say, the languages in Europe, you'll notice that the vast majority of European languages are actually all from the same Indo-European family. Though there are outliers—Basque, Hungarian, Finnish—there is certainly nothing to approach the linguistic diversity of North America.

As such, you can cast aside any assumptions of broad mutual intelligibility among indigenous American languages. In a 1946 article, the influential linguists Edward Sapir and Morris Swadesh presented sample sentences—translations of the phrase "he will give it to you"—in order to highlight the differences between North American languages. According to Sapir and Swadesh, speakers of Wishram, a Chinookan language in Oregon and Washington, said *ačimlúda*, while speakers of Takelma, a language isolate also in Oregon, said *ʔòspink*. For Southern Paiute (Uto-Aztecan; Utah, Arizona, and Nevada) they recorded "he will give it to you" as *mayavaaniak'aŋa'mi*; in Yana (isolate; Northern California) it was *ba·jmasiwaʔnuma*. The idea that these groups could understand one another seems ludicrous on even the most casual inspection.

Nevertheless, the fact remains that the most widespread misconception about Native languages is that there's only one of them.* This is as instructive as any of the linguistic detail I just shared, because for such a nonsensical notion to exist there has to be an incredibly deep and pervasive preconception that the only distinction that matters is the one between Native and non-Native—a preconception so deep and so pervasive that we often don't even realize it's there. This assumption is wildly

---

* Or, perhaps more absurd, that there are two Native languages: "Eskimo" and everything else.

counterproductive, obscuring not only the diversity of Native languages but also the relationship between Native languages and European languages such as English. After all, it's almost easy to overlook the fact that American English actually owes much of its distinctiveness to words it has acquired in the New World.

Our popular understanding of the early history between English colonists and American Indians relies heavily on narratives of cultural exchange and cooperation facilitated by translators of near-mythic proportions. In Plymouth, that translator was Tisquantum (more popularly known as Squanto), a member of the Patuxet tribe; in Jamestown it was Pocahontas, the daughter of a Powhatan chief. Though we often read of their skills with English, we rarely learn about their native languages, Wampanoag and Powhatan. These languages have nevertheless had a notable impact on American English.

Wampanoag (also called Massachusetts) and Powhatan are both members of the Eastern Algonquin subfamily, a group that also includes Munsee and Mohegan-Montauk-Narragansett (which was spoken, among other places, on Long Island). Wampanoag was spoken in and around Boston and Cape Cod, while Powhatan was spoken in Virginia from the Potomac to the James River. Along with Eastern Iroquois languages such as Mohawk, Cherokee, and Oneida, they provided many early colonial borrowings into English.

Some of these borrowings were used to identify unfamiliar plants and animals, giving us English words such as *woodchuck* (Cree), *raccoon* (Algonquin), *skunk* (Abenaki), and *squash* (Narragansett). *Opossum*, the name of what I consider to be a singularly nasty creature, comes from a Powhatan word. William Strachey, the first secretary to the Jamestown colony, recorded the word as *aposoum*, a "beast in bignes[s] of a pig and tast[e] alike." I prefer John Smith's description: "An Opassom hath a head like a Swine, and a taile like a Rat, and is of the bignesse of a Cat."

English has, quite naturally, also adapted words from American Indian languages to describe American Indian culture. *Squaw*, *papoose*, and *wigwam* are of Algonquin derivation. *Tipi*, meanwhile, comes from a

Lakota word for "dwelling."* But there are also Native words that have become wonderfully, quintessentially American. One of my favorites is an Algonquin word meaning "marshy meadow." It eventually gained traction as a dismissive term for an unsophisticated village the middle of nowhere. You probably know it as *podunk*.

The greatest Native linguistic influence, however, is to be found in American place names. Take the Abenaki, an Algonquin people who lived in New England, Quebec, and the Maritime Provinces, and who were particularly important for their contribution to Maine place names such as *Ogunquit*, derived from an Abenaki phrase meaning "a sand bar lagoon," or *Kennebunk*, the combination of the Abenaki words *kenne*, "long," and *benek*, "cut bank."

Wampanoag, the language of Tisquantum, has left traces all over New England. In Wampanoag and other Algonquin languages, a final *-t* is a locative marker (meaning "at"), which accounts for many of the New England names that end in *-t* or *-tt*—for instance, *Swampscott* ("at the red rock") or *Cohasset* ("at the stone ledge"). The notorious *Chappaquiddick* also comes to us via Wampanoag. The island, which is separated from Martha's Vineyard by a narrow strait, gets *chappa* from the word *chippi*, "separate," and *quiddick* from *acquidne*, "island."

The vast majority of state names are also derived from indigenous American languages. Some, such as *Alabama*, *Illinois*, *Kansas*, and *Missouri*, are versions of tribal names. Others are more localized place names that were appropriated for the larger state. *Alaska*, for instance, comes from an Aleut word meaning "the object toward which the action of the sea is directed"—that is, the mainland. *Texas*, reflecting that area's complex linguistic history, is a Spanish rendition of a Caddo word for "friend." The name *Oklahoma* was originally suggested by

---

* Unfortunately, these sorts of words often get thrown around without thought for their provenance. *Moccasin* and *tomahawk* are Algonquin words and therefore not something you'd use as a descriptor in Alaska any more than you would call a kimono a bathrobe. Sometimes, however, a Native word can become associated with a general concept that is then used cross-culturally. The word *totem* comes from Ojibwe, for instance, but it is used in English for the totem poles constructed by speakers of very different languages, such as Tlingit and Kwak'wala.

Choctaw chief Allen Wright—from the Choctaw *oklah*, "people," and *homma?*, "red"—as an alternative to "Indian Territory."*

Wyoming is a particularly interesting case. Although there has historically been a diverse group of American Indians who have called Wyoming home, the name *Wyoming* actually comes from the same language that was spoken in and around what is now New York City. In the Munsee language, *chwewamink* means "at the big river flat." *Wyoming*, the anglicization of this word, was first used to name a valley in northeastern Pennsylvania before being popularized by Thomas Campbell's poem about the Revolutionary War–era massacre:

> On Susquehanna's side, fair Wyoming!
> Although the wild-flower on thy ruin'd wall,
> And roofless homes, a sad remembrance bring,
> Of what thy gentle people did befall;
> Yet thou wert once the loveliest land of all
> That see the Atlantic wave their morn restore.
> Sweet land! may I thy lost delights recall,
> And paint thy Gertrude in her bowers of yore,
> Whose beauty was the love of Pennsylvania's shore!

Whether due to the popularity of the poem or perhaps to some inherent appeal to the rhythm of the word itself, there are now Wyomings in thirteen other states, Ontario, and New South Wales, Australia.

To be sure, the American place names that have been borrowed from Native languages have something of a phonetic leg up in that they sound different from the boring old Indo-European sounds we're used to. In *Made in America*, Bill Bryson writes, "You have only to list a handful of Indian place-names—*Mississippi, Susquehanna, Rappahannock*—to see that the Indians found a poetry in the American landscape that has all too

---

* There is some debate as to whether *OK*, that most quintessential of American words, also comes from Choctaw—specifically, the Choctaw expression *okeh*, which means something like "it is so." However, most experts seem to agree with Allan Metcalf, the author of *OK: The Improbable Story of America's Greatest Word*, who contends that the word was coined first in English before making its way into Choctaw.

often eluded those who displaced them." Though I don't disagree, I would argue that these names have an emotional resonance—that they have poetry—not because of their sound but rather because so many words from Native languages are words Americans use for "home."

Once I'd generally oriented myself within the universe of indigenous American languages, I was ready to start thinking about the specifics of Crow. On a hunch, I went back to the girls at the visitor center. Without batting an eye, they pointed me toward a bookshelf where, among the usual titles about Custer and the battle, I found a surprisingly extensive selection of books on the Crow language. I bought a heavy blue grammar by Randolph Graczyk and spent the rest of my afternoon poking about in it.

The Crow call themselves Apsáalooke, or Children of the Large-Beaked Bird.* Their ancestors migrated to the plains in search of buffalo in the sixteenth century, leaving a "Land of Many Lakes" (an area thought to be in Wisconsin) for the Dakotas. Here, the tribe split in two, with one band—the Apsáalooke—moving up into the area in eastern Montana that they today call home.

The Crow language is a member of the Siouan family, which includes Mandan, Ho-chunk, Lakota, and Dakota, among others, and extends primarily throughout the Plains, east into Minnesota and Wisconsin, and south to Arkansas and Mississippi. Within the family, Crow is most closely related to the language of the Hidatsa, and based on linguistic evidence, scholars such as the linguist G. Hubert Matthews have concluded that the Crow and the Hidatsa were originally part of one larger tribe before they split nearly 500 years ago. The languages of the Crow and Hidatsa have also diverged in more immediately apparent ways, however. While Hidatsa has only a small group of fluent speakers still living and is struggling to survive, there are still several thousand living speakers of Crow, making it one of the more widely spoken American Indian languages.

---

* The accents over double vowels in Crow words indicate tone. If the accent is on the first vowel, then the tone is rising; if the accent is on the second vowel, the tone is falling.

As I sat in my hotel room in Billings and paged through my grammar, the first thing I noticed is that Crow has—to use something of a technical term—really long words. Much like many other American Indian languages, Crow is polysynthetic, which means that a single word in Crow can contain lots of information. Consider *baawaashbaaléewiawaassaak*, which means "I'm not going to go hunting."* When I was learning Spanish, it took me ages to remember that I could just say *hablo* instead of *yo hablo*, because *hablo* is necessarily first person. I can't even imagine how long it would take me to accustom myself to single words that can contain three verbs, a negative marker, an indefinite marker related to *hunt*, and a declarative marker.

Even more unusual is the typology of Crow. Linguists use the phrase "morphosyntactic alignment" to describe the way a language treats the arguments of transitive and intransitive verbs—what we in English call subjects and objects. Some languages (like English) treat transitive subjects the same way as intransitive subjects: "*she* hits *her*"; "*she* runs." Other languages (say, Basque) treat intransitive subjects the same way as transitive objects. So "*she* hits *her*," but "*her* runs." Then there are the languages that use combinations of these two systems. Crow is one of these languages. Known as an "active-stative" language, Crow is sometimes a *she*-runs language and sometimes a *her*-runs language.

If you grew up speaking Crow, you wouldn't think twice about any of this, but when you're approaching the language from the perspective of an English-speaker—particularly from the perspective of a non-linguist English-speaker—it can seem overwhelming to have to rethink ideas as basic as "subjects," "objects," and even "words."

But the feature of Crow that most intrigued me—in part because I had never seen it before—is something called switch reference. Switch reference was first observed by the linguist William Jacobsen in his

---

* In the *Concise Encyclopedia of Languages of the World*, Graczyk provides a complete gloss of the word:

baawaashbaaléewiawaassaak
baa-w-aash-baa-lée-wia-waa-ssaa-k
INDEF-1-hunt-1-go-want.to-1-NEG-DECL
I'm not going to go hunting.

study of Washo, a language of Nevada. Roughly speaking, switch reference is a grammatical way of distinguishing multiple subjects. If in English, for instance, you were telling a story about multiple members of
the same gender, you would have to use proper names ("she—Jill, I
mean") to keep the story straight. In Crow, however, there are markers
that indicate "different" and "same" subjects, respectively, allowing lis-
teners, readers, and speakers to do away with clumsier forms of clarifi-
cation.

Then there is something called the mirative. A mirative—from
the Latin for "to wonder"—is a grammatical indication of surprise.
There are, of course, many ways to express surprise in language, the
ones most familiar to English-speakers involving intonation, stress, or
the words "get out." But languages such as Tibetan, Korean, or Crow
can encode surprise in the word itself. In Crow this is accomplished
through the use of a suffixal verb, the rough grammatical equivalent
of a spit-take.

Like so many aspects of the Crow language, these are all grammatical tools of eloquent distinction. They also serve to remind us that the
monolithic "how" and exaggerated monosyllables of silver-screen Indians are gross misrepresentations of the complexity and elegance of Native languages; indeed, they would be gross misrepresentations of any
language.

For years the relative isolation of Crow Nation helped keep its language strong. Just over forty years ago a survey showed that 82 percent of students on the reservation spoke Crow as their first language
and that 79 percent of twelfth graders reported being primarily Crow-
speakers. The prospect for future language maintenance at this point
looked extremely promising. By 1995, however, the numbers had taken
a startling turn. Only 25 percent of children ages three to nineteen
were fluent in Crow, while only 50 percent of their parents spoke the
language. Though numbers were higher among tribal elders—85 percent of the students' grandparents spoke Crow—the statistics indicated
that the younger generation was in the middle of a major shift away from
the traditional language. Unfortunately, it's this generation that typically gives the greatest insight into the life span of a language.

I decided to make a visit to Little Big Horn College to find out more about the current state of the Crow language. Located in Crow Agency, Little Big Horn College opened in 1980 as a vocational-technical school with only a handful of students. Today the college has more than three hundred full-time students and is one of the few places in the country where you can study Crow.

Despite my best attempts to get lost in what is not much more than a three-street town, I eventually found the college and made my way to a small office where I met with Tim McCleary, a historian and Crow-language instructor. The son of missionaries, Professor McCleary was versed from a very young age in the business of language study. I liked him immediately. Affable and generous with his time, he seemed only slightly bemused by my interest in Crow grammar, and he was patient as he walked me through the patterns for a few Crow words. The language, he explained, was extremely accommodating to new words. Some of these new words were Crow-English hybrids. A favorite word of his daughter's was *baachúuxinneeted*. The *baa-* is a Crow prefix meaning "one of," and the ending *–inneeted* is an approximation of an English participle. *Chuux*, meanwhile, is related to the sound of "jack." What does the phrase mean in its entirety? "To be jacked up."*

When I asked Professor McCleary about the vitality of the Crow language, his smile dimmed. Nineteen years ago, he told me, the only language spoken was Crow. Three years ago he first started noticing that Crow wasn't being spoken in the hallways. That summer, even though 98 percent of his students were Crow, he had only one primary speaker of Crow in each of his two classes. "There is," he suggested, "a false sense that everything's OK."

By the time I left Crow Agency, I had more questions than answers. I had managed to get a rough sense of the Crow language, and I felt appreciably better informed about Native languages in general. But I wanted to know more about language preservation specifically. Crow has a reasonably strong and visible presence in a decent-sized community, and yet it lost a huge proportion of its speakers in just twenty-five

---

* Susan Stewart, the park manager at Plenty Coups State Park taught me another bit of slang: *eegaawaa*. Used only by women, she told me, it pretty much means "OMG."

years. What would I find in larger language communities—or in much smaller ones?

As I drove out of town, I noticed a smattering of Crow-language signage—above the door to the Laundromat, for instance, is the Crow word *ammaaiisshuuwuua*. The exit off I-90 for Crow Agency, meanwhile, is labeled *Baaxuwuaashe* ("flour mill," a reference to the days when the Bureau of Indian Affairs was also home to the government-built mill). I later discovered that as part of a recent initiative, Crow place names have been added to a number of rest stops and highway signs. Though the public use of the language doesn't approach anything like the density one sees in non-English language communities in major U.S. cities, it nevertheless serves a purpose: you are aware, at the very least, that there is a language other than English here. All in all, it seems a noble effort. Still, I couldn't help but wonder if it was going to matter.

Before I left Montana, I had one more stop to make. I figured I couldn't see two historical reenactments and then leave without seeing the battlefield itself.

It's a strange place, the Little Bighorn Battlefield. Administered now by the National Park Service, the monument's outlying buildings have the generic sensibilities of most workaday federal construction, showcasing all the aesthetic grace you expect from a bureaucracy. As such, the buildings feel resolutely 1950s, inspiring chilly thoughts of Dwight D. Eisenhower, nuclear fallout, and linoleum.

The rest of the park and monument, on the other hand, is spare and mournful. Even on a bright summer day, you can't help but fall into a reflective mood. I was particularly susceptible to this, being the sort of person whose entire day can be ruined by even the most glancing reminder of my own mortality. I remember seeing a single, sad cloud in one far corner of the sky, which was enough to send me spiraling off into melancholy. Searching for some semblance of profundity, my brain skittered about the first few words of a much-loathed Wordsworth poem I'd been forced to learn in high school, and as I approached the monument, I felt with a sudden, horrible certainty that someone was going to start playing taps. With no small amount of dread, I slowly made my way to the memorial.

There are two sets of gravestones at the battlefield. The first form the almost comfortingly regular columns and rows of the memorial cemetery. The others are on Last Stand Hill. Most of the bodies of the U.S. cavalrymen who died here were, grotesquely, left in the open for five years until 1881, when they were gathered into a mass grave. So though there are to this day still a great many unanswered questions about what exactly happened over the course of the battle, the final resting place of each combatant is not in doubt. The gravestones here, unsettlingly weathered and lopsided, mark the exact spots where the men fell.

Custer's gravestone is straighter, bolder, and marked with a small American flag, but it is otherwise no different from the unnamed markers of his brethren. The only text is his rank, his name, the date, and the words "fell here."

Scattered throughout the hill are other, newer stones, polished granite with crisp white engraving. These mark the deaths of Indian warriors. Until very recently, a visitor to the battlefield would not have seen even these small reminders of Custer's opponents. As a matter of fact, until 1991 the monument itself was actually known as the Custer Battlefield National Monument. It wasn't until the appointment of Barbara Sutter, the site's first Native American superintendent, that the name change was enacted and progress began to be made with regard to a greater acknowledgment of Native involvement. The markers were first placed in 1999, and in 2003 the Indian Memorial—a sculpture based on the drawings of a Cheyenne warrior—was dedicated.

For roughly 132 years, then, the only sign of what is arguably the greatest military victory a Native group has ever achieved against the U.S. Army was a solitary wooden marker the National Park Service reluctantly erected in the 1950s. How must that have felt, I wondered, for the descendants of the Lakota, Cheyenne, and Arapaho men who fought there? How did that affect the perceptions of the schoolchildren and tourists who visited? How much has our understanding of Native peoples been guided, purposely or not, by the administrators of government bureaucracy?

Without a doubt, the fate of the Crow language—of any language— rests in large part on matters of education, economic opportunity, and technology. But my time in Montana led me to consider the influence of a more nebulous set of variables: namely, the popular portrayal and understanding of language, culture, and history. The vitality of a language cannot be unrelated to the nature of its representation among its speakers and non-speakers alike. At each stop along my journey, I continued to discover the many ways in which this is true.

CHAPTER TWO

Arizona: Navajo

L ATER THAT SUMMER, I found myself on a remote stretch of High-way 160 just south of the Utah-Arizona border, speeding toward a town whose name I didn't even know how to pronounce. I was heading off to investigate another Native language, one I thought might help an-swer some of the questions I'd come up against in Montana. The Crow reservation had given me a broad sense of the challenges faced by indig-enous languages in the United States. I was hoping Navajo Nation might help me fill in some of the details.

Part of the vast Athabaskan-Eyak-Tlingit language family, the Na-vajo language has linguistic relatives both near and far, from Chiricahua and Mescalero in the Southwest to Gwich'in, Tanacross, and nine other languages in Alaska. The vast majority of these languages are severely endangered or extinct. A few—notably North and South Slavey, Dogrib, and Dene Suline in northern Canada—have speaker populations in the low four figures. Navajo, on the other hand, has more than 150,000 speak-ers and is spoken not only by more people than any other Native lan-guage in the United States, but by more people than all the other Native U.S. languages combined.

I wanted to know what it would be like to visit such a strong and vibrant Native language community. Would it feel like walking into another country? Would English be abruptly replaced with a panoply of new and unfamiliar sounds? Or would it feel like one of the immigrant neighborhoods of New York City, where outsiders are greeted in English but discussed sotto voce in a different tongue? Navajo Nation, I knew, was my best opportunity to experience a Native language not yet on the verge of extinction. So I drove to Arizona, turning northwest at Flagstaff and heading up toward Tuba City and, ultimately, a town called Chinle.

If you're interested in tackling an indigenous American language on your own, Navajo is in many ways your best bet. The sheer size of the Navajo-speaking population has helped Navajo become one of the more abundantly studied and documented Native languages, and there are plenty of language materials to be found even if you're not fond of specialty stores or the dustier corners of libraries. That being said, it isn't exactly what I would call the most accessible of languages.

Given how monstrously subjective such an assessment is, I generally try to avoid labeling languages as "difficult" or "easy." One man's Chinese, after all, is another man's Pig Latin. But I feel comfortable saying that the vast majority of us would consider Navajo to be something of a challenge. I certainly know that when I'm reading about Navajo, I frequently feel like my brain is on sabbatical. Just now, for instance, I was going through a paper suggesting that Navajo transitive verbs encapsulate a sort of relativistic frame of reference. I really wanted to figure out what was going on. I was all set to quote Einstein and work into these pages some pointed commentary about translation and cross-cultural difference and maybe even the twin paradox. But try as I might, I couldn't make sense of it.

Fortunately, however, Navajo is such a fascinating language that even the easier stuff is really interesting. Take Navajo verbs, for instance. In English, we encode information about subject and aspect and tense in our verbs with inflection, and with some exceptions these inflections usually take the form of verb endings. The most obvious difference between the English and Navajo verb is that Navajo—and most other Athabaskan languages—primarily uses verbal *prefixes* to add or change information communicated by the verb.

And it's not just a matter of slapping on an -*ed* (or, in this case, an *ed*-) to let people know that things happened in the past. Navajo verb stems can take a number of different prefixes at once, prefixes that indicate not only subject, aspect, and mode but also object, type of object, and various adverbial functions. Linguists call this kind of morphology a slot-and-filler template, which basically means that you can treat Navajo verbs a bit like a row in a game of Connect Four: first you drop a verb stem in on the far right, and then you slide various prefixes into their respective columns until you have a complete verb.

To give you a better idea of how this works in practice, here's a standard Navajo verb template, as compiled by the linguists Robert Young and William Morgan:

Optional Morphemes														Required Morphemes		
Disjunct Prefixes							Conjunct Prefixes								Verb Stem	
o	Ia	Ib	Ic	Id	II	III	IV	V	VIa	VIb	VIc	VII	VIII	IX		X

Source: Young and Morgan, *The Navajo Language*, 37–38.

Now, every verb doesn't take every prefix, so this is something of an impossibly worst-case scenario. It is nevertheless still intimidatingly different from the verb tables we're used to seeing in our French, Spanish, or even Latin textbooks. But once you familiarize yourself with the ins and outs of each prefix, it's really not so bad.

The verb stem, as you can see, is slotted in on the right. Most stems are one syllable—the stem for "cry," for instance, is -*cha*. Information about the subject of the verb is found in positions III, V, and VIII. For the most basic subjects, you only have to worry about this last position— take the second-person subject pronoun *ni*, slot it in with "cry," and you get *nicha*, "you're crying."*

After that things get more interesting. Position V can be used for the so-called fourth-person prefix *ji-*. This indicates, broadly, a subject

---

* Some verbs require not just the stem in position X but also a mandatory prefix in positions I or VI. So while the verb stem for "play" is -*né*, you also have to include the prefix *na*-. "You're playing," then, is *naniné*.

other than the speaker or the hearer—you could potentially use this to distinguish between two characters in a story. (This serves a similar function to that of Crow's switch-reference markers.) Position III, meanwhile, is allotted for what's known as a distributive plural, used to indicate that the subject or direct object of the verb numbers three or more.

To complicate matters further, Navajo verbs don't really use what English-speakers think of as "tense." This isn't to say that Navajo verbs don't communicate similar information; they just go about it a bit differently. So if you look at position VII, you'll find information about the temporal flow of the action (for example, whether it's ongoing, habitual, or completed), but positions I, II, and VI can make even finer distinctions. The prefix *hi-* (position VIc) can be used, for instance, when three or more subjects act in succession as opposed to in a larger group—the difference between "the chickens flew the coop one by one" and "the chickens flew the coop all at once." The prefix *náá-* (position I) indicates repeated action of a very specific kind. Called a "semeliterative prefix," *náá-* can be translated as "another one" or "one more time."

My favorite feature of Navajo verbs deals not with prefixes but rather with stems. While many verbs—such as *cha*—have only one stem, some transitive verbs require a different stem based on the physical properties of the object they're acting upon. A rock, paper, and scissors, for example, could each require the use of a different verb stem. Young and Morgan (names you'll grow extremely familiar with if you have even the most cursory interest in the Navajo language) identified twelve categories of verb stem—known as "classificatory verb stems"—each loosely grouped around certain common physical qualities. There are groups of "solid roundish objects" such as apples, eggs, and balls; "mushy matter" such as lard, dough, and scrambled eggs; and "slender flexible objects," which include not only strings of beads and pieces of rope but constellations and the words in a language.

Of course, it's all fun and games until you actually have to learn to speak the language. The existence of classificatory verb stems in Navajo is surely cause for no small amount of angst for students of the language. And it's probably no less vexing for instructors. I know it has at the very least presented some interesting challenges for Rosetta Stone's Endangered Language Program, which was asked by Navajo Nation to assist in the creation of language-learning software. Danny Hieber, a content editor for Rosetta Stone, blogged about the difficulties involved with teaching the Navajo verb "to be sitting there" through pictures. Because the verb stem changes depending on the physical properties of the object in question—it is different for a man; it is different for a computer; it is different again for a newspaper—programmers were forced to include many more examples than they would have had to for a language such as English. Although I can't imagine that I would be able to figure out the rules of Navajo grammar under such conditions, I can freely admit that it's more accessible than flipping through a book by Young and Morgan.

Luckily for me, I don't have to worry about midterms or final grades, so instead of being bogged down by complexity I'm free to find in Navajo verb structure an intriguing emphasis on clarity and specificity. To be sure, an English-speaker can get across the same information communicated by a single Navajo verb thanks to our fine stock of adverbs. I can't help but wonder, though, if maybe precision is somehow more central to the Navajo language and if that's ultimately why I find the language so intimidating. Maybe I'm just more comfortable with ambiguity.

I thought about this frequently during my time with the Navajo, because as I learned more about the Navajo language and Navajo history, I began to draw some very unambiguous conclusions and then, almost immediately, to pull back from them. I like to think my skepticism with regard to simple explanations is born of common sense, but the truth is that vacillation is a convenient crutch for an insecure mind. It took a trip to Navajo Nation for me to realize that it would be a disservice to everyone involved to shy away from the straightforward—indeed, even obvious—analyses.

And so it was in Navajo Nation that for the first time I began to form some genuinely strong opinions about the state of language in America.

Extending into four states and spanning an area that, at over 27,000 square miles, is approximately the size of West Virginia, Navajo Nation is the country's largest expanse of Native-controlled land and home to nearly 170,000 of the tribe's 300,000-plus members. My home base on Navajo Nation was a town called Chinle, one of five agencies on the reservation. I stayed there for largely practical reasons: it's relatively centrally located, it's near a gas station, and it's home to the only Holiday Inn on Navajo land.* But I also came to Chinle because I wanted to take a tour of the town's lone attraction, Canyon de Chelly.

Inhabited for nearly 5,000 years, Canyon de Chelly—whose name comes from the Navajo word for canyon (*tséyi*) and does not rhyme with *jelly* but instead is pronounced more like the French *chez*—is home to the longest continuous human settlement anywhere on the Colorado Plateau. Today about eighty or so families still live in the canyon.

Most of the tourists who visit come to gawk not at the canyon's present inhabitants but at its past dwellings: the ruins of Anasazi settlements in the canyon date back nearly a thousand years. These pueblo dwellings were constructed along the walls of the canyon and, at times, seemingly into the walls of the canyon. The most famous are the White House ruins, a structure believed to have been built around 1060 CE and abandoned just over 200 years later. These ruins, two levels of tumbling adobe brick that were once covered with the white plaster that gave the ruins their name, probably once housed about twelve Anasazi families.

The White House ruins are located in the only part of the canyon that is open to the public. To see the rest of the canyon, as I did, you have to enlist the services of a Navajo guide. My guide, an easygoing Cowboys fan named Oscar, took me down to the canyon in a Jeep. As we drove over the canyon floor, he detailed the history of the canyon and the Anasazi and Navajo settlements in the area, pointing out ruins and petroglyphs by reflecting the sunlight with his rear-view mirror. Every so often we would spot in the distance one of the group tours run by another local hotel and would watch as red-faced tourists rumbled by in monstrous open-air buses that reminded me of nothing so much as a southwestern duck boat. Every time we saw one, Oscar chuckled to himself. He told me he called those tours "shake and bake."

Midway through the morning we stopped at the White House ruins and picked up some cold drinks. Sipping a Diet Coke, I soon lost myself in a dreamy contemplation of the polychromatic canyon walls and rock formations. And then I heard the words "Canyon del Muerto."

---

* I am brand-loyal in very few ways, but I happen to feel very strongly about the cinnamon rolls served at the Holiday Inn Express free breakfast.

"What did you just say?" I asked Oscar, no longer feeling quite so dreamy or contemplative.

"The Canyon del Muerto. It's just over there," he said, pointing. "That's where you find Massacre Cave."

My stomach dropped. I had a feeling I was no longer going to be able to spend my time stupidly admiring the view.

The Canyon del Muerto, I learned, was not nearly as grim as its moniker. It was named in 1882 when a Smithsonian expedition found a number of burial grounds in the area. For a moment I felt a stab of hope. Maybe for once I'd get through the day without stumbling across a profoundly depressing bit of history. Unfortunately, the story of Massacre Cave was not so benign. Worse, it turned out to be an ominous prologue to what is surely the darkest chapter in Navajo history.

By the eighteenth century Canyon de Chelly was already an important Navajo population center. The Spanish were also well established in the area by this point, but their settlements were typically located some distance from Navajo settlements, and at first interaction between the two groups was fairly limited. Which is not to say they weren't aware of one another. The first Spanish references to the Navajo date all the way back to 1626, when Fray Gerónimo de Zárate Salmerón, a Franciscan priest, first wrote of "the Apache Indians of Navaju."*

But perhaps not unexpectedly, as the years went by relations were not always cordial between the two groups. The Navajo would on occasion raid New Mexican settlements, and Spanish soldiers frequently captured Navajos and sold them into slavery. In 1805 these tensions boiled over. As part of a series of military operations designed to strengthen Spain's presence and discourage increasing Navajo aggression, a number of Spanish troops entered Canyon de Chelly, determined to make a show of force. To their surprise, however, the canyon was deserted. They were alone.

---

* The word *Navajo* itself appears to come from the Tewa word *navahú*, which means a "large area of cultivated fields." (The Spanish appreciated the agricultural skills of the Navajo from very early on—in a 1630 letter to the king of Spain, Fray Alonso de Benavides called the Navajos "very great farmers.") The Navajo, however, call themselves Diné, or "the People."

Or so they thought. As a matter of fact, a group of women, children, and elderly Navajo were hiding in a cave in an adjoining canyon. According to Navajo oral tradition, this group gave away their position when an old woman, thinking herself safely out of firing range, began shouting insults at the Spanish forces—in Spanish. The Spanish attacked, and though the Navajo attempted to hold them off, their defenses were no match for the Spanish guns. More than a hundred Navajo died. You can still see the marks the bullets left in the stone in what is today known as Massacre Cave.

But this wasn't the last time the Canyon de Chelly was visited by hostile forces.

At the time of the Civil War, Navajo lands were part of the New Mexico and Utah territories, and Canyon de Chelly had become known as something of a Navajo stronghold. General Edward Canby, the regional military commander, was convinced that the only way to control the Navajo and put an end to hostilities was to forcibly remove them from their traditional lands. In 1862, Canby handed over his command and his convictions to a general named James H. Carleton, a man who would become one of the most—if not *the* most—reviled figures in the history of the Navajo people.

Carleton's philosophy toward indigenous peoples was fairly representative of American thinking at the time: he advocated the "civilization" of the Navajo. He believed that once the Navajo were exposed to English and Christianity and separated from their traditional culture they would abandon any raiding campaigns and set aside their differences. "The old Indians will die off and carry with them the latent longings for murder and robbing," he wrote. "The young ones will take their places without these longings: and thus, little by little, they will become a happy and contented people."

He also believed there was gold to be found in the area. But I'm sure that never factored into his thinking.

Carleton eventually decided to relocate the Navajo about 300 miles east to a new reservation in a place called Bosque Redondo. Despite being advised that Bosque Redondo was remote and difficult to supply and, moreover, that the Pecos River was prone to flooding and too alkaline to be used for drinking or irrigation, Carleton requested congressional authorization to build a fort here. Around this fort—which was named Fort Sumner—he established a forty-square-mile reservation.

Unsurprisingly, the Navajo were reluctant to move. Carleton needed a new strategy. "The Navajo Indians have got to be whipped," Carleton explained in an 1863 letter. He ordered Colonel Kit Carson, a famous frontiersman, to find a way to force the Navajo to Bosque Redondo. Carson's men burned fields, chopped down orchards, and confiscated livestock and food. But even this was not enough to force the Navajo to Bosque Redondo. Instead, many retreated to Canyon de Chelly.

And so in early 1864 Carson and his men advanced on Canyon de Chelly, the Navajo's last stronghold. Carson ordered the complete destruction of any settlements in the canyon.*

It was this attack—in concert with Carson's promise not to harm anyone who surrendered—that finally persuaded most of the Navajo to turn themselves in. You could say, then, that it was in Canyon de Chelly that the Long Walk of the Navajo officially began.

Between 1863 and 1866, 9,000 Navajo and Mescalero Apache were relocated to Bosque Redondo; roughly a third died during the walk and confinement. At Fort Sumner, the Navajo found barren land and clueless agents. There weren't enough blankets, firewood, or food. Disease ran rampant, and Comanche forces attacked regularly. To this day the Navajo call this place Hwéeldi—"place of suffering."

In 1868 a treaty was finally negotiated that allowed the Navajo to return to their traditional homelands. This treaty—the Treaty of Bosque Redondo—ended hostilities between the groups, freed the Navajo from their captivity at Fort Sumner, and established the boundaries of the new Navajo Indian Reservation.† But though the experiment at Bosque

---

* It is not entirely clear how enthusiastically Carson followed Carleton's orders. Carson had ignored Carleton's commands in the past, and the first time Carleton had asked Carson to go after the Navajo, Carson had tried to resign. Even so, reports of Carson's comparatively humane treatment of his prisoners hardly absolve him of his part in the campaign.

† This original reservation consisted of about 5,200 square miles, but since then it has been gradually expanded by executive order and congressional act. Navajo efforts to reclaim the bulk of their traditional lands represent the most successful such Native campaign in U.S. history.

Redondo was over, General Carleton wouldn't be the last government official to try to force cultural assimilation. The series of hardships to be visited upon the Navajo by the U.S. government was just beginning. The next time, however, the government would target not only the Navajo people but also the Navajo language.

I had known when I arrived in Chinle that there were a few places I wanted to go. I knew I'd go to Canyon de Chelly and swing by tribal headquarters in Window Rock. I knew I'd go to the interactive museum in Tuba City and to Monument Valley and the Hubbell Trading Post in Ganado. What I didn't expect was to spend so much time looking at and learning about schools. But it is in the Navajo schools of past and present that the recent history of the language is to be found.

The history of Navajo schools begins after the Civil War, when President Ulysses S. Grant appointed "peace commissioners" to bring an end to the Indian Wars. This 1868 report provides a fairly detailed view of the sorts of ideas these commissioners came up with:

> Naturally the Indian has many noble qualities. He is the very embodiment of courage. Indeed, at times he seems insensible of fear. If he is cruel and revengeful, it is because he is outlawed and his companion is the wild beast. Let civilized man be his companion, and the association warms into life virtues of the rarest worth. Civilization has driven him back from the home he loved; it has often tortured and killed him, but it never could make him a slave. As we have had so little respect for those we did enslave, to be consistent, this element of Indian character should challenge some admiration. . . . Through sameness of language is produced sameness of sentiment and thought; customs and habits are moulded and assimilated in the same way, and thus in process of time the differences producing trouble would have been gradually obliterated. . . . In the difference of language to-day lies two-thirds of our trouble.

Such statements seem particularly preposterous in light of the fact that, just a few years earlier, the country had been in the grip of a vicious war fought between two groups that spoke the same language. Nevertheless, the government was set on its course. The Indian would be "educated."

That this was a strategy born of no small amount of self-interest is obvious. The schools that the government established for the Navajo and other Native children were not pure acts of charity or social responsibility. The need to civilize the country's Native population was, rather, treated as an issue of national security. Educational matters even factored into diplomatic negotiations. In the Treaty of Bosque Redondo, for instance, the government extracted a promise from the Navajo that for the next ten years they would send their children to reservation day schools built and run by the government.

These schools were just one part of the educational reform efforts undertaken by the Bureau of Indian Affairs (BIA). The U.S. government also built dozens of boarding schools both on and off reservation land to help advance their general strategy of assimilation. The first of these Indian boarding schools, the Carlisle Indian Industrial School, opened in Pennsylvania in 1879. It was founded by Captain Richard Henry Pratt, the man who famously said, "A great general has said that the only good Indian is a dead one, and that high sanction of his destruction has been an enormous factor in promoting Indian massacres. In a sense, I agree with the sentiment, but only in this: that all the Indian there is in the race should be dead. Kill the Indian in him, and save the man."

Many Native families were understandably hesitant about sending their children away, but the government brooked very little opposition. If families were unwilling to send their children voluntarily, then officials found ways to encourage compliance. In 1883, for instance, the government threatened to withhold rations from any Crow families who refused to send their children to school. The next year, nineteen Hopi men were sent to Alcatraz for the same infraction. In some instances the authorities simply ignored the parents' wishes and forcibly removed the children from their homes.

Once they arrived at these boarding schools, willingly or no, the children typically had their hair cut and their clothing taken away. They were given uniforms and new names and were strictly forbidden to speak languages other than English.* Anyone caught "speaking Indian" was punished—sometimes with a slap on the wrist, sometimes with a stick to the mouth. Some students suffered more severe punishments such as having their mouths washed out with soap or being made to stand with arms outstretched and a heavy dictionary in each hand. An early-twentieth-century BIA teacher named Albert Kneale summed up the pedagogical philosophy neatly: "Children were taught to despise every custom of their forefathers, including religion, language, songs, dress, ideas, methods of living."

Manuelito, a Navajo leader during the time of the Long Walk and the Navajos' incarceration at Bosque Redondo, made a famous statement I came across again and again while I was in Navajo country, a statement that drives home just how profound a betrayal these boarding schools represent. "My grandchild," said Manuelito, "the whites have many things which we Navajos need, but we cannot get them. It is as though the whites were in a grassy canyon and there they have wagons, plows, and plenty of food. We Navajos are up on the dry mesa. We can hear them talking but we cannot get to them. My grandchild, education is our ladder. Tell our people to take it."

In 1882 Manuelito sent his two sons to Carlisle Indian School. They both fell ill—one at school, the other as soon as he returned home for a visit—and died.

In the midst of all this misfortune, there were some small signs that education might one day fulfill Manuelito's vision. One of the first of these came in the form of a school founded in 1902 by Katharine Drexel and the Sisters of the Blessed Sacrament.† Located not far from the center of tribal government at Window Rock, St. Michael Indian School is to this day the only Catholic school in Navajo Nation.

---

* Native-language instruction was banned in all government schools from 1800 until 1888. And between 1888 and 1934, Native languages were permissible only in Bible study.

† Katharine Drexel was the niece of the founder of Drexel University in Philadelphia and herself founded Xavier University of Louisiana. She was sainted by Pope John Paul II in 2000.

I visited the town of St. Michaels on a crisp, sunny day in early August. The museum, a former trading post and the first building to be used by the mission, is a small stone structure set apart from the sprawling complex that makes up the convent and school. As I walked up I saw that they were refinishing some of the woodwork on the outside of the building, and I stood frozen in place for several long minutes, trying to decide just how much of an inconvenience I might be causing for the man in charge of the repairs. When he saw me, frozen in place, he gave me a strange look and gestured me inside. I couldn't say if he was wondering why I was standing so still or why I was there in the first place.

As soon as I walked in, it was clear to me that St. Michael's museum is not the most popular attraction in Navajoland. There were two women keeping watch over the exhibits, a smiling middle-aged woman and an extremely quiet older woman I suspected was her mother. While I explored the museum, they sat together and listened to a Navajo-language broadcast on the radio.

Although the land for St. Michael was purchased by the Sisters of the Blessed Sacrament in 1895, it was unused until October 1898, when three Franciscan friars arrived to establish a mission. They moved into what is now the museum and, realizing that their work would be hindered and not helped by an ignorance of the local language, quickly applied themselves to the compilation of an English-Navajo dictionary. They began simply, offering food and coffee to visitors in return for help naming nearby objects. When they had exhausted their proximate vocabulary, they pulled out a Montgomery Ward catalog in order to ask after a wider variety of words. Slowly but surely, they were able to create a small dictionary. This handwritten volume is kept in one of the museum's glass cases, and as I looked at it that afternoon I marveled that something so small and ordinary could once have represented a momentous shift in outside attitudes toward the Navajo language.

The dictionary was far from the friars' only contribution to their adopted community. Father Bernard Haile developed the first Navajo orthography, published a number of linguistic materials, and was considered to speak so well that "he might have been more Navajo than Anglo." Father Marcellus Troester conducted the first census of the

Navajo people. The photographs of Father Simeon Schwemberger provide an unparalleled look into the Navajo traditions of the early twentieth century. And Father Anselm Weber tasked himself with extensive surveys of Navajo territory, personally petitioning the U.S. government for the return of the tribe's traditional lands. His efforts helped lead to the return to the Navajo people of nearly 1.5 million acres of land.

In this way, the mission was over time able to secure the trust and assistance of its neighbors. Similarly, the St. Michael Indian School went a long way toward improving Navajo opinion of outside educators.

St. Michael could only do so much, however. Years later the community was still faced with high dropout rates and levels of illiteracy and was still struggling to find an education system that would work with and not against its culture. At this point there were three kinds of schools in Navajo country. There was the Washingdoon Bi'ólta' ("Washington's school"—a BIA school administered by the federal government) and there was the Beligaana Bi'ólta' ("little white man's school"—a public school administered by the local school district). Then there was the Eeneishoodi Bi'ólta' ("the school of those who drag their clothes"—a missionary school). Eventually the Navajo decided they needed a fourth kind of school: a Diné Bi'ólta'—a Navajo school.

The first of these schools was established in 1966 in Rough Rock, Arizona, an isolated town about thirty miles from Chinle. Rough Rock Demonstration School was the first BIA school in the country to be operated by American Indians, and it utilized both Navajo and English for classroom instruction. It was a revolutionary idea. More important, it was the start of a trend.

Today Navajo Nation is a leader in educational innovation among Native communities. It is home to schools such as Tséhootsooí Diné Bi'ólta', a unified Window Rock immersion program where students in grades K–8 receive at least half of their instruction in Navajo. Navajo Head Start, meanwhile, provides Navajo-language instruction for low-income preschoolers. And Diné College, with an impressive main campus at Tsaile and seven additional sites throughout the reservation, is the largest—not to mention the oldest—tribal college in the country.

In Canyon de Chelly I had seen where the Navajo had been relieved of the power to control their own destiny. But in St. Michaels I saw where they began to take it back.

The next day, feeling a bit weary of language politics, I decided to play tourist. I tossed my grammars and papers in a corner of my hotel room and headed north, unencumbered, toward Kayenta, the Utah border, and Monument Valley, the most popular attraction in Navajo Nation.

The Navajo call Monument Valley Tsé Bii' Ndzisgaii, "Valley of the Rocks"—which is an incredibly accurate yet astoundingly insufficient name for a 90,000-acre expanse of buttes, mesas, and cinematic vistas. Though the tribe has recently finished construction on a new hotel and visitor center, the park itself is refreshingly free of tourist claptrap. The only way you can identify the road down into the valley is by the fact that the rocks on the road are slightly smaller than the rocks not on the road.

From what I could tell, most visitors opt to take a guided tour through the valley. This, frankly, seems sensible. It's rough going down in the valley, and not everyone is as devil-may-care with their cars as I am— and even I thought twice about it. As I looked down into the valley and considered just how much of a difference there is between all-wheel drive and four-wheel drive, I began to have visions of *Into the Wild*. I mean, the way down was like 75 percent boulders on a 50 percent grade. There was, I realized, a very real chance that my trustworthy little Subaru might go in and never be able to get out.

That's when I saw that a caravan of tumbledown RVs had decided to brave the trail in front of me. I'd noticed throughout my time in the Southwest that an extremely popular mode of transportation was the rental RV, easily identifiable by its giant 1800-RV4RENT logo and the shambling incompetence with which it was driven. As I watched the RVs descend into the valley, it became rapidly clear to me that under no circumstances should an RV be driven in Monument Valley. The handling, the size, the questionable structural integrity—on all counts it is singularly unsuited to the terrain. You might as well try to climb a mountain in five-inch heels that are five sizes too big.

But no one had stopped them from going in. And as I watched, astonished, nothing was able to stop them from coming out. It wasn't pretty, but they managed, one after the other, to grind their way up out of the valley. I felt a little ashamed I'd questioned my own car's ability to do the same. So I put my Subaru into gear and started—gingerly— down the trail.

Images of Monument Valley have been featured in dozens of TV shows and movies, from *Stagecoach* to *Forrest Gump* to *MacGyver*, so even my first visit to the valley inspired more than a slight sense of déjà vu. The most iconic formations are a pair of majestic sandstone buttes that have been weathered down in mirror image to resemble a pair of mittens. But everywhere I looked—every sweep of reddened stone, variegated and luminous in the desert sun—felt familiar. In Monument Valley it was as if I'd just fulfilled a wish I didn't even know I'd had.

I immediately went to work filling my camera's memory card. For a shitty photographer with delusions of grandeur, Monument Valley is a dream—you can point and shoot at anything and get something that looks like a postcard. But even in the presence of such astonishing natural beauty, a large part of my mind was still back in Chinle.

I was enjoying my time in Navajo Nation, but I didn't particularly take to Chinle, and it wasn't until I went to Monument Valley that I realized why. Though Canyon de Chelly manages, at times, to approach the sort of natural incandescence of Monument Valley, the rest of Chinle feels like it might as well be in another world, a world made up of an unprepossessing accumulation of hotels, gas stations, and fast-food restaurants. Chinle is almost wholly lacking in what I would call small-town charm; even its non-commercial structures have a decidedly institutional feel. If some towns have a hum of activity, Chinle has a muted rattle of despair.

I'm sure you could argue that my perceptions were colored by my research, that my opinions of Chinle are just a reflection of my growing awareness of the role the U.S. government played in the diminution of Native-language populations. But I didn't feel this way anywhere else in Navajo Nation—my glorious day in Monument Valley reminded me of that. On the contrary, many of my expeditions to towns and sites across the area underscored for me the resilience of the Navajo people. The Navajo have, after all, fought for over a century against government restrictions and inequity, and they have done so as successfully as any other Native group in the country. Their culture hasn't faded into the background; there are Navajo newspapers, Navajo radio stations, Navajo museums, and Navajo schools. The Navajo are emphatically not a people who have been given, either now or in the past, to resignation or capitulation.

When you visit Navajo Nation, then, it's difficult to believe that its language could be in peril. As in nearly every part of the country, you encounter very few non-English-speakers here—the only one I met was the old woman at the St. Michaels museum. Nevertheless, the Navajo language has a very public presence, whether you're taking a tour of Navajo schools or just taking in the usual sights. You would be forgiven for thinking the Navajo language is secure. Though the Crow language made itself known to me only when I went in search of it, here in Navajo Nation the language practically leapt up to beg my attention. I heard Navajo at gas stations and in restaurants; I saw it on signs, T-shirts, and newspapers. KTTN 660, the only radio station I was able to pick up with any reliability, broadcast in both English and Navajo. And everyone I met spoke at least a little Navajo and was happy to try to teach me a few words. They were typically even gracious enough to try to keep a straight face when confronted with my hopeless pronunciation.

But Chinle—grim, down-on-its-luck Chinle—is the kind of place that can wear down even the most determined optimist. As I am typically able to manage only the most mild optimism even on my best days, I found myself wondering if all the good intentions and cultural pride in the world would be enough to overcome the lingering damage of government policies and the not-inconsequential challenges of reservation life. Would language really be a priority for people who were struggling to make ends meet? Even more, was it possible to invest a language with new vitality and significance after decades of oppression and disdain? It seemed to me a monumental task even under the best of circumstances.

As it turns out, my fears were not unfounded. The Navajo are, in fact, currently in the midst of a rapid and massive language shift. A 1990 study found that fully half of Head Start children were monolingual English-speakers—this just twenty years after 90 percent of Navajo children were reporting no preschool experience with English. A survey by the Window Rock school district found that the proportion of kindergartners fluent in Navajo dropped from 89 percent in 1979 to 3 percent in 1989. Deborah House, an instructor at Diné College and the author of *Language Shift Among the Navajos: Identity Politics and Cultural Continuity*, reports that at the college "the use of the Navajo language is otherwise not particularly marked. It is much more common among the staff members—janitors, maintenance and cafeteria workers, and secretaries. Navajo-speaking faculty and administrators rarely use the language of school unless they wish to signal solidarity or to mark an event as Navajo; English is by far the norm."

Language instruction must be considered partially to blame for this, though not necessarily in the ways you might think. While the curriculum at the early Indian boarding schools was ultimately designed to eradicate Native languages, they were anything but immediately effective. For one thing, many Navajo were kept out of school. For another, the schools were understaffed and underfunded, surely one of the few instances in history when substandard schools might actually have had some side benefits. The boarding schools did, however, inflict extensive psychological trauma, trauma that led many Navajo to associate their native language with punishment, humiliation, and disgrace. Many of these students have elected not to teach their children the language in order to spare them a similar fate.

The current generation has a new set of psychological challenges. In a series of interviews with Navajo teenagers, sociologist Tiffany Lee found that the source of language-related shame has shifted. "Interestingly, absent from the students' counter-narratives were direct expressions of shame for their heritage language," she writes. "Instead, students revealed expressions of embarrassment of their own limited Native-language ability, not necessarily embarrassment or shame with the language itself." This nevertheless reinforces the cycle of language deterioration as younger Navajo avoid using their language just as previous generations did, albeit for a different reason.

Meanwhile, the high visibility of Navajo-language instruction in schools and the extensive publicity surrounding language efforts conspires to convince parents that they needn't bear the burden of passing the language on at home. The schools are there to shoulder the instruction; public rhetoric implies the problem is well in hand.

Though the Navajo have an impressive array of language programs in place in their schools, despite their best efforts only 10 percent of Navajo pupils are currently receiving language instruction, and then largely in supplemental programs. Even standout programs have not been able to guarantee long-term and widespread success. In spite of its early achievements, Rough Rock faced heavy criticism and significant challenges both inside and outside the community, and its model has not been widely replicated.

But even if the Navajo had 100 percent enrollment in programs like Rough Rock, it's not clear to me that their language would be invulnerable. It can't be ignored that the deterioration of the Navajo-speaking population is due in no small part to the economic advantages afforded by speaking English, advantages that intensified when government policies incapacitated the Navajo economy.* English is, as House notes, "the language associated with access to power, status, respect, prestige, and economic benefits in both professional and private life." Though the government may no longer pursue an active policy of assimilation through education, today it has an even more powerful tool at its disposal. By contributing to the economic hardships that exist today on Navajo and other reservations, the government can ensure that for Native men and women throughout the country, English isn't a choice—it's an obligation.

---

* I refer particularly to the forced livestock reductions of the 1930s and 1940s. While some of these policies may have been well intentioned, their implementation was disastrous.

CHAPTER THREE

Washington: Lushootseed, Quileute, Makah

Now that I've told you about Native languages that are living, it's only natural, I think, to tell you something about Native languages that are dying.

When I first became interested in the subject of American languages, I knew that many of the languages I would eventually investigate would be in decline. This was a reasonable assumption given that I was interested first and foremost in understanding the mechanism of that decline. But I was initially so focused on the genesis of language loss that I neglected to consider the consequences. It didn't occur to me that there might be a difference between the loss of a dispersed population and the loss of the core population. If an American community of French-speakers switches over to English, there are still 110 million or so French-speakers worldwide. When indigenous American languages lose their last American speakers, however, they cease to exist as mother tongues.

It is this latter type of language loss—which I should call, more accurately, language death—that brought me to the Pacific Northwest.

I chose to travel to Washington because with twenty-nine federally recognized Indian tribes and confederations, the state is home to an extremely wide variety of Native peoples and is generally a smart pick for anyone interested in learning more about Native culture. But even more important, it is still home to a handful of Native languages. And all of them are poised on the very brink of extinction.

Washington is a place of impressive natural splendor no matter when you go or how you get there. But if you go at the right time and come from the right direction, if you pick the perfect environmental and geographic context, the Pacific Northwest isn't just a treat for the eyes—it's practically a balm for the soul.

I approached from the southeast—driving out of Nevada into Idaho, up through Oregon and west toward Puget Sound—on a day that started out so hot and dry I could feel the liquid leaching from my lungs. Had I been willing to backtrack, I could have stuck to interstate travel, but I was tired of seeing the same truck stops and travel plazas, so I decided to take a more direct route up through the Independence Mountains along a series of two-lane state highways.

This took me through the Duck Valley Indian Reservation, which straddles the border between Idaho and Nevada. A fair amount of the land on this reservation serves as an open cattle range, and the road is thoroughly marked to make sure motorists are aware of this fact. Outside of Yellowstone and a few deer-clogged parts of Missouri, I'd never driven through an area where animals strayed with any regularity onto the road, so I took these warnings with a grain of salt. I figured "Caution: Open Range" was more of a suggestion, like *So maybe keep an eye out just in case, but honestly, this is a really big place. And it's not like there's much grass for the cows to eat on the highway. So you probably don't have to worry. Anyway, they're just cows, right?*

I reconsidered my stance soon enough. As the car came around a curve, I slammed on my brakes, my front bumper coming to a stop about eighteen inches from the masticating jaw of a prodigious steer. I blanched; I like to imagine he sneered. Over the next thirty minutes I navigated around dozens of cattle, most of whom serenely positioned themselves in such a way as to cause maximum inconvenience. It was their road, they seemed to be saying. I was just passing through—very, very slowly.

Then, just as my initial adrenaline spike began to level off, I came to the bugs.

From a distance it looked like a thin layer of ochre had been scattered across the highway. As I got closer, though, I noticed the dust was moving. And then I was hit with the smell. Though I may be able to identify all manner of cockroaches, water bugs, and bedbugs, outside New York I'm at a bit of an entomological loss. So I can't tell you if they were locusts or cicadas or grasshoppers or what. All I know is this: they swarmed, they jumped, and they smelled like an unholy mixture of vomit, fecal matter, and monosodium glutamate.

At first it wasn't too bad, but as I drove through bug slick after bug slick, rolling with a molten crunch over thousands of insects, the stench crept in and took up residence inside my ventilation system. I shut off the air-conditioning and closed the vents, a last resort on a 90-plus-degree day, but the heat made things worse. I found a bottle of Febreze and desperately sprayed it everywhere I could. When that had no effect, I sprayed it again at my shirt, my hair, and my face. But in the end, all I could do was get through the area as quickly as possible. Then I pulled over to the side of the road and threw up.

I washed the car three times in Boise, but it would be weeks before the smell completely disappeared. As I made my way north, however, as ragged hills yielded to rolling fields and then, at last, to an almost otherworldly viridescence, I found that I minded the smell less and less.

It probably also didn't hurt that I was finally able to open my windows.

Regardless, I was happy to be heading to Washington. At that point I'd been on the road for more than a month straight, and I was sick of it. I was sick of the long hours, the lumpy beds, and the greasy food. The cattle and the bugs had been the questionably flavored icing on the really smelly cake. I wanted nothing more than a cool breeze, a bit of rain, and the hospitality of my yoga-loving, healthy-eating friends in Tacoma. Only then, I decided, would I even start to think about language again.

As it turned out, though, I started thinking about language even before I arrived in Tacoma.

The first time I visited the Pacific Northwest I was five years old. My parents had been invited to some sort of mysterious economists' gathering in China, and I was on my way to Vancouver to spend the summer with family. My uncle Gary drove down and picked me up in Washington state, and a few minutes into the trip I chirped, "Mount Rainier!"

Gary looked around in confusion. As far as he could tell, I couldn't see Mount Rainier from where I was sitting. But, he noticed, we had just passed a sign that *read* Mount Rainier. *No*, he thought, *she's too little to be reading. Jim probably just thought it would be funny if he taught his daughter a few local names and had her play a little joke on Uncle Gary*. He drove on.

As I continued to call out names—"Sunnydale!" "Pacific Highway!" "Kingdome!"—my uncle was increasingly impressed. Not because he thought I was figuring any of it out on my own, but because with each new passing recitation, what he was sure was a prank became a more elaborate one. (In all fairness, this does sound like something my father would have done.)

But then I said something that convinced him otherwise: "Puyallup!" And that's how my uncle realized that I could read.

Or so the story goes. I have absolutely no memory of this, of course. I can confirm that I was obnoxious and precocious, and to this day I retain a moderately irritating habit of reading road signs and billboards aloud. So I don't doubt that some version of these events occurred. But there's no way I sounded out Puyallup. I know this because twenty-three years later I had to be taught how to pronounce it.

Puyallup, a city of about 35,000, is located ten miles or so southeast of Tacoma. By the time I started seeing signs for Puyallup, I'd been on the road for far too many hours, and my brain was laboring under the strain of not one but two separate stops at McDonald's. Unsurprisingly, I initially supposed what must be the worst of all possible pronunciations: "poo-yall-UP," a vague threat, certainly digestive, possibly southern, and decidedly unpleasant. In my defense, however, that's kind of how it's spelled.

That night my friends in Tacoma were in the process of telling me about their new neighbors when all of a sudden I heard a few unintelligible syllables.

"What did you just say?" I asked.

"Pyoo-AL-up?" my friend said.

"Yes . . . that."

"It's a city not too far from here," she told me. "Took me weeks to figure out how to pronounce it. I didn't quite feel like a local until I could."

"So it's like the Houston Street of the Pacific Northwest?"

"Something like that, yes."

I paused, considering. "Can you say it again? And slowly."

No matter how you say it, Puyallup is something of an enigma. In a 1921 issue of the *Washington Historical Quarterly*, Edmond S. Meany, as part of a series on Washington place names, cites two possible translations of the word *Puyallup*. The first—"shadow from the dense shade of the forest"—dates back to an 1880 address by Elwood Evans, an early Washington politician and historian.

The second translation first appeared on June 30, 1916, when the *Tacoma News* published the interpretation of Henry Sicade, a prominent member of the Puyallup Indian Council, the grandnephew of a chief of the Nisqually, and the grandson of a chief of the Puyallup. (Or, as the paper put it, an "educated Indian.") He suggested that the word Puyallup came from *pough*, meaning "generous," and *allup*, meaning "people."

I found evidence of a third translation in, oddly enough, the *Chicago Daily Tribune*. On December 18, 1955, the paper ran an article—"Indians Named Puyallup, and This Is Why!"—that related the following: "Local wits enjoy telling gullible strangers about the city's name. They say it came from the Indians who put raw oysters on the back of their tongues and then said the word, 'Puyallup.' This guaranteed the oyster going down on the first try." I am to this day unclear as to how that qualifies as wit.

As you might expect, the only translation to gain popular traction is the second: "generous people." This is, at least, the translation I found scattered throughout travel guides, newspaper articles, and the Internet, where it is often asserted with such confidence that I almost overlooked the near-complete absence of supporting evidence.

The study of language is a particularly messy endeavor, even for a social science. The discipline is on one level intensely abstruse and on another almost universally approachable. Which is to say that you don't have to be an expert in linguistics to be an expert in language—even if it's only one language. There are, then, a great many people who feel perfectly justified in passing along their own language-related trivia and opinion as if it were hard, scientific fact.*

Consequently, I think a great many of us have a hard time separating linguistic fact and fiction, so overwhelmed is any legitimate information by grammatical flimflam and etymological sham. I know for my part I've been taken in over the years by more than one tall tale. I was three years into my study of Chinese before I realized that the word for "crisis" did not, in fact, also mean "opportunity." Only recently did I discover that my reflexive urge to correct "10 items or less" is not at all borne out by historical usage. And I'm sure that in the years to come I'll find a legion of other ways in which I've allowed myself to be swindled.

I've tried my best, however, to develop a reliable method for snoping out what's what, and as I've done so I've begun to better understand the conditions that allow for the widespread dissemination of linguistic fraud. The obscurity of a language is the first of these conditions; it's hard to disprove a claim in the absence of actual fact. But just as important is what I like to think of as the cocktail party quotient: the more likely a story is to serve as entertaining small talk, the more likely it will be repeated, regardless of its accuracy. Over the years, these two factors have ensured that the languages of Native America have been particularly fertile grounds for an astonishing amount of made-up shit.

The Puyallup originally spoke a dialect of language called Lushootseed (known variously as Puget Salish, Whulshootseed Salish, or Skagit-Nisqually), which is part of the larger Salishan language family. Although Salishan languages were at one point spoken throughout the Pacific Northwest—in Washington, Oregon, British Columbia, Idaho, and even parts of Montana—the population of Salishan-speakers is today precariously low, and most Salishan languages in the United States and Canada are nearing extinction. Most estimates of the Lushootseed-speaking population are given not in triple digits or even in double digits, but rather in handfuls.

The number of people looking to learn Salishan languages is similarly small, which means the demand for language-learning materials is com-

---

* Not that I would know anything about this.

paratively low. And since most materials tend to be produced not for a general audience but for an academic one, if you're not a professional linguist or dedicated amateur, Salishan language resources are few and far between—not to mention largely incomprehensible. You certainly can't turn to Google Translate in a pinch.

After some digging, however, I was able to get my hands on some basic Lushootseed reference materials, including a dictionary and a collection of educational newsletters published by the Puyallup Tribal Language Program. I was less than surprised to discover that despite its overwhelming and persistent popularity, "generous people" might not be the only correct translation of *Puyallup*. Or even *a* correct translation.

I got lucky with the newsletters. Written to encourage interest in the language among schoolchildren, each month's edition typically consists of a few basic phrases, a short article of some local interest, and a word search. A few issues, however, also parse important vocabulary, providing information on each of the word's constituent parts. It was here that I found a decidedly mundane translation of *Puyallup*.

puy	-al	-əp
curve or bend	be located at	bottom

No other information was provided. So I was left with two possibilities, either "bend at the bottom" or "at the bottom of the bend." A quick look at a map helped clarify matters: Puyallup is, as you might be able to predict, located just south of a bend in a river. Based on this translation, I could see how Puyallup might originally have been a simple place name with the basic, geographically descriptive meaning "at the bottom of the bend of the river." Later, the name could then have been adopted for the Indian tribe that historically inhabited the area, the dialect spoken by said tribe, and the river that, however elliptically, gave the location its name. This made sense to me. A definition of "generous people" would be plausible only if the sequence of attribution were reversed—if *Puyallup* first served as the name of the people and then was used as the name of the place.

The traditional name of the Puyallup Indians, however, is not Puyallup but S'Puyalupubsh. Although the tribe translates this word as "generous

and welcoming behavior to all people (friends and strangers) who enter
our lands," their language program suggests otherwise:

s-	puy	-al	-əp	-abš
(nominalizer)	curve or bend	be located at	bottom	people of

In other words, the traditional name for the Puyallup Indians was "people
of the place at the bottom of the river bend"—or, even more simply,
"people of Puyallup."

I was reassured by the unassuming nature of the translation. But just
to be sure, I turned to the Lushootseed dictionary, the result of years of
collaboration between the distinguished if relatively little-known linguist Thomas Hess and Vi Hilbert, an elder of the Lushootseed-speaking
Upper Skagit tribe. Here, I confirmed the geographical reading. I looked
up *Puyallup* and found myself redirected to *puy*—"curve, bend." A note
went on to explain the meaning of *S'Puyalupubsh* in the driest of fash-
ions: "They are called the people of the bend because their river is full
of bends."

This is hardly the stuff of cocktail-party banter. Which is exactly
why I believe it.

It seems likely that "generous people" is a folk etymology of very
long standing, probably since even before 1916. But it's worth pointing
out that Henry Sicade, the source of this translation, did dedicate his
life's work to education. He doesn't seem like the kind of guy who'd try
to pull a person's leg just for the sake of leg-pulling. Moreover, his translation was plausible enough to gain widespread credence within the
Lushootseed-speaking community. And the *-allup* of *Puyallup* could
easily be linked to *alap*, which has the rough meaning of "you folks."*
Though I never did find a *puy*-type word that might mean something

---

* Technically, Hess and Hilbert classify *alap* as a second-person-plural clitic. A clitic,
very broadly, is a morpheme that is more independent than an affix but less independent than a stand-alone word. Although a clitic has independent meaning, it's usually
mushed up with another word. The *'m* in *I'm* or the *'s* in *she's* would be two such
examples.

like "generous," I don't doubt one exists provided you're willing to accept a vague enough relationship.

The confusion surrounding Puyallup puts me in mind of Lake Chaubunagungamaug in Webster, Massachusetts. The lake gained some degree of notoriety on account of its full name, which is acknowledged as the longest place name in the United States: Chargoggagoggmanchauggagoggchaubunagungamaugg. Its renown was augmented by its widely asserted translation: "You fish on your side; I fish on my side; nobody fishes in the middle."

In a 1990 letter to the editor published in the *New York Times*, this translation was roundly dismissed by Ives Goddard, one of the foremost experts in Algonquin languages and curator emeritus in the Department of Anthropology at the National Museum of Natural History. Not only was the forty-five-letter name partly the result of a cartographic error, he wrote, but the translation itself was also the fanciful elaboration of a newspaperman named Lawrence J. Harvey. (In his defense, Harvey made no secret of his fabrication.) Goddard acknowledged that Nipmuck, the language that gave us Chabunagungamaug, is "very poorly known," but he nevertheless felt confident in suggesting that a more accurate definition of the name might be something like "lake divided by islands."

So we have on one hand the careful, considered opinion of a highly respected linguist. His proposed translation is straightforward and descriptive, sensible characteristics considering the fact that the lake itself probably predated a need for territorial negotiation. On the other hand, we have a reporter with no linguistic credentials who freely admitted that he made the thing up. But his version is way more fun. Guess which one shows up most frequently?

Linguistic data very rarely factor into plausibility when it comes to popular translations of words from indigenous American languages—or any languages at all, for that matter. It's understandable. Quirky, memorable stories are more fun. Who wants to go digging for a more boring truth? I can't help but think, however, that languages such as Lushootseed, Nipmuck, and Mi'kmaq are particularly prone to willful misunderstandings for reasons beyond their mistake-masking obscurity.

Consider, for instance, the pervasive myth of the however-many

Eskimo words for "snow."* It's clear that one reason this fiction has proven to be so irresistible is that it makes for good copy. But I wonder if it would have been quite so pervasive if it didn't also dovetail with the idea that Native peoples have a unique and profound relationship to nature. I wonder if Lake Chaubunagungamaug would be such a novelty if not for the cliché that a single word in an Indian language corresponds with a prolonged stream of English. I wonder if linguistic fallacy reveals as much about the perception of the culture of the language as it does about the language itself.

In his letter, Ives Goddard specifically condemned "supposed literal translations that encourage the stereotype that unwritten languages can only use simple-minded logic and elaborate explanations to communicate even fairly simple ideas." His plea seems to have fallen largely on deaf ears. Fourteen years later, the very same paper published a new translation of the lake's name, courtesy of Paul Macek, a local historian: "English knifemen and Nipmuck Indians at the boundary or neutral fishing place." Today, as far as I can Google, incidence of Macek's definition already far outstrips Goddard's.

This is an aspect of language death I hadn't previously considered. It isn't just the language that is lost but also control of the linguistic narrative. This isn't to say that misconceptions about widely spoken languages never crop up. And linguists have as little luck turning the tide against these fallacies as Goddard has had with Lake Chaubunagungamaug. But it is substantially more difficult when you don't have a written corpus to consult or extensive data to cite, leaving endangered languages far more vulnerable to distortions from cultural and ethnic stereotypes.

It was with this in mind that I made plans to visit my next destination, a town called Forks. I hadn't originally set out to go to Forks, but once I realized how close I was, I couldn't resist. And so, on a chilly, rainy

---

* There is not, by the way, a single language called Eskimo. Nor, for that, matter are all Alaskan/Arctic languages called Inuit. The Eskimo part of the Eskimo-Aleut language group includes both Inuit and Yup'ik languages. The Inuit prefer not to be called Eskimo; the Yup'ik don't object to the use of *Eskimo* as a catchall term, but they definitely prefer not to be called Inuit.

morning, I headed west to the Olympic Peninsula and the town that teenagers—and teenage vampires—made famous.

I told myself I was heading to the area because I was interested in the Quileute language. And it's true that I wasn't *un*interested. Linguistically, Quileute is something of an outlier, unrelated to any of the other languages in the Pacific Northwest. In other ways, however, the language is tragically representative of Native languages in the area. Down to its last few speakers, Quileute faces imminent extinction.

My plan was simple: I'd roll into town, grab a bite to eat, and visit the Quileute reservation at La Push. If I had time, I'd check out the Timber Museum. And then, just before I left, maybe—just maybe—I'd take a quick peek at a couple of the town's more popular tourist attractions.

Suffice it to say, not two hours after I arrived in Forks, I found myself sitting in the back of a giant tour bus emblazoned with the words "Dazzled by Twilight."

Forks is a small town of just over 3,000, located about fifty miles southwest of Port Angeles, the nearest sizable city. Originally a busy little logging center, until recently Forks was most famous as the birthplace of Leann Hunley, an actress on *Days of Our Lives*. But then, in 2003, an aspiring writer named Stephenie Meyer Googled something like "the rainiest place in the U.S." The Internet gods sent her to Forks, and so she decided to set her stories there. The rest is history.

Today, the *Twilight* series is a worldwide cultural phenomenon, and fans from all over flock to Forks to pay pilgrimage to the books' real-life milieu.

When I decided to go to Forks, I'd thought I had some idea what I was getting into. I was no stranger to—or enemy of—pop-culture compulsion. I mean, I grew up with *Star Trek* and *Buffy* and *The X-Files*. I'd been there; I'd read the fanfiction. But as soon as I drove into town, I started to get a sense that this was not at all going to go as I had expected. First there was the sign on the Olympic Suites Inn: "Edward Cullen Didn't Sleep Here." I remember laughing because I assumed it was meant to be bitchy—like, obviously Edward Cullen didn't sleep here because he is a fictional character. Later I was informed that the joke was actually that Edward Cullen didn't sleep there because he is a vampire, and vampires don't sleep. *Obviously.*

Tourism in Forks has skyrocketed over the past few years, and the town has largely embraced its good fortune. Almost every hotel, restaurant, and shop I saw had some sort of *Twilight* merchandise or advertisement. Even the local pharmacy; even the local Subway. To give you an idea of the level of frenzy that Forks was able to inspire in its visitors, one of the most popular things to do in town, as far as I could tell, was to visit the town welcome sign. It reads: "The City of Forks Welcomes You." That's it. Nothing about *Twilight.* Nothing about Edward Cullen. Even so, every time I drove past I saw a steady stream of visitors posing for photos in front of the sign. I even have one of myself, looking mildly bemused.

At my first stop, the Forks Chamber of Commerce, I watched as four separate staff members—each of whom sported at least one piece of *Twilight*-related flair—struggled to keep up with customer demand, frantically distributing maps and ringing up merchandise. Even though it was fairly early in the day, when I went over to take a peek at the guest book I saw that dozens of people had already been in. Many of the visitors were from Washington, but I also spotted entries from France, Spain, Switzerland, and China.

In the comments section, nearly everyone identified their position on the Edward-Jacob spectrum. There were more than a few exclamation points involved.

Outside, a group of people were crowding around "Bella's truck," an old-fashioned red pickup that had been installed in the parking lot. It wasn't the truck used in the movies. It was just an old pickup that was by virtue of a sign and some geographical happenstance enjoying a second life as a tourist attraction. When I saw it I very nearly let out a groan of dismay. You see, I hadn't actually been expecting much from Forks beyond a bit of comic relief. But once I saw that stupid truck I knew I wouldn't be able to get away without thinking about more serious questions of popular narrative and representation.

Before I left, I decided to check out the Forks Timber Museum just next door. When I opened the door, the woman at the front desk looked up in surprise, shielding her eyes against the light. "Are you sure you mean to be here?" she asked, not unkindly.

No, I found myself thinking. *I'm really not.*

The Quileute Indian Reservation is a single square mile of land about fifteen miles west of Forks. The main population center on the reservation is the village—such as it is—of La Push, so named due to its proximity to the mouth of the Quileute River. In the nineteenth century, French traders frequently came to the area, and many of their words were incorporated into Chinook Jargon, the local lingua franca. One of these words was "mouth": *la bouche* became *la push*, and so the settlement got its name.

Quileute is one of only two Chimakuan languages—the other, Chemakum, has been extinct since the 1940s. Its primary linguistic claim to fame rests in its sounds: Quileute is one of only five known languages in the entire world that contains no nasal sounds. So no *m*, no *n*, no *ng*.

More intriguingly, Quileute is one of several area languages that uses a very peculiar type of systematized wordplay. The renowned linguist and anthropologist Edward Sapir first observed this phenomenon among the Nuu-chah-nulth (also known as the Nootka). They would, he noticed, regularly change the consonants in certain words depending on certain physical characteristics of either the person being addressed or the person being discussed. The same thing happens in Quileute. For instance, if you were talking to someone who's cross-eyed, you'd put a ƛ- in front of every word. If, though, you were talking to a hunchback, you'd use the prefix *v-*. Short men, funny people, and those with difficulty walking all get their own initial sounds. Whether this might indicate a language accustomed to individual differences or extremely opposed to them, I couldn't begin to say.

Due to their remote location, extremely compact territory, and, no doubt, their small population, the Quileutes weren't initially subject to quite the same level of bureaucratic scrutiny as some other tribes. Their language nevertheless suffered the same misfortunes as so many other Native languages, beginning with the establishment of the first tribal school in 1882. By the mid-1970s, the population of native Quileute-speakers had dwindled to fewer than fifteen, at which point the tribe established a committee of elders and experts to spearhead preservation efforts. Even so, the number of native speakers continued to fall, from ten in 1977 to six in 1990. The best estimate is that there are three, maybe four native Quileute-speakers still living today.

Even though it seems impossible that Quileute will ever again be a mother tongue, the language is not yet completely lost. The tribe stepped up its preservation campaign in 2007 with the Quileute Revitalization Project, focusing on documenting the language and creating and disseminating language-learning materials. And recently the language has received a boost in interest from an unexpected source. Like the Quileutes' home, the Quileutes' language is also benefiting from the *Twilight* bump.

I caught the *Twilight* tour bus on North Forks Avenue, the town's main drag. I was a full five minutes early, but I was still the last one to arrive, and the girls on the bus gave me a bit of the stink-eye as I crept toward the back. *Great*, I thought. *Just like high school.*

The tour was run out of a store called Dazzled by Twilight, the brainchild of Annette Root, a *Twilight* fan who first came to Forks as a tourist herself. When she arrived was shocked by the lack of *Twilight*-related retail presence, and so, displaying an enviable amount of foresight, she moved in and literally set up shop. When I visited Forks, Dazzled by Twilight was a spacious storefront crammed with T-shirts, perfume, and paying customers. They also ran up to four popular tours a day, at $39 a person. At the time, I was not surprised to discover they were planning to expand and upgrade. Who knows how long it will last, but I imagine they're something of a small empire now.

Our guide was a forcefully outgoing man named Travis who had previously cut his teeth running tours of Hollywood. His was an impressively slick performance, but his smooth, practiced delivery seemed slightly out of place in a town such as Forks. I couldn't help but wonder, every so often, if I'd somehow stumbled onto a studio back lot.

As we got under way, Travis played the crowd like a pro, knowing exactly how to elicit the maximum amount of adolescent glee. Early on he asked a very important question: "So who here is Team Jacob?"

Now, in a situation like this, normally I would just not respond. I really don't go in for audience participation in any way, shape, or form—it gives me hives. But I was sitting on a bus with a dozen fifteen-year-olds *going on a* Twilight *tour.* I was more than a bit out of sorts from the get-go. And so I found myself raising my hand. I also found I was the only one raising my hand.

That's when they hissed at me. They actually hissed at me.

"Whoa, tough crowd," Travis said with a grin. "So I guess we're Team Edward?" The bus responded with riotous cheers. I sank farther into my seat.

The tour took us all over Forks: the police station, the hospital, and a succession of houses that had been for whatever reason identified as the main characters' residences. At each stop, the girls would scramble off the bus to take pictures, and time and time again, I found myself intrigued by their casual indifference toward matters of fact and fiction. Take the house of Bella Swan, the series heroine. Now, I have no idea how it was selected. Stephenie Meyer didn't visit Forks before publishing *Twilight.* I can't imagine she was able to base Bella's house on a real house. And even if she did, *Bella herself isn't real.* But this doesn't matter to true fans. Travis told us the story of how one morning the owner of the Swan house had walked into the kitchen to find a complete stranger standing there in awe.

"Oh, don't mind me," he said. "I just wanted to see Bella's kitchen!"

Once we finished our circuit of Forks, we headed toward La Push. As we crossed over into Quileute territory—"No Vampires Beyond This Point"—the soundtrack switched over to Warren Zevon's "Werewolves of London." I perked up. I love that song. I actually love that song so much that I said as much out loud.

"Oh, so do I."

I turned to my right. A woman was smiling at me. The one woman over forty—actually, the one woman over thirty. She was there with her pre-teen daughter, a dimpled girl in a *Twilight* T-shirt who was excited to the point of insensibility, and she looked vaguely relieved to find me there.

I think I probably looked relieved to find her, too.

About two thirds of the way through the film *New Moon,* Jacob Black, werewolf and member of the Quileute tribe, says something to Bella

Swan. And no one knows what it is—all anyone knows for sure is that it's in Quileute.

When Stephenie Meyer chose to set *Twilight* in Forks, her decision had nothing to do with the town's proximity to any Indian reservation, much less La Push. According to her, she chose Forks first and foremost for its vampire-friendly climate. Only after she began researching the surrounding area did she learn about the Quileutes. And only after she learned about the Quileutes did she start thinking about werewolves.

There surely are many different accounts of the Quileute origin myth, but one of them goes something like this: the being known as K'wati (or the Transformer) went to the mouth of the river by La Push and saw two timber wolves, and he decided to transform these wolves into people. In the version of the story I read, K'wati then made the following pronouncement: "For this reason you Quileute shall be brave, because you have come from wolves. In every manner you shall be strong."

Note that K'wati did not then add, "And the strongest and most shirtless among you will also periodically change *back* into wolves. Then, with very little effort, you will be shockingly and disproportionately famous."

La Push and the Quileute tribe have been thrust into the spotlight just as much as Forks, if not more so. Basic though the tourist infrastructure of Forks may be, it's significantly more developed than that in La Push, which is little more than a handful of weathered buildings crouched near the water. Even so, the reservation is seeing a tremendous influx of visitors. Quileute merchandise—both authentic and otherwise—is selling like mad, the weekly drum circles held at the community center have been opened to the public, and when I visited, the tribe's Oceanside Resort, a picturesque collection of cabins, motels, and campgrounds, was positively bustling.

And with the inclusion of a single Quileute phrase in *New Moon*, the interest in the Quileute people and culture has been extended in some small way to the language as well. This interest was stoked due to the fact that everyone involved with the movie refused to provide a translation.

As curiosity grew and entertainment media began asking about the mysterious line, the cast and crew—*New Moon* director Chris Weitz and actor Taylor Lautner in particular—repeatedly demurred, suggesting instead that hard-core fans "ask a Quileute."

Which, naturally, they did. In force.

Shortly thereafter, the Quileute Nation posted a statement on its Facebook page:

> Dear Fans: Thank you for all the calls and emails regarding the scene in the movie where Jacob whispers to Bella in Quileute. Please know, we would love to translate the phrase for you, but out of respect for Jacob's feelings for Bella we are unable to at this time.

In the absence of any knowledgeable guidance, fans have turned to increasingly implausible online speculation. Consensus appears to favor one of two options, either "I love you" or the more oppressively saccharine "stay with me forever." Rarely, however, does anyone offer any proof or analytic support for their preference apart from "I read it online so I know it's true." I saw requests for "people who speak Indian," and I saw assertions that the phrase is in Mohawk. I read one post that seemed to imply translation was as simple as typing an English word in a Quileute font.

But, to be fair, I'm not sure anyone really can figure it out without expert—and willing—help. For one thing, no one seems to agree on what was actually said. I've seen three separate transliterations ("kwop kilawtley," "kwopkalawo'li," and "que quowle"), none of which appear to be written with Quileute spelling conventions. Even if there was a specific phrase to translate, you can't exactly run down to Barnes and Noble and pick up a Quileute dictionary.

The *Twilight* franchise has certainly made celebrities of the Quileute people and their culture, and I can only hope that the economic windfall is compensation enough for what I suspect will be years of putting up with stupid questions about werewolves, vampires, and throwaway werewolf lines in vampire movies. And though I'm not a fan of the *Twilight* books, even I can admit that it's fairly miraculous that because of these books there are thirteen-year-olds saying things like "I want to learn Quileute." In a country where indigenous languages are essentially ignored among non-Native populations, this is something to celebrate.

The *Twilight* industry in Forks serves as a reminder, however, of the tenuous boundaries between reality and fantasy. It is important to be aware that even the most genuine interest does not guarantee a language or culture will be represented fairly or thoughtfully. I suspect that many of the fashionable young people who appropriate Native dress in indefensibly disrespectful ways do so, unknowing and unthinking, because to them Native culture is "cool." Put simply, in American culture there is more misinformation about Native culture than there is information. I wish the Quileute tribe luck steering its flood of new fans and visitors toward the latter and not the former.

When you drive west from Seattle on Highway 101, you skirt the Olympic National Forest on your way north to Port Townsend before jogging to the east. Then a few miles past Port Angeles the road splits in two. If you're looking to see temperate rain forest and up-close views of the Olympic Mountains, stick to the southern route, which takes you through Sappho, Beaver, and eventually down to Forks. But if you're looking for something more, then the northern route—State Route 112— is for you.

It's this road that will take you to the end of the world.

And it's this road that took me to my last stop in Washington state, a place called Neah Bay.

I've navigated some pretty spectacular roads in my time, chief among them Highway 1 along the Pacific Coast, the Blue Ridge Parkway in North Carolina, and the Beartooth Highway in Montana and Wyoming. Along the way I've developed a system for determining the comparative caliber of the landscape. It's not that I'm interested in rankings or that I'm looking for reasons to be underwhelmed. But if I'm in the most beautiful place I've ever seen, I want to be aware of that fact. I want to be able to feel the moment the entire balance of my life experience shifts ever so slightly toward the sublime.

So I use something I call the Fuck-Me Factor.

It's very simple. The louder and more profane my reaction, the more impressive the scenery. Your standard ocean view, for instance, would typically elicit an appreciative but family-friendly response, something like "cats and dogs" or "goodnight, nurse." An alpine waterfall or stirring sunset merits something closer to "crap" or maybe "crap-damn." By the time you get to your heavy hitters—the Grand Canyon, the Rocky Mountains, the first glimpse of Manhattan after a trip to Massachusetts—I've usually left behind all semblance of gentility: "fuck," "holy fuck," "fucking shit," "fucking hell." It's my version of a heartfelt sigh. The last thing I manage to say before I'm finally struck dumb by sheer emotion is typically "fuck me."

As soon as I turned onto SR 112, I basically turned into a character from *Glengarry Glen Ross*. By the time I reached Sekiu, I was out of words. When I finally pulled up to my cabin on a beach about six miles southeast of Cape Flattery, I had lost my breath. It was then and remains to this day the most beautiful drive of my life.

With the foothills of Olympic Mountains to the south and the Strait of Juan de Fuca to the north, the road is just a sliver of pavement, a tenuous ledge between forest and sea. It is slow going, and not only on account of the highway's twists and turns—there's also the view to consider. Time and time again I found my eyes drawn one way or another, either down toward the ocean or up into the trees, only to realize with a start that I did still need to pay some attention to the road.

The highway ends in Neah Bay, a tiny town of about 800 and the largest settlement on the Makah Indian Reservation. The main industries in Neah Bay are fishing and tourism, but apart from the museum, the general store, a few motels, and some tiny shops and restaurants, there's not much to the town. A few dogs ran alongside my car as I turned off the main road and headed toward Hobuck Beach.

There isn't a particularly wide variety of lodging options in Neah Bay, so even though I'd read a few excellent reports of the Hobuck Beach Resort, I wasn't expecting much. I was staying in a cabin, sure, but I figured it would be something like the "cabins" I'd been forced to sleep in on high school camping trips: knotty wood, spiderwebs, an insidious damp that sticks to your socks for days. I'm not averse to the outdoors—quite the opposite—but at the end of the day I do appreciate a spot of indoor plumbing. I figure that untold multitudes of men and women have labored for centuries to harness the powers of hot water, so it's up to me to show my appreciation for their efforts by using it.

I was thrilled when I discovered that my cabin was a neat little one-bedroom house with a kitchen and full bath. From the living room, I could hear the ocean; from the front porch, I could see it. I grabbed my coat and walked the thirty seconds from the door to the beach, a half-moon of sand and sea grass flanked by wooded hills. I took off my shoes and stood in the surf as the sun set. I watched the waves turn gold.

It was at this moment that I began to think very seriously about never leaving the Olympic Peninsula.

Though it was midsummer, by the time I got back to the cabin, the evening had turned chill. I turned up the heat and curled up on the couch with *First Lessons in Makah*.

This slender volume—more of a booklet, really—was the reason I'd come to Neah Bay. The Makah language is part of the larger Waskashan family, a group of languages indigenous primarily to Vancouver Island (which sits just across the strait from Neah Bay). Although languages such as Haisla, Kwak'wala, and Nuu-chah-nulth can still boast native-speaking populations, Makah, the southernmost language of the family, now exists solely as a second language. Ruth E. Claplanhoo, the last native speaker of Makah, died in 2002 at the age of 100.

The phonetic inventories of Makah and other Wakashan languages are renowned for their use of consonants, which is a nice way of saying that they use lots of sounds that don't exist in English. There is the letter *ł*, which my book informed me is "an *s*-like sound with the tongue in the position of *l*." Or *x*, which is "an *h*-like sound with the middle of the tongue raised." I was guided in the pronunciation of an entire set of consonants with the instruction "A glottal stop is produced simultaneously with the consonant. This closure in the throat must be maintained until after the closure in the mouth is released."

I honestly had no idea what to do with any of that, so I decided to set pronunciation aside and move on. Only then did Makah begin to reveal its secrets—like its particularly fascinating way of dealing with something called evidentiality.

In English I can simply say, without qualification, "The sky is blue."

Although I could certainly explain how I know this or why I believe it, it's not grammatically necessary to back up declarative statements with supporting evidence. But in Makah there exists a series of suffixes that deal very specifically and precisely with the question of how a person knows something. Adding -*wa:t* to a verb, for instance, indicates hearsay—the difference between "The sky is blue" and "I heard that the sky is blue." If you're looking at something from afar and aren't quite sure of what you're seeing, you can use -*cadił*: "The sky looks blue—I think."

Evidentials have always been a favorite linguistic subject of mine. If I were ever to go back to graduate school, I imagine I would probably want to write a great many papers on comparative political discourse in languages with and without evidentials. Just imagine, for instance, how different the experience of watching Fox News and MSNBC might be if the anchors' every declaration included this kind of information.

It was in my reading about evidentials that I found—from an article written by William Jacobsen, who also happens to be the author of my Makah primer—what must be one of my all-time favorite bits of linguistic data. As part of a discussion of lexical suffixes that act like evidentials, Jacobsen cites the following pair of sentences:

ƛ̓a·ci·w̓alic
"You're getting fat."

ƛ̓a·ci·wiƛ̓kuwic
"You look like you're getting fat."

I spent a long time thinking about which statement would annoy me more.

Makah, like Crow, Navajo, and so many other indigenous languages of North America, is polysynthetic. Which means, again, that a single word can oftentimes be broken down into a relatively large number of linguistically meaningful parts. (The smallest of these parts, by the way, is what's called a morpheme.) This doesn't mean that a curt utterance in Makah necessarily translates into a mouthful of English. But it does mean that a word in Makah can be extended by a series of affixes and thereby take on a more elaborate meaning. Take ƛaƚa·wač'ak. When parsed out, it becomes:

ƛaƚa·w	a	č'ak
go along	(epenthetic*)	device for

So one word in Makah—ƛaƚa·wač'ak—becomes four words in English: "device for going along." This is a fairly simple example. It becomes more complicated with a word such as a ƛa·ƛa·kʷaƚx̌adub.

ƛa·	ƛa·	kʷaƚ	x̌ad	u	b(a)
(reduplication)	perpendicular stick-like object	separate forcefully	extreme point	(epenthetic)	thing

A literal translation would be "stick-like object with separated grooves on one end."

I'm often charmed despite myself by the level of description a single word in a polysynthetic language can contain. But I try to remember that the literal translation isn't necessarily the most appropriate translation. Because although a ƛa·ƛa·kʷaƚx̌adub is a fairly specialized bit of fishing equipment—a finger rest for a harpoon—a ƛaƚa·wač'ak is something much simpler: a paddle.

Literal translations are incredibly useful for the linguist and language student, but if translators rely too heavily on them, polysynthetic languages can seem to evince a lack of sophistication—a dangerous perception, particularly when that language belongs to a people also routinely stereotyped as "primitive." Now, English is a far more analytic (or isolating) language, which means that its ratio of morphemes to words is closer to 1:1. So it's hard to come up with a precise parallel to illustrate

---

* An epenthetic is a sound that is slipped onto or into a word without changing its meaning. You see it fairly often when adding affixes: sometimes the root and stem clash a little bit in your mouth. Think about plurals of English words ending in an "ess" sound—you don't say *glasss*, but rather *glasses*.

what I mean here. But imagine if translators of English insisted on breaking down each word not into morphemes but into its etymological parts. A word like "telephone" could be literally translated as something like "far-off sound thing." Which sounds completely ridiculous, of course.

It's easy to forget that my sense of a language in translation is very different from the sense a native speaker of that language would have. I would have a very different perception of a person depending on whether they use "far-off sound thing" or "telephone," "going-along device" or "paddle." I know it seems obvious when I spell it out that a dumb-sounding translation does not imply a dumb language—or, worse, dumb speakers of that language. But given the way the Makah language has historically been treated by outsiders, I don't think it's the worst thing in the world to belabor this point.

Although Europeans first landed on the Olympic Peninsula in 1774, the Makah didn't come into contact with the new arrivals until 1788, when an English captain and fur trader by the name of John Meares dropped anchor off Cape Flattery. The Makah called the outsiders *babaɬids*—"house-floating-on-the-water people." It would take nearly seventy years for the outsiders to decide what to call the Makah.

The Makah don't use the name Makah—or at least they didn't used to. Instead they call themselves qʷidičča?a·tx, "the people who live by the rocks and seagulls." They are hardly the only group in the country to be saddled with an exonym that, like so many other tribal monikers throughout the country, bears little resemblance to their traditional name. Remember, after all, that the Crow are also the Apsáalooke and the Navajo the Diné. Sometimes these names are mere accidents of fate. Sometimes, however, they are accidents of misunderstanding. Take, for instance, the Nuu-chah-nulth, a closely related tribe that lives on the western coast of Vancouver Island and was for many years known as the Nootka. Helma Ward, a Makah elder, told anthropologist Patricia Pierce Erikson the story of how the Nootka got their name:

> They were asked, "What is your people's name?" They responded, "nootka." They thought the men wanted to get out of where they were. So they were saying "nootka," telling them to go out around

the island. But the men decided to stay. So they stayed and were fed. The next day they were told again how to leave—"nootka"—go out around the island. So they've been called Nootka people ever since.

By comparison, I suppose the Makah should be relieved. Their adopted name may come from another language, but at least it doesn't mean something so wholly unrelated.

The name Makah was codified in 1855, when the governor of Washington Territory and members of the Makah Tribe signed the Treaty of Neah Bay. Among other provisions, the treaty established the boundaries of the Makah reservation—a mere 28,000 acres of the 700,000 acres the tribe had traditionally inhabited—and codified tribal fishing rights. The treaty was written in English only, and whether it was due to intent or ignorance, government officials elected to use the word maq̓a·, the Klallam name for the tribe. It means, depending on your source, "generous with food" or "well-fed." Makah has been the "official" name of the tribe ever since.

For the Makah, then, the Treaty of Neah Bay marked not only the beginning of reservation life, a time when the U.S. government would involve itself in every aspect of daily life, from trade to agriculture to education, but also the first time the United States tried to undermine their language.

The interaction between English and Makah started off innocently enough. One of the first European Americans to live among the Makah was a man named James Swan, the author of *The Indians of Cape Flattery*, the first ethnographic work on the Makah. Swan (no relation to Bella) first visited Neah Bay in 1859 as part of his travels throughout the Olympic Peninsula. Eventually he settled in the area, and in 1862 he was hired as the reservation schoolmaster. Over the next four years he compiled his monograph, which included an extensive Makah word list.

Though a dedicated amateur, Swan was no linguist, and his translations were sometimes unreliable—he wrote, for instance, that qʷidičča?a·tx meant "the people who live on a point of land projecting into the sea." This was due in part to the fact that the Makah were not uniformly supportive of his endeavors. Many years later, Helma Ward—the same elder who told researchers the story of "nootka"—was working as a language specialist for the Makah Cultural and Research Center. After working with Swan's materials, she remarked, "We had to go through and fix Swan's vocabulary. It was full of bum words. Swearwords. People were giving him the wrong information just to be mean to him."

Even so, Swan's lists were used to teach English to Makah-speakers—and Makah to English-speakers.

But not all efforts on behalf of language education were so feckless or relatively benign. Consider the case of C. A. Huntington, an agent assigned to the Makah reservation in April 1874. In his first annual report to the Commissioner of Indian Affairs, filed that September, he wrote of his plans for the children of Neah Bay:

> I have taken the buildings at Bahada Point two miles distant from the nearest Indian camps. Here I propose to separate the children entirely from the homes and as much as possible from the ideas and habits of their parents. I propose to take them entirely out of barbarous surroundings, and put them into the midst of a civilized, Christian home. . . . In connection with all this, I shall make it my first endeavor to teach them to speak the English language, not by the slow process of letters and books, but by the usage of common parlance. The Indian tongue must be put to silence and nothing but the English allowed in all social intercourse.

With enough effort, one might be able to locate a well-meaning humanitarian sentiment in that statement, but all I see is disdain for non-white, non-Christian culture. Unfortunately, it was this attitude that permeated the schools that Makah children were sent to. Like the other Native students at assimilationist schools throughout the country, Makah children were threatened with punishment for any outward expression of their native culture and language.

Mary Lou Denney's account of her father's time in school is typical:

> When he was caught [speaking Makah], they took him outside and it was raining. The weather was very bad and they put him to a

harness and they had to walk around just like animals when they were, I don't know what they would do, but anyway they just kind of walked in a circle and they were chained. . . . They didn't have a coat on, just their clothes that they wore to class. He said he'll never forget that because there were some pretty sick kids that were having to do the same thing. So him and my mom decided that they wouldn't allow us to go through that kind of treatment and that we would learn the English.

The Makah language might well have died out completely were it not for the intervention of Mother Nature. But in 1970 a series of powerful waves exposed hundreds of centuries-old artifacts near Ozette, a largely abandoned Makah village about twenty miles south of Neah Bay. Over the next eleven years, archaeologists uncovered more than 55,000 artifacts and 40,000 structural remains from the site, a village that had been buried and amazingly well preserved by an eighteenth-century mudslide. Reporters flooded the area, eager to see for themselves "North America's Pompeii."

The local community came together to participate in the dig, to aid with cataloging and identification, and to ensure that their cultural legacy remained in their control. Tribal elders spent hours sifting through the archaeological inventory, explaining what the objects were and how they were used, and dredging up long-forgotten facts and stories. Regular school trips to the site sparked interest not only in archaeology but also in traditional Makah culture. Soon enough the tribe declared its intention to establish a museum.

The Makah Cultural and Research Center (MCRC) opened in 1979. It sits on the eastern end of Neah Bay, just across the street from the sign welcoming visitors to the reservation. The exterior is squat and unassuming, but inside is a world-class anthropological museum. The Makah employed an exhibit designer from the staff of the Royal British Columbia Museum in Victoria, but a group of eight tribal elders largely determined the thrust of the design, and instead of trying to maximize the quantity of artifacts on display, the tribe chose to focus on presenting the clearest and most compelling cultural narrative possible. Though only about 1 percent of the Ozette artifacts are shown at the museum, the exhibits provide a remarkably clear and compelling introduction to Makah culture, surely an indication of the epic scope of the full collection.

Today the museum is an unqualified success. It is the tribe's main tourist attraction, drawing more than 14,000 visitors a year, and it plays a major role in the community with regard to matters of cultural and historical preservation. It is also, as I discovered, home to the Makah Language Program.

Beginning in the 1960s, the Makah fought to put their language and culture back in their classrooms. Although Makah was eventually offered to students as an elective, it took the energizing effects of the Ozette dig to generate interest in large-scale plans for language study and instruction. The renewed vitality paid off. In 1978, the tribe received a grant of just over $90,000 from the National Endowment for the Humanities to put toward language preservation efforts. The first act of the newly established Makah Language Program was to establish an official orthography and train native speakers in its use.

Soon, elders were working side by side with teachers to develop an appropriate language curriculum. In 1984 the program offered Head Start and elementary-school instruction. In the 2009–10 school year, classes covered grades K–12, and Makah III, the most advanced course to date, was offered at the high school level for the first time.

At the MCRC I met Crystal Thompson, an animated young Makah woman in her late twenties who was in her seventh year with the Makah Language Program. One of four part-time teachers on staff, Crystal taught Head Start through fifth grade. In addition to their teaching duties, Crystal and her colleagues made up what is essentially the Makah version of the Académie Française. In the absence of any living native speakers, these are the tribe's linguistic authorities, so when a need arises for a new word, the task falls to them. When I spoke with Crystal, she had recently been thinking over a word for "toolbox." She and her fellow teachers eventually decided on *babuksac*—"working container."

Crystal told me about her classes, about how she loved when parents called up after hearing their children speak their language for the first time. She also told me about her students and how shy they could be at first, particularly the younger ones.

"How do you handle it?" I asked.

She smiled. "I just tell them, 'I'm not asking you to be perfect; all I want you to do is try. You can't do anything wrong in here.'"

Native language instruction in the United States has come a long way from the assimilationist educational policies of men such as Richard Henry Pratt and C. A. Huntington. Today there is a wide range of strategies being utilized to nurture existing languages and preserve the remains of dead and dying ones. There are Head Start programs that focus on early learners and high school courses that are offered as electives. There are schools such as Rough Rock that offer bilingual instruction, and schools such as the Pūnana Leo "language nests" in Hawai'i that offer full Native language immersion. Tribal colleges and other postsecondary institutions provide the opportunity to gain advanced linguistic expertise.

None of this would have been possible without some efforts on the part of the U.S. government. The Native American Languages Act of 1990, for instance, declared that it was "the official policy of the United States government to preserve, protect, and promote the rights and freedom of Native Americans to use, practice, and develop Native languages." While the initial act was mostly something of a symbolic gesture, it was amended in 1992 to include a grant program under the auspices of the Department of Health and Human Services. The Esther Martinez Native American Languages Preservation Act of 2006 further amended the act and authorized three-year grants for Native language nests, survival schools, and restoration programs.

Since 1994, the Administration for Native Americans (ANA) has provided grant money to tribal governments and Native Hawaiian groups for the development of language programs and learning materials. Between 2000 and 2007, the ANA provided $56 million for 254 language preservation projects.

Although government support is a welcome and perhaps even necessary condition for successful language preservation efforts, the future of Native languages also relies on the dedicated efforts of individuals such as Leanne Hinton, the founder of the Breath of Life project in California, or Jessie Little Doe Baird, 2010 MacArthur Fellow and director of the Wampanoag Language Reclamation Project. After training at the Massachusetts Institute of Technology, Baird worked to compile a wide range of Wampanoag learning materials—a monumental feat given that Wampanoag has been extinct since the late nineteenth century.

Science, too, is playing its part, as technological advances facilitate not only the preservation of Native languages, but also the acquisition of them. Rosetta Stone, for instance, established a corporate grant program to help develop software for languages such as Mohawk, Inupiaq, and Navajo. You can download an app for your Android phone that will help you learn Caddo; you can use the Cherokee syllabary on your iPad.

Even so, it might not be enough. Linguist Michael Krauss estimated in 1998 that of the 175 indigenous languages still spoken in the United States, 90 percent were at risk of extinction. "The sad irony is," Krauss writes, "that even as U.S. policy has changed explicitly to recognize and support indigenous languages as a national asset . . . parents are still abandoning their heritage language in favor of English. This process is occurring at such a rapid rate that we stand to lose more indigenous North American languages in the next 60 years than have been lost since Anglo-European contact."

Now, there are those who might ask whether this is really so bad. Why *should* these languages be preserved? In the United States, there is absolutely an economic benefit to being fluent in English. You could argue, then, that there is an economic cost to focusing on instruction in any other language. And so, by emphasizing the preservation of these indigenous languages at the expense of English proficiency, we may be further hobbling economically disadvantaged Native communities in order to satisfy the whims of privileged academics or bleeding-heart activists.

You could argue on the other hand, however, that each language is an invaluable resource, that every word is a layered little gem of human history, culture, and cognition. You could argue that the loss of a language is an irrevocable and incalculable loss to all humankind.

Where do I stand on this? Well, I love language. I like to ferret out its surprises and then tuck them away like a flower in a book so that every so often, when I'm overwhelmed by the gross inadequacies of daily life, when someone corrects another person's grammar just to be nasty or

I happen to hear Rush Limbaugh express an opinion about women, I can turn back to my collection and exclaim over the mirative or the classifica-tory verb or the evidential suffix, and remember that the human brain can do extraordinary things. So yes, of course I think languages should be preserved.

I'm not suggesting anything extreme. I'm certainly not recommend-ing that Native access to English instruction be somehow restricted. Admittedly, I don't know of any empirical work that explores the economic, cultural, or psychological benefits of indigenous language preservation and revitalization. But I do consider it a moral imperative to make sure something is done to preserve as much of these languages as possible. Even if you take the Darwinian view and argue that a lan-guage that can't survive on its own shouldn't survive you can't pretend that current state of Native languages in the United States is somehow "natural." These languages are not in danger due solely to the gradual encroachment of a language better suited to our particular time and place. They are in danger at least in part because the U.S. government undertook a systematic campaign to put them there.

Just as there is more than one Native language and one Native culture, so too is there more than one Native experience. The last thing I want to do is imply that suffering at the hands of the government is the sole defin-ing characteristic of that experience. Nevertheless, whichever way you look at it, this country did some seriously bad things that have had some seriously bad ramifications. Here are just a few facts: the life expectancy for men on the Crow reservation is forty-four years, on par with coun-tries such as Afghanistan, Sierra Leone, and Zimbabwe. Due without a doubt to the slipshod regulation of uranium mines, teenage Navajo girls are significantly more likely than the average American girl—some say as much as seventeen times more likely—to be stricken with cancer of the reproductive organs. The suicide rate for male American Indians and Alaska Natives ages fifteen to thirty-four is three times higher than the national average.

Is this all the government's fault? No, of course not. But it is definitely mostly the government's fault. Government policy directly limited the ability of Native communities to determine their own linguistic (and non-linguistic) fate. Language preservation can return at least some part of that choice by making sure the resources are available for future revitalization efforts.

Makah elder John Ides put the history of indigenous American languages in stark terms: "*Not* learning a language is also a native experience." But it is important to remember that this is not the be-all and end-all of Native language in the United States. Throughout the country there are communities of Native peoples, children and elders, linguists and educators, who are fighting to mitigate the effects on their language of generations of systematic and deliberate oppression. The languages of Native America serve as a testament to the fact that sometimes the study, instruction, and preservation of language isn't always a dry and fusty thing. Sometimes it is, in every word and phrase, an expression of hope.

People typically come to Neah Bay for three reasons: to fish, to see the museum, and to hike to Cape Flattery. I don't like boats, and I'd seen the museum, so I figured I'd head out to the cape, the northwesternmost point in the continental United States

Cape Flattery was first sighted by James Cook on March 22, 1788. Cook thought he saw an opening between the cape and a nearby island, "which flattered us with the hopes of finding a harbour." As he got closer, though, he dismissed his initial judgment, and instead of heading toward what was indeed the entrance to the Strait of Juan de Fuca, he and his ship sailed north to the west coast of Vancouver Island. Before he left, he christened the disappointing cape Flattery.

Today, Cape Flattery feels nearly as remote as it must have felt to Captain Cook. To get there, you drive west of Neah Bay, pass the Tribal Center, and then turn onto a gravel road, which takes you to the head of the Cape Flattery trail. The hike to the ocean is only three quarters of a mile, a fairly easy walk down a succession of well-kept paths and cedar boardwalks. It should probably take most people about a half hour, but I found myself lingering as I made my way through the trees, hardly able to decide if I wanted to use my eyes or my camera.

The forest was still and slightly dark, and the sudden, public expanse of the cape crept up on me. One minute I was caught in a private thick of green; the next I was on an outcropping with a crowd of fellow tourists. I was expecting a vast sweep of ocean, but I didn't realize that just half a mile off the cape is Tatoosh Island, the location of John Meares's first meeting with the Makah chief who gave the island its name. The island is soon to be returned to the Makah, I was told. For years it was used by the Coast Guard, but they don't need the lighthouse, not anymore.

There were ships in the distance, too. As I began the hike back uphill, I wondered where they were headed—to Port Angeles, or maybe to Tacoma. Every ship that passes through the Strait of Juan de Fuca passes Cape Flattery, which means that I had stood on the very first point of land that an eastbound vessel would see.

The end of the world, I was reminded, is only a matter of perspective.

CHAPTER FOUR

Louisiana: French and Louisiana Creole

T HE EXPLORATION AND COLONIZATION of the Americas precipitated a rapid decline in indigenous language diversity that continues to this day. However, it also ushered in a new era of European
language diversity.

As a result of the fierce competition between European countries for
land and resources in the New World—not to mention for the services of
skilled navigators—there were from the very first expeditions a variety
of languages in what is now the continental United States. Ponce de León
brought Spanish to Florida; Verrazzano brought Italian and French to
the Atlantic Coast; Henry Hudson brought English and Dutch to the
Northeast. Swedish settlers, meanwhile, found their way to Delaware,
and the French moved south from their initial positions along the St.
Lawrence River.

Although English was the majority language in the colonies from
very early on, population growth in nineteenth-century America was
not limited to any particular language. As Richard Bailey points out, at
the time of the American Revolution, more than a fifth of European
Americans spoke a language other than English. By 1800, 17 percent of
the population of New York and New Jersey was Dutch and 9 percent of
Delaware was Swedish. A full third of Pennsylvania was German.

There was for a long time a popular belief that languages separated from their home countries, like a bud nipped from its stem, ceased to develop. This phenomenon was called colonial lag, and there were many—including, notably, Noah Webster—who argued in particular for its applicability to American English.* But though the colonial languages in the New World might have been isolated from their homelands, these languages were not unaffected by their trip to the New World. Colonial lag is, as linguist David Crystal says, "a considerable oversimplification." Language, even in isolation, continues to change.

But, more to the point, these languages were not always isolated from *other* languages. So not only do you see borrowings between languages in the early history of the Americas—such as the Dutch words that are still spoken in New York City, or the Algonquin vocabulary we use for plants, animals, and places—you also see entirely new language varieties. By this I mean the contact languages known as jargons, pidgins, and creoles.

The Dutch in New Netherland, for instance, developed a simplified version of the Unami language (known as Delaware Jargon) that they later taught to Swedish and English settlers. Various forms of Trader Navajo allowed English-speakers to engage in commerce on Navajo lands. In the Pacific Northwest, an estimated 100,000 speakers of more than 100 different languages at one point spoke Chinook Jargon, which borrowed words from local indigenous languages, English, French, and even Cree and Hawaiian. In the southeast, Mobilian Jargon, a pidgin based on Muskoegean languages, was the local lingua franca.

Given the maelstrom of language interaction that characterized the New World colonies, it is easier than it should be to overlook influences neither Native nor European. But as any student of early American history knows, population growth in the Americas was not due solely to European colonization. It was also fueled by the importation of African slaves. And the languages these slaves brought with them had their own lasting impact on the linguistic topography of the Americas.

These are the languages that I want to explore next—the languages

---

* This idea lives on today in the relatively common perception that there are isolated pockets in Appalachia that still use Elizabethan English. (There aren't.)

that provide a glimpse into the history and experience of Africans in America.

When I first began thinking about African language in America, I was initially drawn to obscure, isolated tongues. I made plans to visit Brackettville, Texas, the home to a small community of Afro-Seminole-Creole-speakers, and I thought about going to Nantucket, where I might learn about Cape Verdean Creole. At that point I was still more interested in peculiarities than in universals, in the sorts of destinations that might pique the interest of New York's more jaded travel editors. This is why I almost didn't go to Louisiana.

There I was, flitting about the country collecting grammars and vocabulary and piles and piles of informational brochures from, frankly, some of the least exciting tourist destinations I could find, yet I seriously thought about skipping right over Louisiana, the home of zydeco, crawfish, and the go-cup. It just seemed like such an obvious destination, no more creative than name-checking *Citizen Kane* on a list of best-ever movies or saying that if I could have dinner with anyone in the world, dead or alive, I'd choose Jesus.

My initial hesitation also stemmed in part from my ideas about what kind of language could be found in Louisiana. French is the first language I ever studied, beginning all the way back in 1986, when I was still figuring out how to tie my shoes and get my underwear on without falling over. The languages I studied later in life proved to be slippery little bastards, secreting themselves just out of cognitive reach the moment I turned my attention to anything else. As soon as I started Chinese, I forgot Greek; as soon as I dove into Italian, I forgot Chinese. Once I began taking Spanish lessons, everything else was shit out of luck.

Except for French. It's been more than ten years since I have spoken or read French in anything but the most desultory manner, but my stodgy textbook French will be damned if it's going anywhere. While I struggle to say much in Chinese beyond *nǐ hǎo*, I can still remember all seven words in French that end in *-ou* and take *-x* in the plural.* I can't say if it

---

* *Bijou* (jewel), *caillou* (stone), *chou* (cabbage), *genou* (knee), *hibou* (owl), *joujou* (toy), and *pou* (louse).

sticks because I started learning it while in a critical period of development, because I studied it for so long, or because it was my first attempt
at a second language. Maybe I am, despite my assertions to the contrary,
just a bit of a Francophile. But whatever the reason, bits of French have
been in my brain for long enough that it has long since ceased to seem at
all exotic to me.

What's more, I grew up in a city whose French roots are, 364 days a
year, in evidence in the most mundane manner possible: in the flat, mid-
western pronunciations of French place names. St. Louis is littered with
French—DeSoto, Laclede, Bellerive, Lafayette, Soulard, Gravois—but
you'd probably never know it to hear it. Only on Mardi Gras does the
city suddenly remember its seventeenth-century affiliations, at which point
St. Louisans spontaneously rediscover a recognizable pronunciation
for five very important words: *laisser les bon temps rouler.*

All in all, I just didn't think French was that interesting. Why, I
thought, would I go out of my way to get somewhere not so very different from where I grew up to learn about a language I've had in my head
since Ronald Reagan was president?

Tellingly, I had not stopped to think that the French of Louisiana
might be any different from the French of my elementary school. At that
point it still hadn't occurred to me that the notion of a singular Louisiana
French might be a grotesque oversimplification—much less that any of
these varieties of French might have anything to do with the African diaspora. These things wouldn't happen until much later, until I made my
way to places such as Vacherie and Lafayette and Natchitoches.

How, then, did I end up in Louisiana? Did I have a change of heart?
Did I stumble on some previously undiscovered language primer? Was
it just on the way from Miami to Montana? No, I ended up in Louisiana
pretty much because I really wanted to go to New Orleans. (I read a
bunch of Anne Rice as a kid. Sue me.) Once I got there, however, I realized that the history of French in Louisiana is far more complex than I'd
originally thought, and my quick jaunt to New Orleans became a more
thoughtful journey through the prairies and bayous of Louisiana.

In 1718, Jean-Baptiste Le Moyne de Bienville and the French Mississippi
Company decided to found a city. They had no residents, no structures,

and no exact location, but they did have a name: La Nouvelle-Orléans, an opportunistic choice intended to honor the French regent, the Duke of Orléans. Once they settled on a location, they began by building an eleven-by-seven-block district next to the Mississippi River. Today this area is known as the Vieux Carré (literally, "old square") or, more familiarly, the French Quarter, and in addition to being the oldest section of New Orleans it is arguably the most famous. It is in the French Quarter that you will find Jackson Square and the St. Louis Cathedral, Antoine's and Café du Monde. And each year during Mardi Gras, it is the French Quarter that hosts much of the outsized revelry the city is so famous for.

Though the French Quarter has always been the oldest part of New Orleans, it has not always been the most well favored. Over the years the French Quarter has had, to put it mildly, some ups and downs. First there were fires. The Good Friday fire of 1788 destroyed 856 of the city's 1,100 buildings; six years later another fire destroyed 212 more. But after each fire, the residents rebuilt. And, in fact, some of the precautions taken against future fires—reliance on materials such as stucco and brick, close-set buildings with shared firewalls—have contributed to the quarter's unique architectural character.

Then there were bureaucrats. In 1836, in an attempt to deal with the problem of rising tensions between the city's Anglo and French populations, the city government divided the city into three autonomous districts.* As historian Carl Brasseaux has pointed out, this isolation did not serve the French Quarter well. The reduced tax base resulted in a reduction of government services, and over the next forty years the area—and its language—fell into decline. "By the end of Reconstruction," he writes, "the French Quarter was a glorified slum." But, again, there was a sad sort of silver lining to this cloud. Because residents of the area couldn't afford to replace the eighteenth-century construction

---

* The demarcation between Francophone and Anglophone areas can still be seen on any map of New Orleans. The traditional boundary of the French Quarter on the southwest is Canal Street, and many of the street names change from Franco to Anglo as you cross this street: Chartres becomes Camp, Decatur becomes Magazine, Treme becomes Liberty.

with more-modern structures, the French Quarter was able to retain what we now think of as its historic charm.

Today the French Quarter is, in parts, spectacularly picturesque, with creeping wisteria, eighteenth-century Spanish-influenced architecture, and a sense that at any moment Blanche DuBois might come floating around the corner. In other parts, though, like so many major tourist attractions, it's a big, smelly armpit of a place. Bourbon Street is particularly awful, full of roving bands of drunken tourists and shops full of cheap plastic crap. Mardi Gras beads seem to be constantly underfoot, like those last bits of sand you can never get out of the crotch of your bathing suit. It's like the worst parts of the Vegas Strip, only fatter.*

But if you're looking for some lingering signs of French, you'll find them here. Though French hasn't been the majority language in New Orleans for many decades—indeed, today more residents speak Vietnamese than French—its influence is everywhere in New Orleans and most particularly on the streets of the Vieux Carré.

Most of the French I came across was my favorite kind of French: culinary French. Consider, for instance, trout meunière, trout dredged in flour and served with a lemon and brown butter sauce. The name here comes from the French for "miller's wife," a nod to the preparation's rustic simplicity—and, presumably, dependence on flour. At Galatoire's on Bourbon Street, trout meunière amandine—almond-encrusted trout meunière—is the single most popular entrée.

Then there's *pain perdu*, or "lost bread," which fans of cable food shows know is a fancy term for French toast and a great way to use up old bread. *Étouffée* comes from the French for "suffocated" or "smothered" and is most frequently seen in the company of the words *crawfish*, *rice*, and *roux*. *Beignet*, French for "fritter," is the name of the official state donut of Louisiana.† For such a delicious treat, its etymology is surprisingly unappetizing: from what I can tell, *beignet* can be traced back to the same French word that gave us *bunion*.

---

* If I still sound vaguely traumatized, that's because—to my everlasting regret—I chose to stay just off Bourbon Street while in New Orleans.

† Massachusetts, by the way, is the only other state with an official donut (theirs is the Boston cream).

Once I ventured outside the kitchen, however, I started to notice that many of the French-inspired phrases I stumbled on in New Orleans felt decidedly awkward. Take the phrase "make dodo." Derived from the French *faire* ("make") and *dormir* ("to sleep"), "make dodo" is used—as is *faire dodo* in Quebec and France—to tell young children to go to sleep. (In Cajun country, *fais dodo* is instead used as a name for the dances thrown once said children are safely in bed.) This literal borrowing of the meaning of *faire* also shows up in phrases like "make ménage" ("clean the house") and "make groceries" ("go grocery shopping").

And as in St. Louis, French has granted New Orleans the dubious gift of unpredictable pronunciation. Sometimes words of French origin will have French pronunciation: *praline*, for instance, is pronounced "PRAH-line"; *gout* ("taste") is pronounced "goo." But other times the pronunciation will be Americanized: *Decatur* is "duh-KAY-ter"; *Fontainebleau* is "fountain blue." And then there are the pronunciations that I much suspect were made up solely to confound outsiders. Why else would you accent the second syllable of *Burgundy*? Or pronounce *Burthe* "byooth"?

New Orleans French doesn't just reflect the local heritage, it reveals the local personality. It's delightful but just a little hard to follow, like an excessively elaborate secret handshake. New Orleans is the same way. I've never been to a city so simultaneously gregarious and reticent. You're welcome to attend the festivities, but forget about the after-party. I bet you could live half your life in New Orleans and still not feel like a local. On your first visit, you can't help but feel that you might benefit from some footnotes.

All things considered, I was beginning to wonder if French in Louisiana wasn't a little more complicated than I'd thought.

Ironically, the more I explored the French Quarter, the more I began to be aware of languages other than French. Given that from 1763 to 1801 New Orleans was part of Spain, one of these languages was, unsurprisingly, Spanish. You can still see Spanish throughout the French Quarter—just look closely at the decorative tiles that memorialize the old Spanish street names. You can also find Spanish in two of Louisiana's most well-known and idiosyncratic words: *picayune* and *lagniappe*.

Picayune is probably best known in the United States as part of the name of the largest daily newspaper in New Orleans. It also, of course, shows up regularly on SAT lists as a word meaning "worthless" or "petty." Both uses stem from the word's older, Spanish usage. *Picayune* was the name for a half real, the smallest unit of currency in Louisiana under Spanish rule. By the time the United States took control of New Orleans, a picayune was worth 6¼ cents (one-sixteenth of a dollar). This also happened to be the exact price of one of the city's papers, which was, accordingly, thereafter known as the *Picayune*. The paper merged with the *Times-Democrat* in 1914 and has been the *Times-Picayune* ever since.

Another particularly characteristic Louisiana word is *lagniappe* (pronounced "LAN-yap"). *Lagniappe* derives from the Spanish *la ñapa* and means, roughly, "a little something extra thrown in for free" or, perhaps more succinctly, "gift with purchase."* In *Life on the Mississippi*, Mark Twain writes of his first encounter with lagniappe:

> We picked up one excellent word—a word worth traveling to New Orleans to get; a nice limber, expressive, handy word— "Lagniappe." They pronounce it lanny-yap. It is Spanish—so they said. We discovered it at the head of a column of odds and ends in the *Picayune* the first day; heard twenty people use it the second; inquired what it meant the third; adopted it and got facility in swinging it the fourth. It has a restricted meaning, but I think the people spread it out a little when they choose. It is the equivalent of the thirteenth roll in a "baker's dozen." It is something thrown in, gratis, for good measure. The custom originated in the Spanish quarter of the city. When a child or a servant buys something in a shop—or even the mayor or the governor, for aught I know—he finishes the operation by saying:
>
> "Give me something for lagniappe."
>
> The shopman always responds; gives the child a bit of liquorice-root, gives the servant a cheap cigar or a spool of thread, gives the

---

* The Spanish, in turn, comes from the Quechua *yapay*, "to add." Quechua, an indigenous South American language, is an official language in Peru and Bolivia and is spoken by upward of ten million people.

governor—I don't know what he gives the governor; support, likely.

Without Twain I likely never would have realized the true sense of *lagniappe*. In my experience the word was thrown around, willy-nilly, by souvenir shops looking to gild their less popular merchandise with a sort of vague regional flair.

But the most important Spanish I learned in New Orleans by far was a third word: *criollo*. Its etymology is fairly straightforward: a diminutive of the past participle of *criar* ("to breed," "to raise [children]") and possibly borrowed from the Portuguese *crioulo*, *criollo* can ultimately be traced back to the Latin *creāre*, "to create." The history of its meaning, however, is far more complicated. From Spanish and Portuguese the word made its way into French and eventually to English. We know it today as *creole*. And very few of us seem to agree on what it means.

When I hear the term *creole* bandied about, Inigo Montoya's voice frequently pops up in my head. "You keep using that word," I hear him say. "I do not think it means what you think it means." It's not that *creole* is necessarily hard to define. It's that *creole* is hard to define uniquely. It can describe groups of languages and groups of people, or specific languages and people within those groups. To make sure things are as mixed up as possible, it's also thrown about as a generic descriptor of the cuisine and cultures of Louisiana and the Caribbean. Sometimes the word flirts with even broader definitions: any tomatoes grown in Louisiana, for instance, could be called creole; the same goes for seemingly any spice blend containing cayenne.

If you'd asked me before I visited New Orleans what *creole* meant, I would have given you a largely linguistic explanation followed by the glancing acknowledgment that "it probably applies to some folks in Louisiana, too." But on my second afternoon in the city, I found myself rushing to keep up with a fast-talking tour guide in a top hat who had promised to show me "Creole" New Orleans. He dragged me and an equally harried family of four from one end of the quarter to the other, pointing out landmarks, rattling off dates, and somehow in the middle of all this leading me to the conclusion that I was going to need to draw a much more complete picture of what constituted "creole" if I hoped to understand the languages and peoples of Louisiana.

The first way you can use the word *creole* is to describe language.

Though there is some scholarly disagreement on the precise mechanism by which creoles are created, this is generally the way things are thought to happen: first, speakers of two or more languages come into regular contact with each other and need to find a way to communicate.* They begin to simplify their speech. Soon they are regularly adhering to a set of basic words and to a set of basic rules for using those words together. Sometimes these languages—known as pidgins—become so widespread that children learn them as their first language.† The children develop the pidgin language, enriching its vocabulary and structure. This relatively more sophisticated, stable, and standardized pidgin is what we call a creole.

The SIL Ethnologue currently lists eighty-two creoles throughout the world, languages such as Papiamento, a Spanish- and Portuguese-based creole and the official language of Aruba, Bonaire, and Curaçao, and Tok Pisin, an English-based creole spoken natively by well over a million people in Papua New Guinea. With nearly 8 million speakers, Haitian Creole is the most widely spoken creole in the world. But there are also more localized and short-lived examples, such as Unserdeutsch, a German-based creole that developed in a New Guinean orphanage.

Any language is going to serve as a repository for information about its speakers' culture and history, but contact languages such as pidgins and creoles are revealing in a more immediate and specific fashion. Creoles don't just tell you which languages interacted; they tell you *how* those languages interacted. For instance, if a pidgin or creole exists at all, you know that at some point there were two groups who needed to communicate. But you also know that for some reason neither group was willing or able to learn the other's language.

---

* Some would argue that this first requirement is actually *more than two* languages.

† A jargon is similar to a pidgin, albeit with an even more limited usage and lexicon. Jargons and pidgins are perhaps best thought of not as separate phenomena but rather as two ends of a continuum.

The words and structure of the language lend further insight, as the composition of a pidgin or creole vocabulary is an indication of the relative social, political, and economic power of each language group. The more power one group has, the more accommodating the other group will tend to be. From time to time a creole will develop that borrows words equally from both (or multiple) languages, but this is far more the exception than the rule, because the conditions for creole creation have throughout history most frequently occurred in the context of colonization. Indeed, most creoles are based on the languages of major colonial powers—Dutch, English, French, and Portuguese. And so the majority of the words in these creoles come from the colonial languages in question (i.e., the vocabulary of Papiamento is largely Dutch-inspired; the vocabulary of Tok Pisin is largely English-inspired).

A creole, then, is not just a remnant of historical necessity. It's also a linguistic encapsulation of the power dynamics of colonization and cultural exchange.

The cultural definitions of capital-*C Creole* are just as revealing. According to the most recent scholarship, the term has been in use in Spanish and Portuguese since the mid-sixteenth century, when it was used primarily to distinguish African-born slaves from slaves born in the New World. In his primer on Louisiana French, historian Carl Brasseaux wrote that as the use of *criollo* and *crioulo* expanded, so too did their definitions. Furthermore, these definitions varied from place to place. "In South America," Brasseaux writes, "native-born whites eventually came to apply the term exclusively to themselves. In the sugar islands, on the other hand, the term *Creole* was applied to natives of all racial backgrounds."

It is this latter definition—New World–born—that predominated in the early days of New Orleans. At first the use of Creole was inconsistent and relatively non-specific. Anthropologist Virginia R. Domínguez identifies what she called "the earliest published reference to Creoles in Louisiana proper" in Jean-Bernard Bossu's *Travels in the Interior of North America, 1751–1762*. In 1751, Bossu wrote, "There are four types of inhabitants [in New Orleans]: Europeans, Indians, Africans or Negroes, and half bloods, born of Europeans and savages native to the country. Those born of French fathers and French, or European, mothers are called Creoles. They are generally brave, tall, and well-built and have a natural inclination toward the arts and sciences." As New Orleans grew in numbers, nationalities, and native tongues, so did the need for distinctions beyond "born over here" and "born over there." The meaning of *Creole* eventually became a sort of terminological lever, a way for one group to distance itself from another group—often one it considered somehow less desirable.

In the late seventeenth and early eighteenth centuries, the English-speaking population of New Orleans grew steadily, a trend that accelerated when the United States acquired New Orleans as part of the Louisiana Purchase. Soon, and perhaps naturally enough, tensions developed between the city's new and established populations. It was in this environment that Creole became a way to distinguish between the descendants of the original French and Spanish settlers and the more recent arrivals from Anglo America.

Given the modern-day usage of the word, it's easy to assume that Creole identification was dependent on race, but according to Domínguez, it wasn't until the late 1800s that the term *Creole* began to evince a strong racial component in New Orleans. By this time the country was busy persecuting and restricting the rights of black Americans, and there was an ever-growing perception outside Louisiana that *Creole* was synonymous with *mixed-race*. Many assumed even the whitest-looking Creoles had some African heritage in their background. White Creoles worried about the effects such assumptions would have on their status, rights, and privileges, and eventually they began to separate themselves from the rest of the Creole community, avowing an all-white definition of Creole. The black Creole community, meanwhile, continued to call themselves Creole, a distinction that sometimes put them at odds with the Anglophone blacks they were increasingly identified with.

Creole is, then, depending on whom you ask, a dividing line between French and Anglo, white and black, white and light-skinned black, light- and dark-skinned black, or some combination thereof. Today it can also be used to distinguish among whites with French heritage: while Creoles are descendants of the original French and Spanish settlers, Cajuns are descendants of Acadian refugees. And these are just the conventional definitions. I suspect that the tourist industry likely has its own, wildly different set of meanings.

The confusion engendered by the term is, I think, a testament not only to the historical complexity of Louisiana's racial and ethnic makeup but also to the shifting demands placed on race as a descriptive construct. Before the Civil War, the population of Louisiana wasn't a simple collection of black and white but was rather a grab bag of Anglo, French, Spanish, Caribbean, African, Isleño, Acadian, German, and Native American. Moreover, many of these groups intermingled, creating a wide variety of potential racial identities, an environment reflected in the state's race-related vocabulary. Historian Gary Mills looked at records in colonial and antebellum Louisiana and found extremely specialized terms for mixed-race individuals. Some, such as *octoroon* (one eighth black ancestry) and *quadroon* (one quarter black ancestry), are relatively familiar and were in fairly common use outside Louisiana. Others, such as *sacatra* (seven eighths black ancestry) and *griffe* (three quarters black ancestry) are more obscure. Taken together, these terms provide some indication of the relative frequency of—if not the typical attitudes toward—miscegenation.

After the Civil War, however, black and white Creoles who had previously shared a single culture and community found themselves retreating to opposite corners, as it were. Some were surely surprised by which corner they ended up in. Though Louisianans had once appreciated the gradations of a multi-ethnic society, the racial distinction that mattered the most in the second half of the nineteenth century was the one between black and white.

It's hardly easy, however, to impose a binary structure on a polyadic system. In a society where races have intermingled long enough that distinctions could be made between sacatra and griffe, where do you draw the line between white and black? Some relied on clumsy systems of physical differentiation such as the "paper bag test," which grouped people depending on whether their skin was lighter or darker than the color of the bag, or the "comb test," which tested whether or not a comb could be run through a person's hair. But Louisiana lawmakers—like many other lawmakers throughout the country—largely favored an "any black is all black" definition.*

Ultimately, the word *Creole* is confusing not just because it has so many meanings but also because the racial definitions that underpin those meanings are almost laughably insufficient, not to mention potentially misleading. I admit that until I went on my Creole walking tour, I simply hadn't realized Creoles could be white. To be fair, in Louisiana the term *Creole* is used most commonly as a term of self-identification by men and women of French-speaking African descent. But I assumed this was the only definition.

Before I went to New Orleans, race was not something that had factored much into my thinking of Louisiana French. Or, to be more accurate, I hadn't been aware of the ways in which race had factored into my thinking. But once I began to think more about the state's racial diversity I also began to think how that diversity played out in its languages. How, I wondered, was white Creole French different from black Creole French—if it was different at all? What did each language have to teach me about the histories of these groups?

I had come to New Orleans expecting to find the French of my high school textbooks and hometown street signs. I had found instead a language of tourism and commerce, words seemingly kept alive for their market value. If I wanted to understand what life in Louisiana was like for French-speakers past and present, I knew I'd have to move beyond *meunière* and *étouffée*, to look past the French-language equivalent of Mardi Gras beads and souvenir T-shirts.

In other words, it was time to go find some real Louisiana French.

It was, unexpectedly, a stripper who pointed me in the right direction.

After one particularly exhausting day spent tromping about the streets and alleys of New Orleans, I decided to call it quits and go find a place

---

* This definition persisted at the legal level far longer than you might expect. In 1970 the Louisiana State Legislature passed Act 46—"Designation of race by public officials"—which allowed those classified as white to have as much as $\frac{1}{32}$ of "Negro blood." That is to say, you could have one black great-great-great-grandparent and still be white; you could not have two. This law wasn't repealed until 1983.

near my hotel to get a drink. I chose a bar by following one of my few hard-and-fast travel commandments: thou shalt not drink in an establishment playing trance music at deafening volume. On Bourbon Street this is surprisingly difficult, but eventually I spotted an unobtrusive little establishment just around the corner from the worst of the chaos. When I poked my head in the door, I heard nothing but the low murmur of human voices. Safe enough, I decided, and stepped inside.

The bar was busy but not crowded, and I was instantly comforted by the fact that everyone was drinking a real drink. There were no light-up cocktail umbrellas or neon blue concoctions in evidence, just shot glasses and bottles of beer. Grateful beyond words to spot signs of civilized life, I dumped my bag on a rickety table and ordered a Bud Light and a grilled cheese. I was midway through my sandwich when I realized the customers at the bar were eyeing me askance.

"What?" I asked, wondering if my shirt was on inside out or something disgusting was stuck to the side of my face.

A slip of a girl in a Saints jersey threw back a shot, wiped her mouth with the back of her hand, and smiled. "I'm Jerri! And we're wondering what you're doing here."

"Drinking," I muttered, a little nervously.

"Yes, but why *here*? What's wrong with the stuff around the corner?"

I just looked at her, trying desperately to figure out if I was going to make friends or lose them by revealing my deep-seated dislike of Bourbon Street. Would they take it as a sign of good taste? Or would they take it as a sign of bad taste? Or, worst of all, would they just think I was rude? Luckily, Jerri decided to interpret my silence—whatever it meant—as a friendly one. She turned around on her stool and planted her feet on the rungs. "So," she said. "What brings you to town?"

Jerri, a dancer at a nearby club, was one of the nicest, most bubbly young women I'd met in a long time. Soon enough, she revealed that this bar was where many of the locals who worked on Bourbon Street came before and after their shifts. The fact that I had stumbled in was apparently enough to recommend me, and soon she was treating me like an old friend. She told me about her apartment and her family and the Cinderella tattoo she wanted to get—to match her Tinker Bell tattoo, she said—and how she had to wear knee socks at work because her shins were so bruised from crawling around on the floor. Even her glum-mest disclosures were delivered as cheery exclamations: "Bachelor par-ties are the worst! But I sure need the money! Because my little sister's having a baby!"

Slightly flummoxed, I sputtered out a loosely related collection of con-versational gambits. I told her about the time the women's rugby team had tried to recruit me, that I just couldn't think of the Rams as a true St. Louis team, and that I was interested in Louisiana Creole.

At this she perked up. "Oh! Well we'll have to figure out where to send you to hear some, then!"

Her roommate, a student and part-time bartender, looked over. "There's no Creole spoken in New Orleans. Not anymore."

"Who's from Louisiana?" Jerri challenged. "You or me?"

"Yeah?" retorted her roommate. "And who's a linguistics major? You or me?"

They bickered good-naturedly for a few minutes before Jerri turned back to me, shrugging apologetically. "I guess you'll have to venture outside the city." She smiled brightly. "Sorry!"

Soon enough, Jerri and her friends headed off to work. I finished my beer and went back to my hotel, dodging the dipsomaniacal hordes I met along the way. They were heading out for a night on the town; I was turning in to look at some maps. I couldn't help but feel a slight twinge of envy.

But only very slight.

The next day I drove west out of the city, taking I-10 past Louis Arm-strong Airport before cutting south to the surprisingly unassuming state highway known as Louisiana's Great River Road. As I sped along the sinusoidal path of the lower Mississippi, I wondered how it was that I had so far barely registered the river's existence. Part of it must be, I thought, that even four years after Hurricane Katrina there were still so many re-minders in New Orleans of the destruction wrought by the storm. I'd seen homes and businesses that had yet to be rebuilt; throughout the French Quarter the souvenir shops were selling Katrina-related memo-rabilia, each promising with sly conviction to donate a portion of the price to rebuilding efforts; my hotel lobby was strewn with brochures for Katrina tours.

I spent some time agonizing over these tours. In theory, part of me could see the value in exposing as many people as possible to the full extent of the disaster. This was the same part that wondered if I myself wasn't doing New Orleans a gross disservice by not visiting its harder-hit sections. The rest of me, though, recalled with a flush of shame a time I had been walking through a hard-up village in British Columbia. I'd been taking too many pictures that day, and when I passed a house that was just shy of derelict, its front yard filled with broken furniture and toys and tools that caught the early evening light just so, my first thought had been to lift my camera to my face. *Pretty*, I remember thinking.

In the end I didn't go on a Katrina tour, and I'm glad I didn't. I didn't want to be a tourist to a tragedy such as Katrina. But I wouldn't say I have anything to be proud of, either. I still could have gone by myself, found someone to take me, or even volunteered some time. Instead I gave some money and bought a collection of *Times-Picayune* columns, telling myself there was nothing wrong with timidity but growing ever more certain that it must be my most contemptible trait.

This is what Katrina can still do, years later, even to someone so minimally acquainted with New Orleans and the Gulf Coast. I suspect that many visitors have a similar experience. There's no middle ground here: you're either not thinking about Katrina at all or you're thinking about it and it alone. So even though the Mississippi is the raison d'être of the whole region, even though I'd surely known it was right there alongside the quarter, just beyond Café du Monde, if I was thinking about water, I wasn't thinking about river flow—I was thinking about storm surge.

But as I drove west though Hahnville and Taft, past Killona and Edgard, I couldn't ignore the river any longer, looming as it did just over my right shoulder. It feels strange to think that a river can loom, but that's what it does here. Anywhere on this part of the Mississippi the river is corseted between hundreds of miles of levees, so even on the Great River Road you can't actually see the Great River. Occasionally massive barges sailed past on their way to the Gulf. They looked as if they were floating though the grass.

I was on my way to visit two historic Creole plantations, one white-owned, one black-owned, both French-speaking. The first was Laura Plantation, an eighteenth-century Creole plantation home just outside the town of Vacherie in St. James Parish, about forty miles east of New Orleans. This stretch of the Mississippi was originally settled by immigrants from Germany and Switzerland, and it is still known to some as the German Coast or La Côte des Allemands. I have also seen it called the American Ruhr; this is a nod not to historical settlement patterns but to the petrochemical plants that line the river between Baton Rouge and New Orleans.

But back in the seventeenth and eighteenth centuries, the area was a center of agriculture, home to some of Louisiana's most lucrative sugar plantations. A few of the grand plantation houses still stand today, restored to their former glory by ardent preservationists who are from time to time funded by savvy corporate donors. Just past the town of Reserve is San Francisco Plantation House, a blue-and-peach monstrosity of architectural opulence that epitomizes the style known as "Steamboat Gothic." Farther upriver is the classic colonnaded exterior of Oak Alley, arguably Louisiana's best-known and best-preserved plantation house. And up in Farrow is Houmas House, the Greek Revival residence that provided the setting for both *Hush, Hush, Sweet Charlotte* and *Mandingo*.

When I arrived at Laura Plantation, I stepped out of my car into the thick soup of Louisiana summer. Having grown up in St. Louis, I'd thought I was well used to humidity, but even I was taken aback by the weather. It felt like the inside of a cooler after a long day on the beach, stuffy and sticky and smelling of wet sandwiches. With a shiver of distaste, I slicked my hair back and held my shirt away from my body. I wasn't just sweating—I was fermenting. I began to wish I'd restricted my curiosity to those language communities established after the invention of air-conditioning.

I hurried toward the visitor center hoping for some relief, but before the perspiration on my brow even had time to cool, I was shuffled into a group of other tourists and placed in the care of a guide named Meze. Somehow managing to exude a kind of energetic serenity that I wish were more prevalent among tour guides, Meze quickly identified herself as Creole, explaining to the group that *Creole* simply meant someone born in Louisiana who was part of the Francophone culture. In my mind Inigo Montoya shook his head but otherwise stayed silent.

She then took us to the front of the house, which I had yet to get a good look at on account of being too busy melting. My first thought was that it didn't look like any plantation house I was expecting. It's squat, for one thing. The main structure is set atop eight-foot brick pillars—I was told the foundation is set at an angle to keep the house from sinking into the soft ground—but above that the house is just two stories high. Though there is a porch that runs the length of the building, the front façade is dominated by the Norman roof, an expansive slant of shingles punctuated by two dainty little dormers. Architecturally, it's almost plain. When a member of my group pointed this out, Meze shrugged and acknowledged that the house isn't nearly as fanciful as many of the "Anglo" plantations. "If you're Creole," she said, "you don't show off your money where you make your money."

This is slightly disingenuous, because the house is without a doubt something of a showpiece. Though the structure is relatively modest, the colors are downright flamboyant, with sunshine-yellow siding and robin's-egg-blue and vermillion trim. In contrast, the lavender railings seem almost understated. This, Meze told us, was another difference between Anglo and Creole plantation life. The Anglos may have built bigger, but the Creoles painted louder.

As we proceeded, the tour turned out to be largely variations on this theme: Anglos this, Creoles that; Creoles this, Anglos that. But I grew quietly frustrated that in all the talk of Creole versus Anglo that there was so little mention of language. Though Meze assured us that Creole was spoken at Laura Plantation until the 1920s, I wanted to know what exactly this so-called Creole was. Was it a dialect of French spoken by a particular class of wealthy plantation-owners? Was it the Louisiana Creole I had come in search of? Or was it something else entirely? And, for the love of Jonathan Lipnicki, why could no one else in my group help me out by asking a few of these questions for me? I was becoming a nuisance.

Mostly, I was worried there might not be straight answers to my questions. Creoles and pidgins present a number of challenges to linguists and other scholars, not the least of which is that in their early stages they are rarely ever written down. This is particularly true of the contact languages of the early Americas or any other languages that predated the development of systematic linguistic field methods. So if you're interested in the early history of languages such as, say, Mobilian Trade Jargon, Michif, or Palenquero, usually the very best documentation you can expect comes courtesy of the observations of missionaries, traders, or adventurers—in other words, men and women with even less formal linguistic training than I.

Luckily for me, Laura Loucoul—the plantation's namesake—left a few hints to go by.

Laura was the great-granddaughter of the plantation's founder and, eventually, owner of half the family business. In 1885, still in her early twenties, Laura met a man from St. Louis named Charles Gore, and after a lengthy—and secret—betrothal, they married. At this point Laura sold her share of the farm and moved with Gore to what is now St. Louis's Central West End. Much later, at the behest of her three children, she began writing down her recollections of her life in Louisiana. Her memoir, published as *Memories of the Old Plantation*, was completed in 1936, but it remained private until 1993, when it was discovered in the possession of a Gore family friend.

Laura's memoir focuses primarily on the history of her family and on the details of everyday life in antebellum Louisiana. Nevertheless, she reveals enough that I was able to infer a rough sense of the type of French used by Laura and her family. It seems clear to me that they must have spoken a mostly standard French, a variety the linguist Michael Picone has termed "Plantation Society French." Like many other wealthy and socially prominent families of the time, the Duparc-Locouls kept in close contact with European French, both socially and culturally. Of course, they weren't very far removed from their roots to begin with: Guillaume Duparc, the family patriarch, hailed from Normandy, and his wife, Nanette, was only the second generation of her family to be born in Louisiana. Nevertheless, each succeeding generation was careful to maintain connections with France through marriage and travel. Guillaume and Nanette's daughter Elisabeth married a man from Bordeaux; their granddaughter Aimée also married a Frenchman and lived in Lille and Paris before returning to Louisiana. Of Laura's three first cousins, one returned to France, one married a French consul, and the other became a French consul.

The family also relied on education to reinforce ties with France and, consequently, the standard French dialect spoken by the educated elite. Many wealthy Creole families of the era sent their sons to school in France and their daughters to Catholic schools, and the Duparc-Locoul family was no exception. Between the ages of thirteen and eighteen Laura's father, Émile, studied at a military college in Bordeaux. Laura's mother, Desirée, meanwhile, was sent to a convent in Louisiana where she acquired, according to Laura, a "perfect command of both English and French." And Laura's cousins, themselves born in Paris, received daily instruction from one Monsieur Medout, a French professor hired by Laura's aunt for the express purpose of supplementing her children's language skills. Even Laura, who admits to being no more than a mediocre student (and who initially got less than perfect marks in French at her New Orleans boarding school), uses only perfect textbook French in her memoir.

However, just because Laura and her family spoke Standard French, this was not necessarily the only form of French spoken on the plantation— or even the most popular one. Because, of course, the members of the Duparc-Locoul family were not alone on the plantation. Like any other sugar plantation of its era, Laura Plantation built its success on the backs of slaves.

The first slaves in Louisiana were Native American, but the administrators of the French colony soon began lobbying for a supply of African slaves. Nicolas de la Salle, the colony's first commissary, complained that Native slaves were insufficient, as they "only cause us trouble" and "are not appropriate for hard labor like the blacks." Their efforts—which included a proposal to trade Native slaves for African slaves from French Caribbean islands at a ratio of 2:1—were at first largely unsuccessful, and the black population of Louisiana remained exceedingly low until the arrival of the first slave ships from Africa in 1719. Growth thereafter was rapid, and by 1800, just four years before Guillaume Duparc was granted his land along the Mississippi, there were more than 24,000 slaves in lower Louisiana, accounting for 55 percent of the total population.

For most of my time at Laura Plantation the history of slavery was set aside—perhaps not surprisingly—in favor of a more crowd-friendly narrative of female empowerment. In Creole families, Meze explained with a smile, you don't leave the business to the eldest son, you leave it to the smartest child. (Although I suspect that most eldest sons consider these to be one and the same.) As a result, women had a hand in the family business until 1892: after Guillaume Duparc's death in 1808, the plantation and its businesses were left in the hands of his widow, Nanette. And when it was time for Nanette to choose a successor, she skipped over her sons and settled instead on her daughter Elisabeth, who ruled the plantation with an iron fist for many years. As we moved through the house, dutifully admiring the woodwork and décor, Meze regaled us with stories about the women of the Duparc family and their extraordinary business acumen.

But as I listened to the history of Laura Plantation, I couldn't help but begin to wonder at the sort of ruthlessness that such acumen required at the time. Elisabeth, for instance, was singled out as the driving force behind the plantation's early expansion and prosperity. And though Meze never suggested that Elisabeth was a particularly pleasant person—indeed, it seems as if she was roundly disliked even by members of her own family—even those of us inured to the casual horrors of modern industry would be taken aback by some of her methods.

Consider her management of the plantation's slave population. When the plantation commenced production in 1805, there were only seven slaves in residence, six Africans and one Native American. By 1808—the same year Nanette inherited the plantation—this number had risen to seventeen slaves, which included five children and one adolescent. The family eventually decided to invest in the plantation's labor force, but slaves were expensive, and they would need a great many if they wanted to expand the business. Elisabeth came up with a cheaper solution: in 1830, the plantation acquired thirty teenage female slaves for the express purpose of breeding a workforce.

Her plan worked, and by the time of the Civil War she had 186 slaves living in sixty-five cabins behind the main house. But this "success" relied on Elisabeth's ability to treat the men and woman in her employ in the same way she might treat livestock—if not worse. And though this is the most troubling example of Elisabeth's harsh treatment of her slaves, it is far from the only example. Her disdain for her workers was evident in all her behavior: she branded problematic slaves on their faces to make it more difficult for them to run away; she hurled epithets at her least favorite slaves; she had no compunction about separating children from their parents and spouses from each other.

Four of Elisabeth's slave cabins still exist today, standing in dark, cramped, and run-down contrast to the fanciful and celebratory aesthetic of the main house. Had the tour kept to the front and interior of the main house, I might never have known they were there, but out back they are impossible to miss. As Meze led us toward them, relating in low, somber tones the grimmer facts and figures of the plantation's history of slavery, I felt—surprisingly, unnervingly—something close to relief. Finally, I thought, I was getting closer to a fuller picture of life on the plantation.

Moments later I heard my first words of Louisiana Creole: *Compair Lapin*.

The stories of Compair Lapin—or, as most American children know him, Br'er Rabbit—were ultimately popularized by Joel Chandler Harris, who collected the tales while living on Turnwold Plantation in central Georgia. He was probably also the first American folklorist to record the stories. But it was a man named Alcée Fortier who first transcribed the Louisiana Creole versions of the stories. That he did so while visiting the area around Laura is a fact the plantation, its guides, and their publicity materials make much of.

Fortier, later a professor at Tulane University and a president of the Modern Language Association, was born in 1856 to a prominent landowning family that lived not far from the Duparc-Locouls in Vacherie.* In the 1870s Fortier began compiling local folklore as told to him by

---

* In her memoir Laura recounts running into Fortier when traveling home from New Orleans: "Alcée Fortier, a man easily double my age, entered the train and, after saluting Father, took his seat beside me. We chatted the whole two hours until we reached the Vacherie Station on our plantation." Her father, she related with a characteristic hint of impishness, was piqued by the realization that men—and older men at that—were beginning to pay attention to his teenage daughter.

area slaves. *Louisiana Folk-Tales*, published by Houghton Mifflin in 1894, includes Fortier's transcriptions and translations of more than forty stories, bringing to life the French spoken in the slave quarters at Laura Plantation.

Here, for instance, is the first part of Fortier's transcription of "Chien Avec Tigue" (The Dog and the Tiger):

In jou in chien acheté cent poules et in coq, et in tigue acheté cent coqs et in poule. Tous les soi chien la trouvé in panier plein dézef dans so poulailler, et tigue la té trouvé jisse in dézef. Tigue dit chien volé li, et li taché li, li metté li dans in brouette et li parti pou vende li. On chimin li contré in chévreil; li conté li so zaffaire et li mandé li si li pas raison vende chien la. Chévreil la dit non, alors tigue la tchué li. In pé plis tard li rencontré in lion et li raconté li so lhistoire. Lion la dit tigue té gagnin tort, et tigue la dit, "Vous parlé comme ça pasque vous connin vous plis fort qué moin."*

One day a dog bought a hundred hens and one rooster, and a tiger bought a hundred roosters and one hen. Every evening the dog found a basketful of eggs in his chicken coop, and the tiger found just one egg. The tiger said the dog had robbed him, and so he tied him up, put him in a wheelbarrow, and went off to sell him. On the way he ran into a roe deer; he told the deer his story and asked him if he was not right to sell the dog. The deer said no, and so the tiger killed him. A little later the tiger met a lion and told him his story. The lion said the tiger was wrong, and the tiger said, "You spoke like that because you know that you are stronger than I."

---

* A literal modern Standard French translation might read something like this: *Un jour un chien a acheté cent poules et un coq, et un tigre a acheté cent coqs et une poule. Tous les soirs le chien trouvait un panier plein d'oeufs dans son poulailler, et le tigre trouvait juste un oeuf. Le tigre a dit que le chien les lui avait volés, et il l'a attaché, il l'a mis dans une brouette, et il est parti pour le vendre. En chemin, il a rencontré un chevreuil; il lui a raconté ses affaires et il lui a demandé s'il n'avait pas raison de vendre le chien. Le chevreuil a dit non, alors le tigre l'a tué. Un peu plus tard il a rencontré un lion et lui a raconté son histoire. Le lion a dit que le tigre avait tort, et le tigre a dit, "Vous avez parlé comme ça parce que vous savez que vous êtes plus fort que moi."*

The first thing you probably notice about this passage is that the language is quite obviously closely related to French. In fact, if you've studied even a year of Standard French you can probably fumble your way through the Louisiana Creole version of the story. This is particularly true if you read it out loud, as many of the differences are exacerbated by transliteration. When spoken it is much more obvious that *in* is *un* (one) or *on chimin* is *en chemin* (on the way). Sometimes, though, you also need to pick apart the words a bit to recognize the Standard French. *Dézef*, for instance, is more familiar if you keep in mind the French partitive construction *des oeufs* (some eggs).

The passage also displays a few examples of the morphological simplification commonly seen in creole languages. There's no gender distinction, for instance. The words for "lion" and "tiger" take the definite article *la* even though their Standard French counterparts are masculine; meanwhile, "hen" and "wheelbarrow," both feminine in Standard French, are recorded as *un poule* and *un brouette*. The pronouns are certainly also simpler: *li* is used for *il* (the third-person masculine subject pronoun), *le* (the third-person masculine direct-object pronoun), and *lui* (the third-person masculine indirect-object pronoun).

But it's important, as always, to keep in mind that a loss of inflection does not imply a concomitant loss of expressiveness. After all, if it did, we'd have to turn to Old English in order to communicate with any grace. For example, while the verbs in the above passage may look crude to a student used to the frequently irregular conjugations of standard French, this doesn't mean that Louisiana Creole French is without verbal finesse. Consider the phrase "Lion la dit tigue té gagnin tort." I translated this above as "The lion said the tiger was wrong," but to really communicate the meaning of the word *té*, a marker of anteriority, it would be more accurate to say "The lion said the tiger was wrong [before]." Louisiana Creole has a number of these verbal markers, including *ape* (progressive), *ale* (definite future), and *bin* (present perfect), each uninflected proof that in language there is a difference between simple and simplistic.

Generally speaking, however, due to their relative morphological simplicity creole languages tend to be labeled by non-linguists as "corrupt" or "uneducated" versions of the prestige language. Fortier himself acknowledges this tendency in *Louisiana Folk-tales*, emphasizing that

Louisiana Creole "is not merely a corruption of French, that is to say, French badly spoken, it is a real idiom with a morphology and grammar of its own."

It would be naïve, however, to imply that derisive attitudes toward creole languages are just reflections of morphological dissimilarity. It is also without doubt a consequence of the typically subordinate social standing of creole-language-speakers, as it is not typically our habit to judge a man and his speech independently. Even Fortier, an avowed champion of Louisiana Creole, is guilty of this. He writes, "It is curious to see how the ignorant African slave transformed his master's language into a speech concise and simple, and at the same time soft and musical." It is hard to imagine a single sentence that could convey any more efficiently so many of the stereotypes about Africans and African Americans—innate ignorance, noble simplicity, exotic musicality—that persist to this day.

Though Laura Plantation aims to elucidate to its guests the differences between Anglo and Creole culture, ultimately the lesson I took away was that relatively more nuanced attitudes toward race do not preclude racial privilege. Though there are white Creoles and black Creoles and every sort of Creole in between, if a society and economy once depended on the enslavement of Africans, that fundamental bifurcation between free and slave will, it seems to me, linger longer in language—and the way we talk about language—than any of us should like.

The history and culture of the slaves at Laura Plantation may not quite have been reduced to the status of uncomfortable footnote for the benefit of the plantation's tourists, but it was at the very least marginalized as an awkward tangent. The most overt testaments to African culture were the indiscriminately "ethnic" knickknacks for sale in the plantation gift shop. But there were a few more hints of African influence to be found in the stories of Alcée Fortier, a number of which feature the hapless Compair Bouki.* *Bouki* didn't sound like any French animal I

---

* There is a Louisiana Creole proverb that explains Bouki's lot in life: *Bouki fait gombo; lapin mangé li*—"The hyena makes the gumbo; the rabbit eats it." Bouki is, as I like to think of it, a most unfortunate combination of a schlemiel and a schlimazel.

could think of, so I suspected it would turn out to be an African word. Indeed, after a little digging, I discovered that though in Louisiana Creole *bouki* is often translated as "he-goat," in Wolof the same word means "hyena."

Though I knew very little about Wolof, a Niger-Congo language of considerable difficulty for English-speakers, I knew enough to understand why it might be a language of some influence among Louisiana slaves. Under French rule, the African slave trade was highly concentrated in two respects. First, the vast majority of slaves arrived in the early years of the slave trade. As colonial records show, more than 90 percent of the slaves who were brought to Louisiana between 1719 and 1763 arrived before 1730. Afterward, economic and political realities ensured that Louisiana's slave population was largely augmented by natural means—among other factors, it made more sense for slave ships to stop in the Caribbean instead of going all the way to New Orleans—and so for several decades the black population in Louisiana was insulated from outside influence.

This first influx of slave labor also pulled the majority of its captives from a single part of Africa, which in combination with the punctuated importation schedule contributed to a relatively higher level of cultural and linguistic homogeneity in Louisiana's slave population than was seen in other parts of the Caribbean. As documented by the historian Gwendolyn Midlo Hall, two thirds of the first 5,000 or so slaves brought to Louisiana before 1730 were originally from Senegambia in western Africa, an area whose inhabitants were known for their skills as cultivators of rice.

Wolof, you will not be surprised to learn, is primarily spoken in and around Senegal and the Gambia.

I wanted to know more about the African influence on Louisiana Creole, but I figured that maybe Laura Plantation had helped me all it could. So I pushed on to a second plantation, one located deep in the heart of Louisiana, just outside the state's earliest permanent European settlements. This was a plantation owned by Creoles of Color—black Creoles who had managed to throw off the yoke of slavery. Perhaps there I could begin to sketch a more complete picture of this language that was proving so elusive. Perhaps by investigating where Louisiana Creole had come from, I could better understand where it had disappeared to.

This is how I found myself in the town of Natchitoches, about seventy-five miles southwest of Shreveport. I'd been in Shreveport once, many years earlier, and all I remembered about it was the heat, the humidity, and the fact that, in 1971, it released Jared Leto into the world. On my first day in Natchitoches (pronounced "NACK-uh-tush") I was delighted to discover that those seventy-five miles make all the difference in the world. Natchitoches is a picture postcard of a town, a sleepy assembly of wrought-iron balconies and old-brick construction so charming and prepossessing you expect to see a film crew around every corner.

The most striking feature of Natchitoches is the Cane River, a gentle, shimmering arc of water that winds its way through town with a lazy sort of panache. If you spend an afternoon meandering through downtown Natchitoches as I did, you might find yourself wondering about the Cane River. It was like no river I'd ever seen, almost unnervingly placid and still, a Silent Bob where I expected a Jay. This is due to the fact that, as I later discovered, Cane River isn't actually a river at all. In 1839 a man named Henry Miller Shreve was hired to break up a 160-mile-long logjam in the Red River known as the "Great Raft." As Shreve removed the jams over the course of the next thirty years, it was like popping the buttons off a poorly tailored waistcoat. The river, finally able to breathe, unfurled in unexpected and inconvenient ways. At Grand Ecore, just four miles north of Natchitoches, it jumped channels, cutting east as it rushed toward the Mississippi—and cutting off Natchitoches. Eventually the path through Natchitoches became unnavigable, and it was dammed off to form what is called an oxbow lake.

It was Cane River—or Cane River Lake, I suppose—that had drawn me to the area. Historically, Natchitoches is perhaps best known as the oldest permanent European settlement in the Louisiana Purchase. The first Europeans to visit the area were members of DeSoto's army in 1542, and just 150 years later, the French arrived to establish settlements and trading posts. But Cane River is also the center of one of Louisiana's most notable communities of black Creoles. They were notable in no small part because unlike so many of their brethren, they were not slaves. Rather, they were powerful, wealthy, and—above all—free members of Louisiana society.

Slavery wasn't fully abolished in Louisiana until 1865, when the Thirteenth Amendment released the slaves in the thirteen parishes that had been under Union control (and, thus, unaffected by the Emancipation Proclamation). But even before the government put a legal end to slavery there were still a number of ways slaves could gain their freedom in Louisiana. They could, for instance, perform military or public service. Or they could buy their freedom with money earned by working on Sundays and holidays. During the years of Spanish rule, any slave who could prove Indian ancestry was set free by royal decree. Slaves could also be voluntarily freed by their owners; one of the most common forms of manumission was that granted by white farmers to their mistresses and their natural children.

It was this latter route in particular that contributed to the substantial increase of the free black population of Louisiana between the late eighteenth and nineteenth centuries, which grew from fewer than 200 in 1763 to more than 18,000 in 1860. But in the earliest days of colonial Louisiana it was still rare—if not scandalous—for a white slave owner to free his black companion. Nevertheless, this is how the founder of Cane River's Creole community gained her freedom. It is only one of the many extraordinary chapters in the story of the life of one Marie Thérèse, *dite* Coincoin.

Born in 1742 into the household of Louis Juchereau de St. Denis, the first commander of Fort St. Jean Baptiste and the founder of Natchitoches, Coincoin was the daughter of two slaves, one of whom was reputed to be African royalty.* Coincoin herself was renowned as a slave of great distinction. Not only was she clever and loyal, she also was a gifted herbalist who, as legend has it, nursed her owner through yellow fever and even cut her own baby brother from her dying mother's womb.

---

* Sometimes it's difficult to separate the wheat from the apocryphal chaff when it comes to Coincoin, a woman who routinely accomplished the seemingly impossible.

Coincoin was eventually leased to Claude Thomas Pierre Metoyer, a local planter. Whether it was strictly a business arrangement, genuine affection, or some combination of the two no one can say, but Coincoin and Metoyer were nevertheless together for twenty years, during which time Coincoin bore ten children and Metoyer granted Coincoin her freedom. Eventually Metoyer, in need of a legitimate heir, married a white Creole woman (coincidentally also named Marie-Thérèse) and parted from Coincoin. But before he did so, Metoyer granted Coincoin an annuity and sixty-eight acres of land along the Red River. Coincoin, able at last to reap the full benefits of her considerable talents and work ethic, took her plot of land and turned it into something of an empire. Eventually she and her children—all of whom she freed—owned more than 18,000 acres of Natchitoches Parish.

Coincoin was the reason I'd come to Natchitoches. Her son Louis, in keeping with the family tradition of being utterly unwilling to allow fate to be dictated by injustice, somehow managed to become a landowner while he was still technically a slave. His plantation, today called Melrose, is still home to a number of well-preserved historical buildings. One of these buildings is, as they say, not like the others, and it was this structure that drew my attention as soon as I set foot on the plantation grounds on what would later prove to be one of the hottest days of the summer. It looked, I thought—wishing not for the first time that I had a more sophisticated aesthetic vocabulary—like a mushroom house from Super Mario 3.

This building turned out to be the "African House," a structure thought to have been built around 1800, making it one of the oldest extant American structures built by and for blacks. It is also like no other building I had ever seen. The lower structure, two stories of wood and whitewashed brick, is mostly obscured by a massive sloping roof that sits atop the building like an oversized hat. Had I not been told that the architecture was reminiscent of structures found in the Congo, I would have not been able to pinpoint its architectural provenance any more specifically than "Africa." And even that conclusion was driven not by a familiarity with any of the building's features but rather by a lack of familiarity with them. If it wasn't European, I figured, it probably had to be African.

The sweltering heat faded into the background for a blessed few minutes as I considered the ramifications of this. During my time in Louisiana I'd collected African words like crumbs of bread leading to a destination I'd already mapped out in my head. Anything that didn't fit in with my schoolgirl's idea of French—*bouki*, *gris-gris*, *gombo*—was considered proof positive of the language's essential non-Frenchness. When I read that the name *Coincoin* was thought to be derived from the Ewe name *Ko Kwē*, which is traditionally given to a second-born daughter— and then that Coincoin was, in fact, the second of her parents' daughters, I thought it a grand piece of evidence, the sort of thing Perry Mason might coax from a witness in the last five minutes of an episode. *So you see, ladies and gentlemen of the jury, Louisiana Creole is African!*

Common sense dictated that the language couldn't possibly be wholly devoid of African influence. But until I found myself in front of the African House I hadn't stopped to question how much of that African influence still existed, whether it had been preserved by a series of lucky sociohistorical accidents or whether it had given way to other words, to other structures. Was it possible that I had been exaggerating the impact of African languages simply because I was interpreting anything not European as African?

Crap.

I turned on my heel, got in my car, and found a library. What I discovered was less than conclusive. Gwendolyn Midlo Hall, such a helpful resource when researching the details of the early Louisiana slave trade, is reassuring, writing, "The vocabulary of Louisiana Creole is overwhelmingly French in origin, but its grammatical structure is largely African." But the linguists are less enthusiastic. Albert Valdman and Thomas A. Klingler point out that "so far no scholar has demonstrated, with support from carefully documented studies comparing the various French Creoles and various African languages, a clear link between the grammar of a specific African language or group of African languages and a particular French-based Creole language or the entire group."

Now, I don't like to disagree with linguists, because (a) they tend to be extremely clever even as academics go, (b) they're perfectly willing to take to the Internet to pick apart substandard arguments and assertions, and (c) they have an annoying tendency to be entertaining while they do so. But something about this didn't make sense to me. How could a language that was created in large part by the commingling of French and African languages display so few African characteristics?

As far as I could figure, there were only two potential explanations. The first being that linguistic diversity among the African population could have minimized the structural influence of any one African language. But I knew that two thirds of the initial slave stock had come from Senegambia, and though there are a substantial number of languages spoken in that area, most of the languages are from the same family and many of the dialects are mutually intelligible. Though some leveling surely would have occurred, would it really have been so extreme that scholars in the twentieth century would find no evidence of a grammatical link between Louisiana Creole and any African languages? It seemed unlikely.

Which meant I was underestimating the role of French. Because whatever Louisiana Creole once was, over time it wasn't becoming more African or even more English. So it must have been becoming more French—which means it must have been becoming less creole.

I puzzled over this for a few days as I skulked about Natchitoches, taking in the sights and wondering just how many bed and breakfasts could have been used as filming locations for *Steel Magnolias*. Given what I had learned at Laura and Melrose, I could understand how French had continued to exert a pull on Louisiana Creole. Wealthy white Creole families worked hard to maintain ties with France; free black Creoles like Coincoin and her family, meanwhile, were active in local business and society, both of which would have allowed and required the development in the black community of a more standard form of French. But that sort of change would have been limited to the more rarified echelons of society. It seemed to me that there had to be another force at work—so what was I missing?

It came to me over a meat pie. Of course. I was forgetting about the other kind of French in Louisiana. I was forgetting about Cajun French.

I don't mean I *actually* forgot about it, of course. You can't be in Louisiana and forget about Cajun French, no matter whether you're in actual Cajun country or just in some part of the state that would like to sell you overpriced sauces with "Cajun" on the label. But I had admittedly hoped to be able to ignore the language while I was in Louisiana. My brain had enough on its plate as it was. However, I was beginning to realize that any efforts to rein in the scope of my explorations were utterly futile.

Simply put, Cajun French has grown out of the language spoken by Acadians in exile—most experts agree that *Cajun* is a corruption of *Acadien*.* Originally French settlers in Nova Scotia, the Acadians were deported by the British in 1715 for a variety of reasons that range from the pragmatic to the deplorable, depending on whom you ask. Many of the Acadians who were exiled to the United States or shipped back to France eventually headed south to Louisiana, where they settled in and around Bayou Teche. Today practically the entire lower half of the state, centered around Lafayette, is considered part of Acadiana.

Cajun French is a regional variety of French, which is to say it is *not* a creole. It does differ from Standard French in terms of pronunciation, idiom, and vocabulary. There are legions of petty differences between the two. A Cajun French speaker might omit the *ne* of *ne . . . pas*, he's probably ditched the subjunctive and the formal *vous*, and he doesn't call a car *une voiture*, he calls it *un char*. And if he refers to a lady's *galette*—well, he's no gentleman. But though the flesh may be different, the bones of Cajun French are basically the same as those of Standard French. Its nouns are gendered, its verbal structure is mostly the same, and its pronouns are nearly identical.

And as Louisiana Creole has rubbed up against Cajun French over the years, it has in some cases acquired features of this more standard version of French. The linguist Ingrid Neumann-Holzschuh has described this in some detail, noting that as Cajun and Louisiana Creole communities came into more frequent contact over the years—particularly after the Civil War—certain forms of Louisiana Creole began marking gender

---

* The origin of the word *Acadia*, meanwhile, is a matter of some debate. There are those who postulate an indigenous American origin—*cadie*, for instance, is a Mi'kmaq word for "place," which makes for a logical etymology. But *Acadia* also sounds a lot like *Arcadia*, the Greek name Giovanni da Verrazzano's earliest maps gave to the area around modern-day Delaware. It is also a possibility, then, that the name simply migrated north.

and even using two different Cajun verb forms to describe habitual or completed actions. In this case, then, the typical course of language contact has been reversed: the new forms of Louisiana Creole that have emerged feature *more* inflections, not fewer.

It's important, I think, not to lose sight of the origins of creole languages, of the fact that many of these languages are testaments to a time of gross and loathsome inequality. But the circumstances of their creation are hardly the only interesting part of the story—after all, if all we ever knew were the facts of Coincoin's birth, we would remain ignorant of the remarkable accomplishments of her life.

Louisiana Creole and Cajun French are now so intermingled that they are often discussed not as separate languages but as two points on a continuum. At one end is the most creole version of Louisiana Creole, at the other the most standard form of Cajun French. Linguists, ahead of the curve as usual, are ever cognizant of the fact that humankind is rarely amenable to either/or distinctions. With no small amount of chagrin, I realized I'd managed to forget this. By focusing on one end of the spectrum I'd managed to miss the middle ground—I'd been so busy looking for the African influence in Louisiana Creole I'd overlooked the parts that could only be called American. And in so doing I'd failed to notice that these two languages were drawn together not just by a common lexicon and geographical proximity but also by the slow, steady march of emancipation, integration, and assimilation.

The linguistic landscape of Louisiana underwent a series of rapid changes in the nineteenth century, as possession of the territory was passed from Spain to France before finally settling into the hands of the United States. In 1812 the state was formally admitted into the Union and the doors were thrown open to settlers from other parts of the country. Most of these settlers spoke English. By the 1840s the Anglo community was well established politically and economically, and by the time of the Civil War they accounted for 70 percent of the state's total population.

The slave population was not unaffected by this demographic shift. In 1808, the United States banned the importation of slaves, and so— smuggling aside—most slaves that were thereafter brought to Louisiana came from English-speaking areas. Even Creole plantations such as the one owned by the Duparc-Locouls bought English-speaking slaves. A notice published in *L'Abeille* in 1816 identified six of the plantation's runaway slaves as "American" and able to speak "not a word" of French. By the time Laura was born, the English- and French-speaking slaves had begun to take sides. She writes in her memoir that "the Creole negro servants hated the American negroes and made them very unhappy because they did not speak the negro French dialect."

After 1812 English gained significant traction throughout Louisiana, even in heavily Francophone areas. Before the Civil War this could largely be attributed to population transfer. Though Louisiana had been forced to declare English its official language in order to gain statehood, French continued to be used in parish governments, and in 1845 the state legislature even passed a bill declaring French its official language.

But after the war everything changed. In light of the events that led to secession, the federal government began to take a far less permissive stance toward potential sources of rebellion or nonconformity in the former Confederacy. One of its targets was the use of French in Louisiana. The state legislature soon adopted a constitution that required public schools to use English as the language of "general exercises." They also made it illegal to pass legislation requiring the publication of laws, public records, and judicial proceedings in any language other than English. In conjunction with the rising stock of English as a prestige language as well as support for Americanization from the Catholic Church, these efforts precipitated a rapid shift to English.

The Cajun community was somewhat slower to assimilate, relatively isolated as they were by the swampy expanse of the Atchafalaya. But the 1901 discovery of oil in Jennings, about forty miles west of Lafayette, certainly helped things along, creating what Carl Brasseaux calls "unprecedented employment opportunities" for Cajuns in the oil industry. These employment opportunities were open only to those with some level of English proficiency, however, and with such incentives the Cajun community, too, found itself switching to English.

The ever-increasing preeminence of English has been driven in Louisiana—as it was driven in Montana, Arizona, and Washington state—by a variety of factors that include but are not limited to legislation, economics, education policy, and demographic changes. But I was somewhat surprised to discover that speakers of Louisiana Creole and Cajun French were subjected to the same tactics of linguistic humiliation that were used by those seeking to assimilate Native Americans.

The stories are remarkably similar to those I heard or read about while traveling through Native language communities. They involve public shamings, corporal punishment, and persistent campaigns of misinformation, all in an effort to convince the children that their language was "ignorant" or "bad." In a 1999 article written for the American Association of Teachers of French, James J. Natsis compiles a few of these stories. In one, a student was forced to kneel on grains of corn when he was caught speaking French on the playground; in another a student was sent home to write 200 times "I must not speak French on the school grounds." This latter student, ironically, grew up to become an expert on regional Louisiana French.

Just as they were with Native groups, these tactics were extremely successful in facilitating an abrupt cessation in the generational language transfer of regional and creole forms of French. Why would parents want their children to speak a language they themselves were punished for using? While passing through Lafayette I met a woman named Geraldine Robertson, who told me that her mother had prayed in French but refused to let her children speak it. This, for me, really encapsulated the difficulties these parents must have faced. I personally find it impossible to imagine not feeling free to use the same language with my children as with my god. Like so many privileges, it's one I hadn't even realized I had.

Speakers of Louisiana Creole have had to face additional layers of prejudice and disdain. Their language, often referred to derisively as *français nèg* or *gumbo*—is at the bottom of the prestige pole. While there is some comfort to be taken in the fact that Louisiana's social structure is flexible enough for Creole and Cajun to have a chance to influence each other, it is telling that the influence is one-directional. Speakers of Louisiana Creole can "move up" to use forms that are closer to Standard French. Speakers of Cajun, however, do not "move down."

The stigma attached to Louisiana Creole is such that there aren't even any reliable data about how many people still speak it. According to the American Community Survey, in 2005 there were 129,910 French-speakers in Louisiana; 19,105 of these spoke "Cajun," and 7,929 spoke "French Creole." But because many speakers of Louisiana Creole won't actually admit they use it, Census data are in this instance highly unreliable. The best and most recent guess comes courtesy of the linguist Ingrid Neumann-Holzschuh, who estimated in 1985 that there were between 60,000 and 80,000 speakers of Louisiana Creole. But you hardly need Census data or a field report to know that Louisiana Creole is disappearing, and fast. All you have to do is try to find someone—anyone—who speaks it.

Though I uncovered bits and pieces of French throughout Louisiana, despite driving past innumerable signs that read "Ici on est fier de parler français," the only time I actually heard French was on a side trip to Vermillionville, a touristy see-how-the-Cajuns-lived-in-the-old-days sort of place. Apparently this is a not-uncommon experience: the one place where French seems to be gaining ground throughout Louisiana is in the tourist sector.

Louisiana's Francophone community hasn't taken this lying down. For the past sixty years or so they have by and large been extremely active in attempting to reverse the course of language decline. In 1969, for instance, the Council for the Development of French in Louisiana began bringing in French teachers from Canada and France. And in 1984 Louisiana became the first state to require foreign language instruction in elementary schools, a measure primarily aimed at broadening early exposure to French. My favorite effort to bolster Louisiana's French-speaking population was the brainchild of state senator Dudley Leblanc, a man who made a fortune by creating Hadacol, a "dietary supplement" that just happened to contain 12 percent alcohol. Leblanc's grand plan involved importing Acadian women from Canada and marrying them off to single Cajun men. It's exactly the sort of plan you'd expect a consummate politician to dream up. Even if it didn't accomplish its intended results, he surely made a few constituents very happy.

But no matter how well funded or well intentioned the French-language activists of Louisiana may be, I have to think that the lessons of

Louisiana Creole surely apply to Louisiana French. The dynamics of language contact are, ultimately, determined by the pull of prestige. Louisiana Creole cannot help but be drawn nearer to Cajun French; Louisiana French, I suspect, cannot help but be drawn nearer to English. One day it will go the way of the Cane River, drawing out-of-town guests to its tranquil shores while the rush of the main river passes it by.

CHAPTER FIVE

South Carolina: Gullah

ONE THING I NEGLECTED to mention is that when I stumbled across Alcée Fortier's folktales, it was actually the second time I had been introduced to a new language through the stories of Br'er Rabbit.

The first time it happened was nearly a decade ago. I was browsing through Schoenhof's in Cambridge, Massachusetts, the finest foreign-language bookstore I've ever been to and one of the primary reasons I was never able to attain any measure of financial stability while living in Boston. Occasionally I'd go into Schoenhof's with a mission—find a comparative Greek and Latin grammar, pick up a Classical Chinese dictionary, buy *Harry Potter* in French—but more often than not I would simply browse, drifting from beautifully curated shelf to beautifully curated shelf, eavesdropping on the booksellers as they advised their customers with magnificent expertise.

In this way I discovered any number of new languages. I bought primers on Tibetan and Basque and recordings of Irish and Romanian. I pored over kanji, Devangari, cuneiform. And I added to my ever-growing and ever-less-feasible list of languages to study before I die.

It was here, hidden away on a lower shelf in the back room, that I first met Gullah.

Gullah (also called Sea Island Creole, Sea Island Creole English, or

Geechee) is an English-based, African-influenced creole spoken in some form by about a quarter of a million people, most of whom live on or near the Sea Islands, a chain of islands along the coast of South Carolina, Georgia, and north Florida.* Before that day I'd never heard of it. And I probably would have overlooked it then, too, had my boyfriend at the time not spotted the brightly colored cover of a book called *Gullah Folktales from the Georgia Coast*. We began to flip through story after story about the adventures of various animals including—you guessed it—Br'er Rabbit.

When I first saw the folktales I admit I assumed the stories had just been written in a particularly southern dialect of English. But when I looked at the text itself, I was surprised to discover just how much trouble I had with the language. Consider the passage below, which is the opening paragraph from a story about Br'er Rabbit and Br'er Wolf:

> Buh Wolf and Buh Rabbit in a cote de same Gal. De Gal bin rich an berry pooty. Dem tuk tun fuh wisit um. Buh Rabbit, him gone der mornin, and Buh Wolf, him gone der ebenin. De Gal harde fuh mek up eh mine. Eh sorter courage bofe er um. One morning Buh Rabbit bin a mek fun er Buh Wolf ter de Gal, and eh tell um say Buh Wolf yent duh nuttne mo den eh farruh ridin horse.†

As with the Louisiana Creole recorded by Alcée Fortier, the language here is nearly impossible for me to understand if I don't read the words aloud. *Pooty*, for instance, only registers as "pretty" if I say it; otherwise my brain doesn't make the leap. But even this strategy is of limited use. It doesn't, for

---

* Although different terms can be used to describe the continuum of creole dialects along the Atlantic coast, they are not used interchangeably. *Geechee* seems to be a term used more frequently by older generations and in Georgia; *Gullah* is certainly used more frequently in the Lowcountry of South Carolina. *Sea Island Creole*, on the other hand, appears to be favored only by linguists.

† A loose translation: "Br'er Wolf and Br'er Rabbit were courting the same Girl. The Girl was rich and very pretty. They took turns visiting her. Br'er Rabbit went in the morning, and Br'er Wolf went in the evening. The Girl had to make up her mind. She sort of encouraged both of them. One morning Br'er Rabbit was making fun of Br'er Wolf to the Girl, and he told her Br'er Wolf was nothing more than her father's riding horse."

instance, help me with the word *farruh* (which means "father"—or, in this case, "father's"). It took me ages to figure out that "Eh sorter courage bofe er um" meant "She sort of encouraged both of them." And I'm still unclear on the precise meaning of the phrase "yent duh." Even so, because Gullah is so closely related to English, I was able to rough out a translation without too much trouble. Unfortunately, as soon as I realized how easy it was to translate Gullah, I began to lose interest, being at that point still young enough to relish difficulty for difficulty's sake.

Shortly thereafter, I forgot all about Gullah, moving on to other languages (and other boyfriends). But once I began thinking about the African influence on American language, everything came rushing back. This was, I knew, something I needed to explore.

Gullah may not be the best-known language or culture in the United States, but it has certainly, in a few discrete instances, slipped into mainstream American culture. For instance, a number of Gullah words such as *buckra* (white man), *gumbo* (originally, "okra"), and *chigger* (small flea) have made their way into English. (Or, more accurately, a number of West African words have made their way into English via Gullah.) There are also, of course, the stories of Br'er Rabbit and his friends, many of which match almost word for word stories still told today in West Africa. I would also be willing to bet that without even realizing it most Americans know a song that was originally sung in Gullah. "Michael Row the Boat Ashore" was first attested on the heavily Gullah island of St. Helena during the Civil War, and if you look at some of the later verses, it is easy to see the song's relationship to Gullah:

> He raise de fruit for you to eat.
> He dat eat shall neber die.
> When de riber overflow.
> O poor sinner, how you land?
> Riber run and darkness comin'.
> Sinner row to save your soul.

Without a doubt, however, Gullah's most far-reaching cultural influence is found in the story of Porgy and Bess.

In 1925, a Charleston insurance salesman named DuBose Heyward

published *Porgy*, the story of a crippled beggar and the other inhabitants of a section of Charleston, South Carolina, known as Catfish
Row. Two years later Heyward and his wife, Dorothy, successfully
adapted the novel for the Broadway stage, but it wasn't until George
Gershwin expressed interest in writing an opera based on the material
that *Porgy* began its first steps toward long-standing cultural prominence.

Many of the elements of *Porgy* were inspired by real-life Charleston.
Porgy was based on a man named Sammy Smalls, a somewhat less sym-
pathetic character than his operatic counterpart might suggest. As most
Porgy and Bess aficionados in Charleston were eager to tell me, Porgy
was better known for beating up his female companions than attempting
to rescue them from their disreputable circumstances. In fact, I discovered that in 1924 he was arrested for shooting at a woman named Maggie
Barnes. The *Charleston News and Courier* noted that Barnes escaped injury
due largely to Sammy's bad aim.

Catfish Row, meanwhile, was the fictional re-creation of a three-story
double tenement located on Church Street in south Charleston just a few
doors down from DuBose Heyward's onetime residence. Sammy Smalls
and the other residents of Catfish Row were Gullah-speakers, and it was
their speech Heyward attempted to replicate in his novel. These loose
Gullah speech patterns can, in turn, be heard in some of the opera's most
famous songs, particularly those ("Summertime," "My Man's Gone Now,"
"A Woman Is a Sometime Thing") whose lyrics were written by Heyward.

Porgy and Bess debuted in 1935 and went on to garner its share of both
acclaim and controversy. Gershwin's choice to use an all-black cast was
not met with complete equanimity. Although Gerswhin had been offered a grant from the Metropolitan Opera, he chose to stage *Porgy and
Bess* at the Alvin Theater instead. This was in part a practical decision,
but it was also a necessary one, as at the time the Met had yet to feature
a single black performer.*

The production also ran into difficulties when it went on tour. The

---

* Nor would it until 1955, when Marian Anderson first performed in Verdi's *Un ballo
in maschera*.

show's final stop was to be at the National Theatre in Washington, D.C., but problems arose when it was discovered that the theater did not intend to allow integrated audiences to any of its performances. Led by Todd Duncan—the original Porgy and the first African American to perform with the New York City Opera—the cast refused to perform unless the theater changed its policy. Management eventually acquiesced, and so, in 1936, the National Theatre for the first time seated both black and white patrons together.

But perhaps most controversial was the opera's representation of African American life. The plot's more scurrilous elements—gambling, drugs, prostitution, murder—and the depictions of many of the opera's characters also drew (and continue to draw) sharp criticism, particularly in light of the fact that it was a work about African Americans that was written by white Americans. Virgil Thomson, a white composer and critic, put it most succinctly: "Folklore subjects recounted by an outsider are only valid as long as the folk in question is unable to speak for itself, which is certainly not true of the American Negro in 1935."

Many of the same criticisms have also been applied to the language of the show. In the 1930s, for instance, there were plans to stage a production of *Porgy and Bess* with the Negro Repertory Company, an African American theater troupe in Seattle that was financed by the Works Progress Administration's Federal Theatre Project. The production was canceled before it ever got to opening night, however. The actors took issue not just with the show's content but also with having to use the show's "dialect."

This is an eminently understandable reaction. Heyward wrote *Porgy* in part as an exploration of the "noble savage," and he wasn't shy about explaining his reasons for doing so. As he wrote, "I saw the primitive Negro as the inheritor of a source of delight that I would give much to possess." In light of this it's impossible not to be uneasy about Heyward's appropriation of Gullah-inspired speech. Heyward used these words because, for him, they served as inherent intimations of primitivism. The disdain with which this "dialect" was treated—by whites and blacks—got me thinking.

This is why I decided to go to South Carolina. I wanted to learn the words and structures of Gullah, and I wanted to know what the language had to teach me about African American history and culture. And I wanted to visit the Lowcountry communities whose residents could trace their ancestry back to the African slaves who had been imported to work the region's rice fields. I may also have wanted an excuse to eat a little she-crab soup.

Even more, though, I wanted to explore the tensions between Gullah and English. The similarities between the two are both a blessing and a curse. On one hand, even though the languages are not precisely mutually intelligible, speakers of the two are certainly able to communicate with one another. But on the other hand, Gullah is subject to the same prejudices faced by so many other creole languages. The fact that Gullah so closely resembles English has led many to assume over the years that Gullah is just a simplified or corrupted form of English—that it's not its own language, just bad "dialect." And that's an opinion held not only by whites but sometimes by blacks as well.

Just as Louisiana Creole is more than a whittled-down form of French, so too is Gullah more than some slow-witted kind of southern English. But because I'm a native English-speaker and not a native French-speaker, Gullah is the language that I—along with most Americans—am more likely to mistake and misjudge. Ultimately, I wanted to know how that prejudice had affected the Gullah language and community over the years.

And so I made my way to Charleston, the birthplace of Sammy Smalls, the home of Catfish Row, and the first American city seen by many of the ancestors of South Carolina's Gullah population. Here I began to tease out the context that would help me better understand this new language, learning along the way a little history, a little architecture, and—most unexpectedly—a little metalworking.

Originally established as Charles Towne in 1670, Charleston is the oldest city in South Carolina, located on a peninsula that juts out into the Atlantic Ocean near the mouths of the Wando, Cooper, Ashley, and Stono rivers. Today the city is known primarily as a tourist destination, the home of Rainbow Row and a convenient hub from which to visit nearby islands and beaches. But it is also the home to a number of large corporations and is in addition the second-largest container port on the East Coast. It is in this capacity as a port of entry that Charleston first made a name for itself.

During the colonial period, the city made its initial fortune as the center of the deerskin trade, but the Lowcountry climate was particularly well suited to the cultivation of rice and indigo, and soon enough agricultural production accounted for the bulk of the region's economy. As it turns out, however, these two crops are particularly labor intensive, and in order to sustain its growth South Carolina planters needed access to a large and cheap labor pool. They found it in the African slave trade.

When I first arrived in Charleston, though, I was thinking less about slavery than I was about sandwiches.

The last time I had been anywhere near Charleston was for a wedding, so the most recent memories I had of the area were limned by bourbon-tinged recollections of soft lighting and rigid hairstyles. When I drove into town on a Sunday summer night, the aesthetic realities of the I-95 corridor were somewhat less than I might have hoped. I had envisioned a gradual transition from the wooded hills of Virginia to the dense, subtropical landscape of South Carolina. But I saw few giant oaks and little Spanish moss. I did, however, see plenty of gas stations. All in all, it was remarkably unremarkable, and an inauspicious start. I didn't manage to take in even a smidgen of city character that first night. By the time I arrived at my hotel I was cranky and hungry. That's when I made my first disappointing discovery about Charleston: the Panera Bread on Sam Rittenberg Blvd. closes at 9:00 p.m. on Sundays.

Fortunately, I'd engaged the services of a professional for my trip to the city center, so I had somewhat higher expectations for the day to come. On the drive into town I entertained myself with thoughts of brightly painted town houses and quaint cobblestone roads. I knew there was an open-air market to be explored and delicious southern food to be eaten. Charleston is a lovely and engaging city, and I was very much looking forward to my visit.

My introduction to Gullah Charleston came courtesy of Alphonso Brown, the owner of Gullah Tours and the author of *A Gullah Guide to*

Charleston. I had signed up to join one of his midmorning tours, and though I arrived in plenty of time, I still managed to be one of the last people to get there. When I saw that the bus was nearly full, I ran up to Mr. Brown, apology tumbling across my lips. Then I caught my foot on a piece of sidewalk, tripped, and fell flat on my ass.

I was mortified (if not exactly surprised), but Mr. Brown just shook my hand and smiled. He told me a man named Philip Simmons had worked as a blacksmith for eighty years without so much as a sprained finger. Then one day he'd gone outside, tripped on the sidewalk, and broken his arm.

As I boarded the bus I tried to figure out what the moral of the story was. I wanted to believe he was implying that even very clever people tripped now and then. Or maybe that sidewalks are surprisingly treacherous creatures, something I've believed for years. But, rather grimly, I eventually concluded the only thing Mr. Brown could have meant was that I was approximately as coordinated as an octogenarian.

When I found out later in the tour that Philip Simmons was a successful and widely acclaimed local artist, I was somewhat mollified: I was as coordinated as an *extremely talented* octogenarian. For someone who in junior high had been compared to a brontosaurus, this was actually something of a step up.

Much to my delight, the tour began with an introduction to Gullah. But I was astonished to discover that in the absence of a transcription I was almost wholly incapable of understanding even the most basic phrases. My smug assurance that native English skill would render me effectively bilingual was swept aside the moment Mr. Brown slipped into the rich, lilting tongue. No one on the bus had the slightest idea what he was saying.

He grinned at us, having expected as much. I think perhaps this was as much the point of the lesson as were the basic phrases that constituted it.

Soon thereafter we were heading into Charleston, snapping photos or pressing our faces against the window as Mr. Brown showed us historic site after historic site. Charleston is a city that has for more than a century had a majority African American population, and so there's African history to be found around nearly ever corner. The city is home to historic black-owned business, black churches, and former workplaces of black slaves. He took us to 91 Broad Street, the location of the offices that once housed the first black law firm in the United States, and to 5 Magazine Street, the home of the first black American to receive a medical degree. We stopped in front of Avery Research Center, a museum and archival resource that was originally built to house the city's first free secondary school for African Americans. And throughout the city he pointed out to us the work of Philip Simmons.

Simmons, I learned, was born a few miles outside Charleston in 1912, and his career as a blacksmith began at the age of thirteen, when he left school and apprenticed to an ex-slave. As the years passed and horses (and their need for shoes) fell out of fashion, Simmons began to turn more and more to ornamental ironwork, and it was his skill with gates, fences, and window grilles with which he made his living and found some small measure of fame. Over the course of his life his pieces were acquired by numerous Charleston families and businesses, not to mention museums throughout the world.

Mr. Brown took us to Simmons's workshop, which was as modest a place as you could imagine. We stopped in front of a slightly less-than-mint-condition house, behind which was another house that was in the midst of renovations. Behind *that* was the least stable and well-kept building yet, an edifice best described as a shed. It was in this building, which looked like a junk yard packed inside another junk yard that had been moved more than a few times over a number of years, that Mr. Simmons had fashioned his intricate designs. On one wall, nearly indistinguishable from the worn and rusted tools that filled the rest of the shed, was Simmons's cherished collection of nineteenth-century tools.

When I visited, Simmons himself was not in residence. He was living instead at a nearby nursing home, still creating designs to be fabricated by the apprentices to whom he had entrusted his workshop. He passed away just a few weeks later.

But you can still see his work throughout Charleston, in the nested-heart design of the gate at 91 Anson or the lazy, perfect spirals guarding the driveway at 138 Wentworth. In fact, if you've been to Charleston, even if you didn't realize it you've almost definitely seen Simmons's work. He created so many pieces over so many years that he himself couldn't remember them all. In his later years the foundation dedicated to preserving his work would drive Simmons up and down the streets of Charleston in the hope that he might recognize additional pieces he had crafted long ago.

I must admit that at first I was puzzled by the tour's emphasis on ironwork. It was not, I thought, what I had signed up for. But the more I considered it, the more appropriate it seemed. Philip Simmons left an indelible mark on the city of Charleston with surprisingly little acknowledgment for having done so. Here was a city whose history was linked inextricably with the fates and fortunes of its African American population—many of whom, like Simmons, spoke Gullah—a fact that is decidedly underplayed by the city's tourist literature. Frankly, if you go to Charleston today you're more likely to learn about pirates than the city's generations of accomplished African Americans.

The tour served as a reminder of another way in which the lives and legacies of working men and women are overshadowed by those of the rich and powerful, a phenomenon only exacerbated by the representational inequalities of slavery and race. Tourists don't typically want to tromp about town in search of unassuming lengths of iron; they want to marvel instead at the elegant homes of nineteenth-century planters or the formal gardens of the men who signed the Declaration of Independence. If I wanted to understand anything about the role of African language and culture in the region, I was going to have to pay close attention to things that might not ordinarily have caught my attention. I needed to change my frame of reference. Though I'd been to Charleston several times before, I knew now that those visits had shown me just one side of the city. It was time to see the city again, I realized—time to see what I'd missed.

With this in mind, I decided to take a walk. Much later, when I finally made it back to my hotel, I was grimy, achy, and desperately in need of a beer. But I had—to my satisfaction if not to my pleasure—seen things in the city that would forever change the way I viewed it.

I began in the most obvious place, walking down Chalmers Street over by Waterfront Park to visit the Old Slave Mart. The Slave Mart is a relatively new building, constructed in 1859 and located on a quiet cobblestone street that seems an unlikely place for the business of trafficking humans. Before 1856, slaves in Charleston were primarily sold outside the city's Custom House two blocks away, but a city ordinance prohibited the public sale of slaves there, so the trade then moved to "sales rooms" on nearby streets.

One of these "rooms" was the large shed that is now the only surviving slave auction gallery in South Carolina. Originally owned by a man named Thomas Ryan, the shed was once part of a larger complex of buildings that included offices, a detention area, a kitchen, and a morgue. After the slave mart closed in 1863, the auction shed was used as a two-story tenement and an auto repair shop before eventually being turned into a small but intensely affecting museum.

I would absolutely recommend that anyone who visits Charleston makes sure to visit the Old Slave Mart Museum. That said, it's a bit of a downer. By the time I left I was in a genuinely foul temper, having come to the conclusion that the world is more or less a horrible place infested by horrible people. Everything around me seemed tainted by association. The day wasn't balmy, I realized; it was muggy. Those houses weren't charming, I decided; they were out of fashion. And the cobblestone street I had admired just hours before wasn't picturesque. It was a sign of the city's infuriating insistence on clinging to—and dressing up—its past. It should be paved over, I thought. Someone could twist an ankle. I crossed it carefully and with a scowl.

My next stop, the City Jail and Work House on Magazine Street, didn't exactly buoy my spirits. The jail is exactly as sinister and Gothic as you would expect it to be, crenellated and barred and looking as if it has been in this exact state of disrepair since the day it was built. After 1822 any black sailors whose ships were in port were kept here, slave or no, for fear that their very presence could incite rebellion. It was to the Work House, meanwhile, that Charlestonians would bring their slaves to be punished. Sometimes they were merely forced to grind corn by running on a treadmill, but if their owners were willing to pay a twenty-five-cent fee, the slaves would instead be taken into the Whipping Room, where they were stretched and flogged. The walls in the Whipping Room, I learned, were filled with sand to help muffle the sounds within.

Even my trip to the Aiken-Rhett House, one of Charleston's premier historical homes, served as a reminder of slavery. Built in 1818, the Aiken-Rhett House was sold to William Aiken Sr. when the original owner lost five of his ships at sea and had to meet a number of urgent financial obligations. After Aiken's death in a carriage accident, the house was left in the hands of William Jr., a successful businessman and planter and the man who would serve as South Carolina's governor from 1844 to 1846. He and his wife embarked on an elaborate series of renovations and additions, including the construction of a ballroom, an art gallery, and a deeply ostentatious Greek Revival entrance hall, taking an ordinary Charleston double house and turning it into a glittering showcase for one of the state's wealthiest men. Today it's one of Charleston's most popular tourist attractions.

Amazingly, the Aiken-Rhett House has not been changed substantially since 1858, and today the Historic Charleston Foundation is dedicated to its restoration and preservation. The lights still use gas, and the downstairs warming kitchen still contains a pie safe. The bedrooms upstairs don't have closets, instead relying on the armoires that were in fashion before hangers were invented. As I walked through the house I stopped to examine fragile pieces of nineteenth-century wallpaper that preservationists had stabilized with steel pins and Mylar backing. I learned that the grass mats the family slaves used to roll out each summer have been cleaned, protected, and stored away. I wondered idly what I would have to do in my life for someone to want to go to so much effort to save my dirty old rugs.

Eventually I wandered out back to the courtyard containing the stables and the slave quarters, which have the dubious distinction of being some of the best-preserved urban slave lodgings in the country. At the time of the Civil War, William Aiken Jr. owned more than seven hundred slaves. But most worked on his rice plantation on Jehossee Island, leaving only twelve or so to work at the town house.

Some of Aiken's slaves slept above the stables, and some lived in a two-story brick-and-stucco building on the other side of the courtyard.

The paint has long since worn off the stucco, but the doors and windows are painted a discordant, cheery green. The first floor contains a laundry room and the kitchen where the family's meals were prepared before being transferred to the main house for service. In the days when do-it-yourself firefighting techniques were typically limited to the cunning use of buckets of sand, separating the "cooking kitchen" from the "warming kitchen" was a fairly common practice. It is nevertheless telling that the slave quarters, located just above the cooking kitchen, were afforded no such protection.

On the second floor of the slave quarters a hallway runs the length of the building, and at either end are two larger corner rooms with windows facing out onto the courtyard. Between these are three smaller dormitory-style lodgings with windows that open out into the hall. I remember thinking that the quarters on the end seemed reasonably comfortable—they even had fireplaces. But I suspect that was mostly a relative judgment compared to the cramped darkness of the dormitories, because even the larger rooms, which were sometimes used to house whole families, were only a hundred square feet or so.

Not that any of this could somehow pretty up the fundamental purpose of the building. Even if the rooms were spacious or inviting or colorful, they were still built to house slaves. I mean, the privies in the far reaches of the courtyard might have been substantial brick enclosures with fancy Gothic Revival façades, but they were still privies. And they still smelled.

Now, I don't mean to imply that the entire city of Charleston serves as some fetid reminder of some of the more despicable aspects of American history. I was just looking for it that day. And even so I was unable to wholly ignore the wily charms of Charleston's historic architecture. There were other stories to find here, too, in the circular steel plates I spotted every so often on the sides of buildings, indications that they had been retrofitted for greater structural integrity after the earthquake of 1886. (I hadn't even known that Charleston had earthquakes.) Or in all of the features—stucco, cupolas, piazzas—that were designed to keep residents cool in the subtropical climate. I learned that the city's long, narrow houses are the architectural consequence of property taxes levied based on frontage width. And I saw more than a few buildings with blue doors, a decorative practice that in many cases stems from a Gullah tradition that blue houses are protected from evil spirits.* To many this may sound like mere architectural minutiae, but these were the details that helped me better envision everyday life in nineteenth-century Charleston.

That being said, every time I had managed to forget the city's sobering history for a few blissful minutes, I'd invariably stumble across some new disheartening detail. For instance, seemingly every time I went looking for a piece of Philip Simmons ironwork, hoping to enjoy for a brief moment the fantasy that talent and dedication might reliably be enough to build a life on, that's when I'd find another damn cheval-de-frise.

A cheval-de-frise—literally, "Frisian horse"—was originally a primitive anti-cavalry device first used in the Middle Ages. In its most common incarnation a cheval-de-frise is made by taking spikes or spears and attaching them at opposing angles to a central frame. They are portable, they are sharp, and they are nasty. If you're a Frisian looking to impale a few horses and their riders, I definitely recommend you look into them. But as it turns out, there's also a home version for those worried about trespassers. Just run an iron bar atop the length of your fence and affix wicked little spikes to it. It will make your neighbor's barbed wire look warm and welcoming in comparison.

It is this latter-day version of the cheval-de-frise that you find on the fences surrounding a number of Charleston's historic homes.

Even in this modern age of outlandishly conspicuous public security measures, it was disconcerting, to say the least, to see such openly brutal defensive installations. But the incongruence of their location—surrounding impeccably preserved Georgian mansions in a city some declare to be the country's most "well mannered"—is flat-out startling. Unfortunately, the reason for their construction is less startling when you take into consideration the historical facts.

---

* Later, in the Penn Center on St. Helena Island, I found and transcribed the following Gullah advice for those with hag problems: *De Hag / de hag binna / Gullah ooman / Wah ride ya de / Whole night thru / One sho way to / Scay de hag binna / Trim ya house / Haint blue.*

It all started in 1781 when a slave known as Telemaque was purchased and brought to Charleston. Eighteen years later this slave—by then known as Denmark Vesey—won the lottery, bought his freedom, and established himself as a respected freedman and Methodist. By 1822, however, Vesey's fortunes had changed. That year he was arrested and executed for plotting what would have been the largest slave insurrection in American history.

Whether he was inspired by the Haitian Revolution, inflamed by the city's antagonism toward the African Methodist Episcopal Church, enraged at his inability to free his wife and children, or some combination of the three, Vesey took it upon himself to attempt to coordinate the uprising of more than 8,000 slaves. They planned to kill their white owners and take control of the city before fleeing to Santo Domingo. But before his plan could come to fruition, his co-conspirators leaked information to the authorities, and in the end more than a hundred men were arrested. Thirty-five, including Vesey, were hanged.

Residents of Charleston responded by implementing a slew of increased security measures, from the construction of sturdier fences and chevaux-de-frise to the creation of a standing municipal guard (which would eventually be housed at a newly constructed arsenal known as the Citadel). Charleston's most famous example of chevaux-de-frise is found, not coincidentally, at the Miles Brewton house, on the corner of King and Ladson. The house is otherwise known for its exquisite Palladian architecture; Brewton is otherwise known for being one of the leading slave merchants of his time.

The Slave Mart, the Work House, the chevaux-de-frise—these are the most shocking artifacts of Charleston's African American history. In my opinion, however, the most expressive is the statue found in Marion Square, a small park near the College of Charleston. In the square, atop a lofty column, stands a likeness of John C. Calhoun, a U.S. senator and the vice president under John Quincy Adams and Andrew Jackson. The current statue is the second to stand in this location; the first was removed by the Charleston Ladies' Calhoun Monument Association on account of what they considered to be a deformed index finger and inappropriate attire.

Nearly as striking as the statue is the column it rests upon, an addition to the second version of the monument for reasons that had little to do with the aesthetic or moral judgments of the Ladies' Association. This second statue was lifted up to protect it from the city's black population, which had been regularly defacing the monument since its unveiling in 1887. Calhoun may be considered one of the state's most illustrious historical figures, but he was also a staunch supporter of slavery. In 1837, while speaking on the issue of slavery on the Senate floor, he declared it to be a "positive good":

> But let me not be understood as admitting, even by implication, that the existing relations between the two races in the slave-holding States is an evil: far otherwise; I hold it to be a good, as it has thus far proved itself to be to both, and will continue to prove so if not disturbed by the fell spirit of abolition. I appeal to facts. Never before has the black race of Central Africa, from the dawn of history to the present day, attained a condition so civilized and so improved, not only physically, but morally and intellectually.

Many blacks in Charleston today still pronounce Calhoun's name "Kill-houn."* And, revealingly, the column the statue now rests on is—fully, defiantly—eighty feet high.

I find it impossible to imagine that I could live in Charleston without feeling a constant, low-level hum of historical awareness. Charleston is, more than any other city I have ever visited, obsessed with history and preservation. So although Charleston is a bustling, modern place, it still has the character of an obstinate antediluvian. Everywhere I went there seemed to be an implied challenge in the city's character, a championing of the Way Things Used to Be over the Way Things Are. This is not necessarily a bad thing—provided you ignore the fact that human

---

* In his book, Alphonso Brown relates the following story about this pronunciation: "The use of 'Killhoun' was sometimes thought to be a speech impediment. An old lady exclaimed, 'Oh please! We can say "Calhoun," we mean to say "Killhoun"!'"

bondage was a Thing That Used to Be. Charleston may be a city of great houses. But it is also a city of great fences.

After a few days in Charleston I left the city behind and headed to Beaufort and St. Helena, the heart of Gullah country. In Charleston I had focused on context and background. I figured that if I wanted to understand the relationship between English and Gullah, then first and foremost I needed to reacquaint myself with the historic tensions between white and black. But down in St. Helena I hoped to find specifics. I hoped to learn more about the Gullah language itself and the men and women who speak it.

Beaufort, about an hour and a half south of Charleston, is a deceptively sleepy town. Its lush vegetation and antebellum charm may be straight-up Margaret Mitchell, but Beaufort is just five miles from Parris Island, which means that every other weekend, friends and families of Marine recruits stream in to attend basic-training graduation. Accordingly, all the hotels and tourist destinations are filled with Marine Corps merchandise, Parris Island maps, and advertisements for Der Teufelhund, Beaufort's "only military shop."* As a result, the town is an improbable combination of southern languor and military vigor.

I was in Beaufort because it is the gateway to St. Helena Island, home to the Lowcountry's largest Gullah population. The first thing I realized about St. Helena is that it is and always has been an extremely isolated area. Even today there's only one road in and out—your only other option is to swim. Back in the nineteenth century, however, the area was even more cut off. St. Helena's primary industry for decades was agricultural production, and most of its land was under the purview of various plantations. But you won't find the same grand plantation houses here that you might in other parts of the South. On account of the miserable climate and working conditions, few white slave owners lived here permanently. The conditions were so difficult, in fact, that most didn't even try to employ white overseers. Instead that task was entrusted

---

* Der Teufelhund means "Devil Dog," the famed but questionably grammatical German nickname for Marines.

to senior slaves. And the few white farmers who did live on the island fled when the Union Army captured nearby Port Royal soon after the start of the Civil War.

When Union forces took control of St. Helena in 1861, then, they found an island populated entirely by slaves. The Union, eager to reap the product and the profits of the island's cotton cultivation, promptly liberated the slaves and offered wages and land as an enticement to stay and harvest the cotton. Though the initiative—known as the Port Royal Experiment—was ended by Andrew Johnson in 1865, a great deal of property on the island nevertheless made its way into the hands of former slaves. Many of St. Helena's 10,000 residents today live on land that their ancestors worked more than a century ago.

I started my visit to St. Helena at the Penn Center, a non-profit organization dedicated to the preservation of Gullah culture and a historic site in its own right. The center got its start in 1862 when two missionaries— Laura Towne, a Unitarian from Pennsylvania, and Ellen Murray, a Quaker from Rhode Island—decided to found a school for the freed slaves on St. Helena. They were joined by a black schoolteacher from Massachusetts named Charlotte Forten, and soon enough they were holding classes in the dining room of the main house at what had been Oaks Plantation. The school eventually moved into the island's Brick Baptist Church, but when it outgrew that, too, the women were given fifty acres of land by Hastings Gantt, a freedman who would later be elected to South Carolina's House of Representatives. Over the years the center has expanded and shifted its focus from schooling to community outreach, but today it can still be found on this same fifty-acre tract of land.

The Penn Center would be famous enough were it just one of the first schools for freed slaves. But it cemented its status in the history books in the 1960s when Martin Luther King Jr. and the Southern Christian Leadership Council used the complex for strategy sessions. It was here that King planned the Selma-to-Montgomery marches of 1965.

And it was also here that I began to learn about Gullah's relationship to African languages and cultures.

The lexicon of Gullah is so heavily influenced by English that for decades many believed there to be no relationship whatsoever between it and any non-English language, much less any African language. The linguist George Philip Krapp, for instance, wrote in 1924 that it was "reasonably safe to say that not a single detail of Negro pronunciation or of Negro syntax can be proved to have any other than an English origin." These early theories about the development of Gullah largely relied on the assumption that slave owners and drivers would simplify their language when speaking to their charges. Scholars, therefore, believed that the source of Gullah could only be English—or, perhaps, a combination of English dialects.

It is true that some slaves arrived in South Carolina already speaking a form of English. When it was initially founded, Charleston was in large part populated by the sons of successful colonists in the West Indies, particularly those from British outposts like Barbados. And so in many cases the slaves they brought with them had already been exposed to English. But a 1717 tax shifted the slave trade away from the Caribbean and toward Africa, and thereafter the importation of African slaves into South Carolina continued unabated until the start of the Civil War.*

In light of this, it seems inconceivable that Gullah would exhibit no African influence. Moreover, the direct influence of English was surely limited due to the fact that so few white owners or overseers chose to live on their Sea Island plantations. In fact, as linguist Patricia Causey Nichols points out, after 1715 the majority of new slaves wouldn't have had much interaction with English at all. "Instead," she writes, they "would learn the common language in the slave quarters from those who spoke English as a second (or third or fourth) language—all with the imperfections that accompany such indirect learning." And indeed, more recent research has found overwhelming evidence of African influence in Gullah's syntax, phonology, and vocabulary.

Some of the earliest support for the existence of a relationship between Gullah and African languages came from the Gullah tradition of nicknaming. In Gullah communities, many children are traditionally given nicknames called basket names—that is, a name given when the baby is still small enough to sleep in a basket. Many of these names do have

---

* In South Carolina the provisions of the 1808 act that banned the importation of slaves were less than successfully enforced.

English roots, my favorite examples being Beep-Beep ("The individual so nicknamed was saved from possibly fatal injury by the timely sounding of an automobile horn") and Dukey ("The bearer of this name is a great admirer of the actor John Wayne"). But there is far more African influence to be found in basket names than there is English influence.

There is, for instance, a tradition in many West African cultures of naming a child based on the day they were born. Similar names found in Gullah include the name *Aba*, which corresponds to the Twi name *Ya*—in this case, a girl born on Thursday. The Gullah name *Afiba*, meanwhile, is related to the Ewe for a girl born on Friday. *Akaba*, the name of a ruler of the kingdom of Dahomey (modern-day Benin), represents a more direct borrowing of a proper name. Meanwhile, *Birama*, the Mandingo form of Abraham, is a borrowing of a borrowing.

Through naming practices alone, linguists have been able to identify links between Gullah and the African languages Bambara, Bini, Bobangi, Djerma, Ewe, Efik, Fante, Fula, Gã, Gbari, Hausa, Ibo, Ibibio, Kongo and Ikongo, Kimbundu, Kpelle, Mende, Malinke, Mandinka, Mandingo, Nupe, Susu, Songhay, Twi, Temne, Tshiluba, Umbundu, Vai, and Wolof.

But names are far from the only evidence of African influence in Gullah. In his groundbreaking and authoritative work *Africanisms in the Gullah Dialect*, linguist Lorenzo Dow Turner also found links to African languages in Gullah's sounds and structure. He notes, for instance, that the lack of passive voice in Gullah ("he was beaten" in Gullah would be "dem beat im") mirrors the same phenomenon in Ewe and Yoruba. He also observes that in Gullah the word *pass* is sometimes used to indicate comparative degree of adjective, as seen in the phrase "he tall pass me" ("he's taller than I"). Turner found this very same structure—including the use of an equivalent verb—in a number of African languages.

Turner also cataloged a great many African influences in Gullah's lexicon, recording long lists of Mende and Vai words that are used in Gullah songs, stories, and prayers and finding that—almost astonishingly—many Gullah-speakers still counted using African numbers generations after their ancestors had arrived in the United States. Some, as he writes, even counted using more than one African language:

As regards numerals, I interviewed several older Gullahs, each of whom could count from one to ten in a different African language. A few in Georgia could count from one to nineteen in the Fula language. Usually the Gullahs did not know the name of the language in which they counted, but said that they learned the numerals from older relatives or friends. A few, unknowingly, would draw upon two or more African languages in counting from one to ten.

Though Turner's work shows unequivocally that words, sounds, and structures from African languages have been carried over into Gullah, it bears mentioning that Gullah is more than just an African word stew. Gullah is the product of a complex series of linguistic and cultural interactions. And, like all languages, it continues to develop and change with each passing day. Labeling Gullah an "African" language is hardly more meaningful and appropriate than labeling it "corrupted" English. What I find particularly compelling about Gullah's African roots, however, is not their existence (or the extent of their existence) but rather the information this analysis has revealed about the origins of the Gullah people.

If you're an African American who is descended from slaves, putting together a family tree that goes back any further than the twentieth century—much less back to Africa—will likely be a real challenge. It isn't just a matter of pulling up the Census data or logging on to Scotland's People. And despite what the commercials tell you, Ancestry .com might not be of much help. Not only is much of the documentation related to individual slaves convoluted or incomplete, but because many owners deliberately set out to obscure their slaves' genetic relationships, some of it is flat-out wrong.

The Gullah language, though, has helped give its people a better sense of their likely African origins. First, Turner's research identified significant influences from languages such as Mende, Vai, and Fula, all of which are spoken in and around Sierra Leone. Then the historian P. E. H. Hair, building on Turner's work, concluded that 25 percent of Gullah's African names and 20 percent of its African words have their origins in Sierra Leone. And more recently a linguist at the University of Texas named Ian Hancock identified remarkable similarities between Gullah and Sierra Leone Krio, the English-based creole that is today spoken by about 97 percent of Sierra Leone's population. Many of these similarities—which include, for example, the use of the same metaphorical expression for "greedy" (*big eye* in Gullah, *bigyai* in Krio)—are so striking that Hancock concluded the Gullah people must be closely related to slaves from Sierra Leone.

On very rare occasions Gullah has been used to help trace individual families back to specific villages in Africa. When conducting his initial research in the 1930s, Turner recorded a Mende song sung by Amelia Dawley, a Gullah woman who lived in Harris Neck, Georgia. More than fifty years later, anthropologist Joseph Opala, ethnomusicologist Cynthia Schmidt, and linguist Tazieff Koroma went to Sierra Leone to try to pinpoint the exact origin of Dawley's song. Astonishingly, they found a woman living in a remote village who sang a nearly identical song. In Sierra Leone, as in Georgia, the song had been passed down from generation to generation, from grandmother to mother to daughter.

Since 1989 Gullah groups have made three official visits to Sierra Leone, one of which allowed Amelia Dawley's daughter to visit the remote village her ancestors came from. They refer to these trips as "homecomings."

Whenever I think about the wealth of knowledge contained in the Gullah language—remnants of history and culture and even blood heritage—I have to admit that my mind invariably slips back to those grass mats at the Aiken-Rhett House in Charleston. Each mat is carefully cleaned with conservation-grade equipment, then rolled up and placed in a tube filled with inert gas before going into storage. While I don't doubt that these artifacts are instructive and valuable in their own way, I nevertheless can't help but marvel at the distribution of resources. If anyone ever found his or her family in a nineteenth-century floor covering, I would love to hear about it.

Though the Penn Center is the most visible institution associated with the island's Gullah culture, it is far from the only one. During my time on the island I visited the Red Piano Too gallery, a onetime agricultural cooperative that now houses room after room of local art and crafts. Here I found a copy of the Gullah New Testament (*De Nyew Testament*) and learned about Jonathan Green and Sam Doyle, two prominent Gullah artists. I also saw the dining room at Oak Plantation and ducked into one of the island's four remaining Praise Houses, tiny, low-ceilinged structures slave owners built for their slaves' religious services so as to prevent any large, potentially seditious gatherings.

And just across the highway from the Red Piano Too gallery I ate shrimp and shark at a little place called Gullah Grub. It's not precisely what I would call a hole in the wall, but it looked small and empty enough that as I drove up I wondered if maybe it was something of a hidden gem. My oft-ignored opportunistic side perked up and demanded attention, and I found myself putting together a pitch to a travel magazine before I even walked in the door.

I sat down and ordered an iced tea while I took stock of the interior, scrutinizing the decor in the hope it might suggest to me a particularly clever turn of phrase. It took me a moment to realize a TV was on in the background. At first I tried to ignore the noise, absorbed as I was in doing my best Elizabeth Gilbert impression. But after a moment, I realized I was hearing a voice I recognized. I snapped to attention, whipping around to confirm what I already suspected and dreaded.

It was an episode of *Anthony Bourdain: No Reservations*—the one in which he ate Frogmore Stew at Gullah Grub. I felt my momentary fit of ambition wither once more into fretful inertia. One day, I told myself, I was going to meet Anthony Bourdain and ask him to stop bogarting all the best assignments.*

Luckily, the waitress came back at that moment to distract me. I asked her if I should order the fried shrimp or the BBQ ribs, and after looking at me for a long moment, she said solemnly, "See, I have a theory about the shrimp. If you're going to get the shrimp, you'd better get the shark, too."

---

* This was one of four times during my travels I went into a restaurant thinking I might have found something special and unheard-of only to discover that Anthony Bourdain had already filmed there.

"Shark?" I asked. "Seriously?"

"I was born in the city, too," she said, "And when I moved here I wasn't ready for these country ways. The first time they brought shark meat back to the kitchen I said, 'What is that? Are you killing dolphins?' But now I try to eat some shark and shrimp every single day." She paused. "It's definitely better than stingray."

With an endorsement like that, what else could I do but order the shark and shrimp? And it was delicious.

It probably could have made a great magazine piece, too.

The longer I spent on St. Helena, the more I appreciated how out in the open its Gullah culture was. In Charleston I'd felt like I was reading lemon juice on paper: I knew I'd find something interesting there if only I could figure out how to see it. But on St. Helena it was all right there in front of me. Gullah food, Gullah art, Gullah history—just about anything I wanted to learn was there for me to study.

Gullah language, however, was another story.

Oh, I'd learned about it plenty, that's for sure. But I hadn't heard it anywhere on the island. In fact, in all the time I spent in South Carolina I only heard Gullah twice. The first time was on Mr. Brown's tour. The second was in Mount Pleasant, a suburb about seven miles east of Charleston. I was there for the Sweetgrass Cultural Arts Festival, which has been held in Mount Pleasant since 2005. I spent some time there talking to a Mount Pleasant–based basket maker named Marilyn Dingle. She'd been sewing baskets for more than sixty years, and though many in the community no longer practiced the art, she had taught her daughter, sister-in-law, and granddaughter. She told me that it had been the most difficult to teach her sister-in-law, who was left-handed. Throughout our conversation she worked serenely, weaving palmetto, sweetgrass, and bulrush without hardly having to look.

Eventually I asked her if she spoke Gullah. She ducked her chin down and her voice lowered in a chilly, almost defensive way. "Yes, I do," she said. Slightly taken aback by her demeanor, I apologized if I'd been out of line. She looked back up. "Ever since integration," she said, "we stopped speaking Gullah because everyone told us it was bad English." I asked her then if I could hear some, and she let loose a stream of words I couldn't begin to understand. Then we smiled at each other awkwardly until I eventually staggered away.

I knew heading into my visit that when it came to their language, Gullah communities were famously wary toward outsiders. This wariness extends not just to tourists but also to scholars—even those who speak Gullah. Patricia Jones-Jackson, a linguist who spent nearly a decade studying Gullah language and culture on the Sea Islands, recalled how, no matter how hard she tried, she was never able to pass as local:

> In fact, during my first few years on the islands, I learned that I should not try to pass myself off as an islander by an attempt to imitate the Sea Island language. While I may have had the syntax right, I was never able to perfect the accent, and it is the stress and intonation that give one away. When I asked the islanders how they were able to detect such small differences, I was often told, "I ain't know how I de know, but I de know." And they did know.

Now, there's nothing particularly unusual about a bilingual speaker electing to use the language his or her conversation partner speaks most fluently. In fact, it's something of a well-documented phenomenon, and there are all sorts of reasons for it. What interests me, rather, is the fact that so many Gullah-speakers refuse to speak the language even when asked. Take, for example, the story of Emory Campbell, one of the Gullah-speakers who helped translate the New Testament. In an interview with National Public Radio, Campbell spoke of his experience with visiting linguists. "I didn't want to admit that I knew or spoke Gullah," he said. "These two linguists who came into the area to translate the Bible into Gullah pretty much worked alone for the first year or two, before any Gullah-speakers would assist them."

When asked why he didn't want to divulge his knowledge of Gullah, Campbell responded simply, "Well, when we spoke Gullah, we were put down."

The Gullah people aren't just using English to communicate with outsiders; they're avoiding Gullah to protect themselves.

And no wonder: for years the language has been maligned and

disparaged. Before Lorenzo Dow Turner published his research on the African influences in Gullah, there had been little to no reputable research conducted with regard to the Gullah language, and derisive attitudes are frequently found in the works of men who were considered experts on the language. The most prominent work on Gullah was written by an English professor at the University of South Carolina named Reed Smith. He concluded that Gullah was mostly a form of English African slaves had learned from their white masters, and he made sure to pass along an informant's opinion that Gullah "is the worst English in the world."

Meanwhile, Ambrose Gonzales, the son of a plantation owner who grew up speaking Gullah and published a number of pieces on the language in the newspaper he founded, wrote things such as this:

> Slovenly and careless of speech, these Gullahs seized upon the peasant English used by some of the early settlers and by the white servants of the wealthier colonists, wrapped their clumsy tongues about it as well as they could, and, enriched with certain expressive African words, it issued through their flat noses and thick lips as so workable a form of speech that it was gradually adopted by the other slaves and became in time the accepted Negro speech of the lower districts of South Carolina and Georgia.

The tenor of scholarly debate didn't begin to change until Turner came on the scene—and I think it's no coincidence that he was the first African American to study the language. Along with his determined and repeated public avowals that the Gullah language was not simply degraded English, Turner's exhaustive and careful research helped reshape linguistic conceptions not just of Gullah but of all creole languages.

Outside the linguistic community, though, Turner's work had little impact. Consider this excerpt from a question-and-answer session with Supreme Court justice Clarence Thomas. In it, he was asked about his infamous reticence during oral arguments. He responded with a story about Gullah:

> When I was 16, I was sitting as the only black kid in my class, and
> I had grown up speaking a kind of a dialect. It's called Geechee.

Some people call it Gullah now, and people praise it now. But they used to make fun of us back then. It's not standard English. When I transferred to an all-white school at your age, I was self-conscious, like we all are. It's like if we get pimples at 16, or we grow six inches and we're taller than everybody else, or our feet grow or something; we get self-conscious. And the problem was that I would correct myself midsentence. I was trying to speak standard English. I was thinking in standard English but speaking another language. So I learned that—I just started developing the habit of listening.

There are two things about this that particularly drew my attention. First of all, Thomas was born in 1948, just a year before Turner published *Africanisms in the Gullah Dialect*. Even so, popular conceptions of Gullah were still clearly negative enough to instill Thomas with a sense of shame when speaking his native language. The second item of note is that this Q&A took place in 2000—fifty-one years *after* Turner published. And yet Thomas still refers to his language as "a kind of a dialect."

Now, it's unclear just how self-serving this story is meant to be. Feel free to form your own opinion as to whether or not this justifies Thomas's conduct in court. Nevertheless, the way Thomas describes his native language—"a kind of a dialect," "not standard"—provides an indication of the ways in which Gullah is still to this day denigrated by speakers and non-speakers alike.

A lot of people assume my interest in language means that I'm necessarily someone for whom minute quirks of English style and usage are of great importance. I won't pretend I'm not particular about words and the way I use them. But generally I am extremely impatient with gotcha-style grammarians. They are usually wrong, and they are always rude.

More to the point, they create a pervasive culture of insecurity around the use and study of language. I can recall with troubling specificity the times I've been corrected on usage or pronunciation: the use of *nauseous* instead of *nauseated*, reprimands about sentence-starting *hopefully*s, or, most vexingly, suggestions about my pronunciation of the word *often*.

For eighteen years of my life I used *often* without a second thought. But ever since I was corrected there's been a tiny part of me that has to stop and think, then feel insecure for having to stop and think, and finally feel annoyed that I'm feeling insecure for having to stop and think before I can actually say the damn word.

And this is the experience of an affluent white Midland American English-speaker who works with language for a living. For someone who speaks a genuinely non-standard form of English—or, in this case, a language that *resembles* non-standard English—the repercussions of linguistic prejudice can be far more severe, ranging from economic disadvantage to psychological trauma. Linguistic skill is commonly assumed to be correlated with intelligence, and standard usage is commonly assumed to be correlated with linguistic skill. As neither of these assumptions is necessarily true, the implication that standard usage is correlated with intelligence would seem to me to be doubly flawed.

But this is a common experience of creole- and pidgin-speakers in America and throughout the world. They routinely face prejudice and derision born of the mistaken assumption that their languages reflect some combination of simplicity and stupidity. Speakers of Louisiana Creole are demeaned by speakers of Standard and Cajun French; speakers of Gullah are demeaned by speakers of English. And while the existence of a creole language may be evidence of historical social, economic, and political inequalities, the perpetuation of negative perceptions of these languages is a sign of present inequalities.

Even more troubling, as we've seen, the deep and persistent shame engendered by these perceptions is a surefire way to effect language loss. And when a community loses its language, it loses incalculable cultural artifacts. It would be as if someone had walked into Charleston's historic homes and set them all on fire. No more armoires, no more grass mats, no more wallpaper. No more names, no more stories, no more songs. An entire people would lose the chance to know their history.

Faced with the proximate and inescapable pull of English and relatively high-prestige forms of Louisiana French, Louisiana Creole is fading fast. But I hope things will be different for Gullah. Even though it has fewer than 10,000 monolingual speakers and is harder than ever to find, I saw more than a few signs of vitality. Gullah organizations, for instance, are hard at work restoring a sense of linguistic and cultural pride through education- and entertainment-based outreach. Every November the Penn Center hosts Gullah Heritage Days, a celebration that includes performances, activities, exhibits, and symposiums. Additional festivals take place throughout the year in Beaufort, Hilton Head, and other nearby communities. Outside interest in Gullah language and culture is also on the rise, and today you can find a wide assortment of articles, books, and documentaries about Gullah, none of which refer to it as "bad English."

The geographical isolation of the Sea Islands' Gullah populations is also undoubtedly a powerful ally of those in favor of language retention. The island was for many years home to an overwhelmingly African American population that until relatively recently did not have a great deal of interaction with the mainland. It wasn't until 1927 that the first bridge between St. Helena and Beaufort was built, and there are reports from as late as 1949 that some residents of St. Helena had never even been to the mainland. This isolation strengthens the Gullah language in two ways: first, by insulating the island from the influence of English, and second, by protecting its residents from white-majority prejudice. As Patricia Jones-Jackson writes, "Growing up as a black majority almost free from outside social influences, such as racial prejudice characteristic of the white-dominated society in the inland parts of the United States, undoubtedly affected the attitudes and perceptions of the islanders, to the extent that few of them wish to leave the islands today."

And, perhaps just as important, those who do leave the islands eventually come back. Patricia Nichols, professor emerita of linguistics at San José State University, describes this phenomenon as "re-creolization": "Many speakers learn and use [Gullah] as children, move away from their communities for education and jobs where they use a variety of African American English or a regional Standard English, and then return to their communities in retirement when they 're-creolize' their speech."

All in all, when I think back on my time in South Carolina, whether or not Gullah has a viable future as a mother tongue was honestly one of the least of my worries. Rather, what I took away from the Sea Islands and the Lowcountry was an understanding that it isn't only a proximity to English that whittles away the minority languages of America. It is also a proximity to social injustice.

CHAPTER SIX

Nevada: Basque

A T THE SAME TIME that African languages were mixing and melding with French, English, and other languages of the American South, the languages of Europe were extending into the farthest reaches of the country. Between 1820 and 1924, nearly 36 million immigrants came to the United States, first from the United Kingdom and northwest Europe and later from eastern Europe and the Mediterranean. They streamed into the ports of Boston, Baltimore, and New York, making their way by train, by horse, or by foot to destinations throughout the United States. Some of these immigrants made their homes in the nation's cities, settling the neighborhoods that decades later would contribute so much to regional character. There were Poles in Chicago and Hungarians in Cleveland, Greeks in Detroit and Italians in Providence, Russians in Baltimore and Irish in Boston.

Other groups chose to venture out into the great expanse of the American West. These men and women were driven by economic concerns as surely as were the factory workers of the Northeast, drawn not to the garment or automobile factories but to the cheap, plentiful land available to anyone willing to work it. Soon there were Finns in upper Michigan and Czechs in central Kansas; there were Swedes in northern Minnesota and Portuguese in southern Illinois.

And then there were the Germans, who were just about everywhere.

For years, these rural communities and their languages were largely cut off from the rest of America. These immigrants built schools, held religious services, ran businesses, and established local newspapers, all in their native languages. But over time, the same economic forces that attracted so many immigrants from so many corners of the world reduced these language communities to whispers of their former selves.

I've spent years of my life in cities with rich histories of immigration. I'd been to Little Italys and Little Tokyos and Little Indias and Little Seouls. I knew what ethnic neighborhoods and enclaves looked like; I knew what they sounded like. But I didn't have the slightest clue about their rural counterparts. Why hadn't they been able to maintain their language and traditions? What were the particular challenges that they faced? Were there any traces of linguistic heritage still to be found? I decided to find out.

I pulled out my ratty old road atlas and flipped to the big square states. I needed to pick wisely. Though the languages of nineteenth-century immigrants are, on the whole, far more familiar to me than Navajo or Makah, I knew that on this side of the ocean, these languages live on less in conversation than they do in the everyday rituals of American ethnicity. I didn't want to drive eighteen hours to a town whose only lingering ties to the motherland were souvenir shirts that read "Kiss me, I'm One Thirty-Second Slovakian."

To avoid this, I decided to structure this portion of my trip around the loudest, busiest, and most accessible ethnic ritual of all: the big, boozy festival. I figured there was no better way to get to know America's immigrant communities than to party with them. I'd eat my weight in fried food, drink twice as much cheap beer, and hang out with a bunch of old people. And along the way I'd try to pick up on the ins and outs of frontier life in another language.

As soon as I figured that out, I knew exactly where I wanted to go: Elko, a small city in northeast Nevada that has for many years been home to a small community of Basques.

Strangely enough, I'd actually been there before.

The first time I visited Elko I was feeling lucky to be alive. This was due in part to the fact that I hadn't known what snow chains were until I tried to drive across the Sierra Nevada in the dead of winter. I tend to pride myself on my road-tripping know-how, but in this instance I will freely cop to both ignorance and foolishness. Honestly, you have to be more than a little bit crazy to think mid-February is a good time to make the drive east across the mountains into Reno.

I swear it made sense at the time. My husband and I had been living temporarily in California, and we needed to get back to New York. Having made the cross-country drive a number of times, I was experienced enough to know that I should have swung south in the hopes of avoiding the worst weather the winter had to offer. But two things changed my mind: the incredibly dull stretch of I-40 between Amarillo and St. Louis and the incredibly cheap blackjack to be found in northern Nevada. So I decided to take I-80, the country's second-longest interstate highway, which travels all the way from downtown San Francisco to the New Jersey Turnpike 2,900 miles to the east. I figured that it might be tough going from time to time, but at least I'd be skirting the Colorado Rockies, and as far as I knew those were the only real mountains of note in the continental United States.

I was wrong.

When we left the Bay Area the weather had seemed unexceptional. Chilly, a bit gray, but nothing out of the ordinary. A few snow flurries had started to fall here and there by the time we made it to Sacramento, but I still wasn't worried. As I said, I didn't think the Sierra Nevada were real mountains. But then we moved from snowfall to snowstorm, and suddenly I began to take notice of ominous signs that read "Chains Required."

This is when I turned to my husband and asked, "What the fuck are chains?"

About ten miles later I had my answer. A couple of hundred yards ahead, barely visible through the strengthening blizzard, I saw a California Department of Transportation checkpoint. To my right, a dozen or so cars and trucks had pulled over to the side of the road to install snow chains—which are, of course, simply chains that wrap around the tires to provide traction on snow-covered roads. A few drivers had bundled up and ventured outside to install the chains themselves, but most relied on the services of for-hire chain installers, stocky men in Day-Glo vests who hustled ably from vehicle to vehicle.

As we neared the checkpoint, a flashing light drew my attention to a set of instructions: "4-Wheel Drive with Snow Tires OK." I scowled. Not only did I not have snow chains, I didn't have snow tires. In the absence of a roadside auto center, however, I had little choice but to try to brazen it out with my nothing-special all-weather tires. When the car immediately in front of me was turned aside, I figured we were done for. But for whatever reason Caltrans deemed my car safe for travel and waved me through.

I still wonder what they were thinking. I still wonder what *I* was thinking. The storm intensified minutes after we left the checkpoint, and soon I was able to see only about ten feet in front of me. I couldn't have been going more than fifteen miles an hour, but my car was handling like one of those monstrous flatbed dollies they give you at IKEA. To make matters worse, the road was getting steeper and steeper, and I was doing my best not to consider a scenario in which I stalled out and had to get back into first gear on the icy incline.

At this point I normally would take a moment to say a little something about the scenery, the flora or the fauna, or maybe the quality of the road. But I couldn't see anything, not through the snow. Even if I'd been able to, I wouldn't have been looking. My eyes were cemented to the tire tracks in front of me, to the feeble red flicker of taillights in the distance. My left hand gripped the steering wheel so tightly that it would be sore for days; my right hand lurched nervously between the gearshift and my heart.

All in all, I was almost relieved when they stopped traffic until the storm passed. We were stuck somewhere in the middle of a line of other vehicles, far enough back that we couldn't tell if we'd been stopped for an accident that had already occurred or in order to prevent one from occurring. And then we sat there, in the snow, for an hour. Then two. By hour three I was beginning to get concerned, so despite being preposterously underdressed in tennis shoes and my Cardinals hat, I got out of the car and hiked through two feet of snow toward a ramshackle service station in search of some information.

When I got back to the car, my husband asked what I'd discovered. "Well," I said, "I have good news and bad news. The good news is we're only thirty miles from Reno. The bad news is we're two miles from the Donner Pass."

As it turned out, though, there were more bad decisions to be made that day.

By the time we finally got to Elko, I was desperately in need of a drink, so my husband and I rallied and headed to the casino just down the street from my hotel. It was here that I got my first taste of Basque American culture.

We were sitting at a table, nursing a couple of beers over some low-stakes blackjack, when a well-lubricated local sat down next to us and introduced himself. As soon as he found out we were from out of town, he demanded that we try the local drink, something he called Picon (pronounced "PEE-cone") punch.

The classic Picon punch is a combination of grenadine, club soda, brandy, and a French liqueur called Amer Picon. As I discovered later, in America this is considered *the* quintessential Basque beverage, and you can find it throughout the West, particularly at Basque hotels and restaurants. It takes its name from the creator of the liqueur that gives the drink its unique flavor, a Frenchman named Gaétan Picon who in 1837 invented a potent brand of bitters. The liqueur eventually made its way to the western United States, where it was thrown into the punch that now bears its name.

The man brought us back two lowballs from the bar and set them in front of us with a challenging look. "Here," he said. "Our national drink."

I looked at my husband; he looked at me; we both took a sip.

Reader, I nearly died.

It tasted like lighter fluid mixed with battery acid topped with the actual hair of a dog that had bit me. I managed to approximate something like a smile as I thanked our new friend, but as soon as he looked away I slid my glass as discreetly as I could over to my husband. He drained both glasses and promptly passed out. He claims to this day that it was his body's natural defense mechanism.

In his absence I began, tentatively, to make conversation with the other players. And over a long night of cards I learned to my surprise and pleasure that there's more to Elko than blackjack and buckaroos. Elko also happens to be one of the centers of Basque American culture—a thing that, to be perfectly honest, I hadn't even realized existed. At that point, just about everything I knew about the Basque people and language I'd learned from Alan R. King's *The Basque Language: A Practical Introduction*. (Although in my defense, if you're only going to read one book about the Basques, it's not a bad way to go.)

The Basque people come from the region surrounding the geographical crook where France meets Spain at the Bay of Biscay. Called Euskal Herria, Euskadi, or, most frequently in English, Basque Country, the area consists of the Spanish provinces of Álava, Biscay, and Gipuzkoa and the French provinces of Labourd, Lower Navarre, and Soule. The much-larger Spanish province of Navarre, home to Pamplona and its bulls, is also traditionally considered part of Basque Country.

The most important thing to know about the Basque language is that though it is a European language, it is not an *Indo*-European language. This means it's no relation to the sprawling language family that includes (among many others) French, Spanish, Irish, Swedish, Russian, Persian, Hindi, and English. Nor, in fact, is it a member of any other known language family, despite the best efforts of scholars to prove otherwise.

Believe it or not, this is actually one of the more frequent topics of conversation I'm confronted with when I reveal to new acquaintances my interest in language. "Did you know," they ask me, "that Basque is a relative of [Finnish/Japanese/Etruscan/Burushaski]?" Unfortunately, as intriguing as it would be to learn that Basque is related to an obscure language in northern Pakistan, none of these statements is true. Although Basque has certainly borrowed words from other languages (Spanish in particular), as far as we know, Basque marches to the beat of its own drummer. It is that mysterious and fascinating creature known as a language isolate.

It's for this reason, I think, that Basque gets such a bum rap. See, for centuries the Basque language has been widely regarded as an impossible mess, a tangled soup of *x*'s, *k*'s, and *ɣ*'s that's best left to locals—if not best left alone. In fact, if you've only heard one thing about the Basque language, it's probably that Basque is hard. Really hard. So hard that, according to *A Basque History of the World*, the nineteenth-century

Royal Spanish Academy dictionary actually included in its definition of the Basque language the qualifier "so confusing and obscure that it can hardly be understood."

Even the Basques themselves love to boast about how difficult their language is. There is actually a story the Basques tell about the time the Devil tried to learn their language. He had been conducting what I can only assume were routine demographic surveys of the condemned souls under his jurisdiction, and he noticed that Basques were severely under-represented. He decided to visit Basque Country in person and see what could be done to boost recruitment in the area. But first he had to learn the language.

So he found a farmstead in the countryside and settled in to eavesdrop on household conversations until he had learned enough to get on with his business. Days turned into weeks, which turned into months, until eventually, after seven long years, the Devil was forced to admit defeat and leave the Basques in peace. Because after all those years, he'd managed to learn only two words: those for "yes" and "ma'am."

Now, it's possible that this story may be a slight exaggeration.

All told, there are far too many variables involved in the determination of linguistic difficulty for anyone to be able to make an unqualified statement about any given target language. But generally speaking, two languages from a single family will show some very fundamental similarities—in terms of subject-verb-object order, for example, or the basic ways in which words are formed—and two languages from two different families will show some equally fundamental dissimilarities that make one language harder for a speaker of the other to learn. For instance, in an Indo-European language such as English, we're used to thinking in terms of subjects and objects. In Basque, however, a distinction is made between ergatives and absolutives. Ergatives are simple enough—here it's just a fancy word for "subject of a transitive verb"— but absolutives are trickier. They encompass both subjects of intransitive verbs and objects of transitive verbs. This is easy enough for a Basque-speaker to keep straight, but for an English-speaker it's roughly akin to being asked to sort apples and oranges with the understanding that Granny Smiths get lumped in with the Hamlins and Valencias.

Basque has other peculiarities that set it apart: twelve separate nominal cases, a verb tense used specifically for actions that occur after waking up, two entirely different words for "can" and "cannot," and all those *x*'s and *z*'s. But even so, it would be disingenuous to suggest that Basque is objectively and quantifiably among the most difficult languages in the world. The prospect of memorizing twelve different case endings may seem challenging to an English-speaker, but it's nothing when compared with the morphological convolutions of Archi, a Caucasian language whose verbs can in theory have more than 1.5 million possible forms. And though Basque's high-Scrabble-scoring spelling may appear impenetrable, it doesn't present nearly the cognitive challenge of, say, learning to read several thousand Chinese characters.

Frankly, the hardest thing about learning Basque is that you can't get a leg up by knowing a related language because there simply aren't any related languages. And in addition to being a genetic isolate, historically the language has also been geographically isolated, which means that with the exception of Spanish and French, the Basque language has had little impact on the other languages of the world. Even English, which I've always thought of as a bit of a slut for loan words, shows scant evidence of Basque influence—and even these scattered words are of dubious provenance.

Anchovy, for instance, seems a likely candidate for a bit of Basque English, given both the similarity to the Basque word (*anchoa*) and the popularity of the fish in Basque cuisine. But this etymology is an appropriately slippery one, and scholars have not been able to determine whether in this instance we all borrowed from Basque or, ultimately, from Greek (ἀφύη, a generic term for a small fish). The English word *bizarre,* meanwhile, is certainly related to the French *bizarre* ("odd," "fantastic"). However, one etymology cited if not endorsed by the *Oxford English Dictionary* traces it back to the Basque *bizar* ("beard"), a leap made, as one version of the story goes, when French soldiers were astonished to discover that their Spanish counterparts weren't clean-shaven.*

Another English word popularly (but likely erroneously) attributed to Basque is *jingo.* Its similarity to *jainko,* the Basque word for "god," has inspired otherwise unfounded speculation that the English word was

---

* I like to imagine that something similar happens whenever a Yankees hitter looks up at an opposing pitcher and thinks, *What the hell is that thing on his face?*

adopted from Basque sailors, who presumably frequently found themselves either praying or blaspheming. And although the word *honcho* sounds a lot like the Basque *jauntxo* ("political boss" or "young master"), it has its origins not in Basque Country but in Japan.*

There is, however, one English word that is without a doubt related to Basque. That word is *silhouette*, and it was inspired by one Étienne de Silhouette, a French government minister in charge of the country's finances for eight not entirely successful months in 1759. There are several plausible explanations for the word's creation, the relative merits of which depend on your opinion of M. de Silhouette. Some suggest the word was adopted because de Silhouette was known for being a practitioner of silhouette portraiture. Others, noting that a silhouette is literally a poor man's portrait, suggested that the coinage reflected de Silhouette's skinflint reputation. The most pointed interpretation, however, argues that the silhouette is the only kind of portrait you could finish in less time than de Silhouette managed to last in public office.

It is in de Silhouette's name itself that we find the relationship to Basque. Étienne's father, Arnaud, was born in Biarritz, a city in southwest France on the Bay of Biscay and thus firmly in Basque Country. Larry Trask, one of the world's leading experts on the Basque language, outlined the specifics of the relationship:

> [Silhouette] is a French spelling of the Basque surname Zilhueta, a French Basque variant of the surname Zulueta or Zuloeta; this in turn derives from *ʒulo* "hole" (*ʒilo* in part of the north) plus the very frequent suffix *-eta* "abundance of." This surname was doubtless given originally to someone who lived where there were many holes in the ground, or perhaps more likely caves.

In other words, his name meant something like "lots of holes." It's hard to imagine a more appropriate name for a minister of finance.

However you look at it, English has remained largely untouched by Basque language and culture, a not unexpected outcome in light of how little contact the two languages have historically had.

---

* The Japanese word 班長 (*hanchō*) means "group leader."

For centuries the Basques were highly successful fishermen and navigators, playing a key role in the whaling trade and the exploration racket. When Columbus set sail for the New World, for instance, he took a number of Basque sailors with him, and the *Santa Maria* was actually Basque-owned and -captained. Magellan's second-in-command, meanwhile, was a Spanish Basque named Juan Sebastián Elcano. Several months after Magellan was killed by natives on the Philippine island of Mactan, Elcano took control of the only remaining seaworthy vessel, making him (along with a handful of survivors) the first man to circumnavigate the globe over the course of a single expedition.

But for centuries Basque influence in the New World was largely limited to a few isolated parts of eastern Canada. Although it isn't clear whether, as some claim, the Basques actually made their way to the Americas before Columbus did, they certainly engaged in fishing, trade, and settlement off the coast of Canada in the sixteenth and seventeenth centuries, evidence of which can be found in a scattering of place names, a handful of tombstones, and at least two words in the Mi'kmaq language.

When the Basque people did begin immigrating to the Americas in greater numbers, they went first to South America, a natural destination for a people with high levels of Spanish-language proficiency. It wasn't until the mid-nineteenth century that the Basque language and people finally made their way to the western United States. Immigrants were drawn initially by the promise of gold, but in California and nearby states such as Idaho and Nevada they also found work—and, eventually, gained renown—as sheepherders.

Even so, compared to the contemporaneous influx of arrivals from places such as Italy, Germany, and Russia, Basque immigration was less a stream than a trickle. In 1911 the *New York Times* reported on the commotion caused when just 150 Basque-speakers arrived on a boat from France. In no other city were immigration officials better equipped to deal with speakers of foreign languages, but immigrants from Basque Country were so rare that even Ellis Island found itself at a loss. As the paper reported:

> Not within the memory of the immigration agents have so many
> Basques arrived here on a single steamship. About ten years ago

there came to this port about forty of them, and at that time there was no end of trouble in passing them. No one on Ellis Island could understand them, and no interpreter could be found. The situation was finally met by the mate of a steamship who volunteered to interpret for the Government.

Eventually a Spaniard with a working knowledge of Basque was located, but the disturbance and inconvenience was such that the *Times* declared the group "the strangest lot of aliens that has passed through this port in years."

On my first visit to Elko, though, I realized that there were a few parts of the country where Basque language and culture was anything but alien. That night in the casino I heard about Basque dinner houses and Basque folktales. I heard words like *kaixo* and *ʒahato*. I also heard about Basque festivals.

This is why, months later, I found myself returning to Elko. And this time I wasn't just there for the cheap blackjack. I was in town to attend the National Basque Festival.

Or, as locals sometimes call it, the Basco Fiasco.

Whether you approach from Reno, Salt Lake City, or southern Idaho, the first time you see Elko you can't help but be taken aback. Not because Elko is until the last moment hidden from view, but rather because any major settlement in northern Nevada feels highly improbable. The total population of Elko County is somewhere around 47,000 people, which seems like a good-sized community until you consider the fact that the county, the fourth-largest in the continental United States, covers 17,203 square miles. With a population density of under three people per square mile, Elko County isn't just sparsely populated—it's desolate.

Today the bulk of Elko's economy is focused on mining, but the city owes its existence to the Central Pacific Railroad, which used Elko as a distribution hub while constructing what was then the eastern end of the line. Popular myth maintains that the city owes its name to the Central Pacific as well. According to the story I heard at the visitor center, Charles Crocker, a Central Pacific investor, liked naming towns after animals. He pictured an elk, added an *o*, and called it a day. (I should point out, however, that I have been unable to find any other cities along the railroad's route that were named in such a fashion. And I certainly haven't been able to uncover a reason why Crocker might have felt the need to add that *o*.)

Eventually the rail crews left town, heading east toward Promontory Summit to join the Central Pacific with the Union Pacific. By that time Elko was already firmly established as an important center of economic activity both in the immediate vicinity and in the state as a whole. At the time, in fact, Elko was such a central hub that it was chosen as the first location of the University of Nevada. Although modern-day Elko can no longer lay claim to such prominence, dwarfed as it is by Reno, Carson City, and Las Vegas, it is still the largest city in northeast Nevada.

The area is not without its attractions. Whatever else you might say about it, no one would argue that Elko is lacking in character. After all, this is the modern American West, a town of ranchers, miners, and even madams. People out here wear prefer to wear their cowboy hats unironically, thank you very much. Even the local Walmart, so typically a bastion of American homogeneity, feels like a place where Sam Shepard might just be hanging out.

Tourism is driven by the city's gaming and ranching interests, with out-of-town visitors typically looking to gamble or buy authentic cowboy apparel. And though they don't exactly broadcast this at the Chamber of Commerce, there are also more-adult activities for those who are so inclined. This is Nevada, after all, where any county with a population under 400,000 can legally license brothels. But most tourists who come to Elko are probably in town to attend yearly events such as the National Cowboy Poetry Gathering, the Elko Mining Expo, or the National Basque Festival.

The National Basque Festival is a two-day celebration of Basque food, drink, dance, and sport held each year on a weekend in early July. It is not, as I discovered, the only event of its kind. Basque festivals are held each summer throughout the American West, in Boise; Winnemucca, Nevada; Bakersfield; and San Francisco, among other cities. These festivals, which are also known as "Basque Picnics," allow the country's scattered Basque American population to keep in touch with their traditions and one another. Elko has been home to a major yearly festival since 1964, when the Elko Euzkaldunak Club, Elko's local Basque organization, planned its first major summer gathering to coincide with Nevada's state centennial.

Of all the events planned for the festival, I was perhaps most looking forward to the running of the bulls, an event that for several years had opened the weekend's festivities. An adolescent infatuation with Hemingway had left me with a deep curiosity about bulls and the men who run from them, but the closest I'd come to Pamplona was *City Slickers*. And although I assumed that Elko's bull run was a somewhat modest affair, I was nevertheless anticipating a good show. That year's festival coincided with the Fourth of July, and in my experience, though the Fourth may fall short of New Year's Eve and St. Patrick's Day in terms of public shit-facedness, its intimate association with explosive devices ensures an entertaining general disregard for personal well-being.

Unfortunately, it was not to be. That year the running of the bulls was canceled.* At the city's visitor center, I was told this was due to concerns about "safety and street closures." At the Red Lion Casino later that afternoon, however, I heard another story. My dealer, a chatty California transplant named Debbie, passed along a rumor that the man who had been hired to transport the bulls to Elko had been permanently delayed.

"What happened?" I asked.

"Apparently," she said, "he was picked up for a DUI outside Wells."

The elderly man next to me snorted. "With or without the bulls?"

In lieu of the running of the bulls, the festival opened with a kickoff celebration behind the Stockmen's Hotel and Casino. I arrived early, expecting a crowd, but the street was still mostly deserted. A few people had set up lawn chairs on the sidewalk, and just outside the door to the casino I watched as an older man in a red beret struggled to set up an amplifier. Otherwise there was little sign of activity. I decided I was in no real danger of losing my place on the sidewalk, and so I took a walk around to see if anything else was going on.

To be perfectly honest, Elko's immediate landscape is easier to appreciate in the winter. When the world around you is covered with a thick

---

* For those who might be interested, the festival reinstated the running of the bulls in 2011.

layer of snow, it may as well be blanketed in potential. Who can say what
Arcadian splendors might lurk beneath that wintry veil? But come summer there's no hiding the fact that it's just a heap of sagebrush and dust
and heat and haze. I have to imagine that springtime is a real letdown in
this part of the world. But, curiously, it is the very lack of scenery that
makes the view so striking. Out here, the sky is indescribably vast, more
so even than out on the prairie or the ocean. The mountains, though not
so very far in the distance, seem trivial, like the scale drawing of a human in a museum picture of an apatosaurus.

With the notable exception of Stockmen's (which has been tarted up
a bit for tourists), most of the buildings in downtown Elko are physi-
cally unremarkable, short, squat, and built in a no-nonsense style that
could date to the 1890s or to the 1990s. The Basque influence, however,
is marked. In the space of two blocks, you can find the Biltoki Basque-
American Dinner House, the Nevada Dinner House (which advertises
Basque and Italian cuisine), and the Star Hotel and Restaurant. Arguably
Elko's most popular Basque eatery, the Star has been around since 1910
and is the oldest continuously operating Basque hotel in Nevada. That
evening, the sidewalk in front of the Star was swarming with dancers
dressed in red and white, the first signs I had found so far of the festivities to come. The dancers were, I was soon to discover, the festival's
opening act.

I returned to Stockmen's to find that a sizable crowd had gathered in
my absence, tripods and lawn chairs vying for space with tight clusters of
family members, many of whom sported traditional berets and kerchiefs.
As I found a space near the back of the crowd, I noticed that the man in
the red beret was still fighting with the AV equipment. To his right sat a
small band consisting of a tambourine, a clarinet, and a diatonic button
accordion called a *trikitixa*. The ensemble entertained the audience with
the bright, vigorous melodies of the Basque countryside while we waited
for the main performance to begin.

After a few false starts, and several minutes behind schedule, organizers
finally got the microphone working and declared the festival officially
open. Then, at last, the Elko Ariñak Basque Dancers took the stage.
With more than seventy dancers, the Ariñak troupe has been participat-
ing in the festival for over forty years, and it doesn't take an aficionado

to understand their enduring appeal: many of the dancers are adorable little children. The dancers begin instruction at age four, and for performances they wear traditional Basque clothing. Boys wear white shirts and red berets, kerchiefs, and belts; girls wear red skirts and white shirts under black vests and cover their hair with white scarves.

The older children and adolescents were undeniably skilled and enthusiastically received as they performed a number of short folk dances, but it was clear from the response of the crowd that the youngest dancers were the stars of the show. It also became clear that almost everyone in that crowd knew each other—and each other's children, grandchildren, nephews, and nieces. Each child was cheered by name. It felt less like a festival than a family reunion.

Later, a pickup truck pulled up in front of the casino for the evening's weightlifting and woodcutting exhibitions. One of the woodcutters was a young woman who, despite being about half the size of her companion cutter, chopped her way through a demonstration trunk in no time flat. Her name, I learned, was Stephanie Braña, and she had learned the sport at age thirteen from her father, Juan. She was also a total badass.

A student at the University of Nevada–Reno, Stephanie frequently traveled with her father to Basque festivals throughout the United States to participate in woodcutting competitions, and she had been doing so long enough that in Elko she was something of a minor celebrity. Every time she stepped up onto the trunk, the crowd surged and shouted, "Come on, Stephanie!" Today she is one of the top competitive woodcutters on the West Coast.

After the exhibition I watched a pack of girls and boys in Basque garb swarm frantically over the pavement to collect slivers of wood that had flown off the tree trunks. They then presented them to Stephanie for autographs, which she doled out with the efficient amiability of a professional athlete.

Soon thereafter the crowd dispersed in a slow ebb. Families managed to get halfway to their cars before stopping to chat with acquaintances; then they would get only half the remaining distance again before stopping to see someone else; then they would be stopped once more. It was like an impromptu demonstration of Zeno's paradox. I wondered for a chilling moment if, like a creepy old guy on a playground, I was the only person there who wasn't related to someone else. It was all the excuse I needed. I picked my way through the dwindling crowd and ducked into the casino.

My love of gambling began as a childhood obsession with Hearts, which my family would play with cutthroat abandon every Christmas and Thanksgiving. In college at the height of the Texas Hold-'em craze, I developed a taste for poker as well. I soon discovered the thrill of taking other people's money—and a remarkable ability to forget when other people took mine. By the time I moved to New York (a mere 120 miles from Atlantic City, as I was quick to remind my friends whenever we were in search of a weekend activity) I had fallen head over wallet for blackjack.

Blackjack is an appealingly simple game. It's not quite as mindless as slots or roulette, but once you learn the ins and outs of basic strategy, you don't really have to think a whole lot. You don't have to lose a lot, either. Play your cards right, and the house edge in most casinos is around 0.67 percent. Play long enough and bet little enough, and even if you do lose it's probably a reasonable price to pay for the privilege of hanging out, playing cards, and drinking on somebody else's dime.

But the best part about blackjack is that you're playing *with* other gamblers, not against them. And they're probably drinking, too. It's you against the dealer, and it's a surefire recipe for short-term camaraderie. This is basically the only time in my life when I'm not crippled by social anxiety. I knew that if I could find a good table in Elko, I would get a much better sense of the festival attendees than I could standing awkwardly on the edge of a crowd.

Stockmen's doesn't have the polish of a Vegas casino, but it does have something that more than makes up for it: two-dollar tables. I went inside, found a beer and an empty table, and settled in for a long night.

The table didn't stay empty for long. To my right I was joined by a lively group of locals on summer break from college. To my left sat a slightly reserved man from Boise and a woman who seemed far too young to be on such good terms with the casino staff. For the first few shoes I kept my head down and shamelessly eavesdropped. Much of the conversation revolved around one of the college kids. His name was Jake, and his friends were delighted to discover that he had met his most recent girlfriend at a strip club.

Soon enough the group registered my presence.

"Where are you from?" they asked.

I hesitated. Would I rather present myself as a girl from the Midwest or a transplant to the East Coast? I remembered that the group had called Jake a city boy because his family had moved to Carson City. About 50,000 people live in Carson City. The difference between St. Louis and New York City, I figured, was probably going to be negligible.

"I live in New York," I said.

They roared with laughter.

One of the college kids, a lanky blond who was startlingly devil-may-care with his betting strategy, leaned forward. "If you live in New York," he asked, "then why the hell'd you come here?"

"To see the Basque festival."

They laughed even harder.

All of a sudden the girl on my left looked up from her chips. "What is Basque, anyway? Is it, like, a religion?"

For the next several hours, in between increasingly questionable diversions from basic strategy, raucous shouts for more liquor, and impassioned arguments about the relative merits of Boise State and the University of Nevada–Reno, my new friends regaled me with story after story about Basques in Elko. I learned that there was a big difference between French Basque and Spanish Basque, and that in the past the two groups had gotten on about as well as the Sharks and Jets. When a Basque weightlifter stopped by to greet the table, I was given a run-down of his entire family tree, which included a cousin who owned one of the town's Basque dinner houses.

Everyone I met was proud of his Basque heritage in a disarmingly unpresuming way. The conversation was thick with self-deprecation. One player told me with a sly grin that his father had a sign on his wall that read, "You can tell a Vasco, but you can't tell him much." I later discovered he was the grandson of Beltran Paris, one of the first Basque sheepherders to come to Nevada.

I soon discovered that every conversation about Basque life eventually circles round to sheep. Because for years the fates of Basque immigrants—and the vitality of their language—depended largely on the ups and downs of the sheepherding industry.

Contrary to common belief, the Basques didn't go into sheepherding because they possessed some sort of venerable Old World sheep juju. Rather, the Basques first learned to herd large groups of sheep on the South American pampas. They then brought these skills north to California, at the time the center of the U.S. shepherding industry. With the completion of the Transcontinental Railway in 1869, however, the grazing lands of Idaho and Nevada became more accessible to businesses, to established immigrants from California, and to newly arrived European immigrants from the East Coast. Soon, cities such as Boise, Reno, and Winnemucca—not to mention Elko—were home to growing seasonal populations of sheepherders, many of whom were of Basque descent.

Sheepherding was a demanding but potentially lucrative occupation, and the majority of immigrants the industry attracted were young men looking to work only until they were able to earn enough money to make the round trip back to Basque Country worthwhile. Suffice it to say that this did not create an ideal assimilatory atmosphere, and the situation was exacerbated by the extreme isolation characteristic of open-range sheepherding. If herders weren't out on the range, they typically stayed at Basque-run boardinghouses, where they were able to eat Basque food, enjoy Basque entertainments, and speak the Basque language. It was remarkably easy for a Basque to come to the United States, work for several years, and head back to France or Spain without having learned more than a few words of English.

Relations between Basque immigrants and their adopted communities were further undermined by escalating tensions between sheepherding and cattle-ranching interests, and these tensions were amplified by linguistic and cultural differences.

In the late nineteenth and early twentieth centuries, northeast Nevada's sheepherding industry exploded, and by 1901 there were at least 659,000 sheep grazing in the Elko area. Although some Basques were employed by owners of private grazing land or were themselves landowners, many grazed their sheep on public lands or on private lands that were poorly secured. These itinerant herders enraged local cattle ranchers, many of whom felt it necessary to fight back against these "tramps" and "gypsies." Sometimes ranchers turned to politics to protect their land from encroaching herders. They were often successful: the Nevada legislature passed a number of measures that targeted and restricted the activities of itinerant sheepherders. Other times, however, ranchers would resort to less gentlemanly means, and there are numerous accounts of violence between Basque herders and cattle ranchers.

This combination of economic conflict and cultural differentiation eventually—and perhaps inevitably—resulted in ill will being directed at Basque herders not because they were herders but because they were Basque. In *Amerikanuak*, his excellent history of the Basques in America, William A. Douglass cites a number of examples of anti-Basque sentiment that managed to find their way into print. The *Caldwell Tribune* in Idaho, for instance, ran a piece on July 17, 1909, that included the statement "[The Basques] have some undesirable characteristics that the Chinese are free from. They're filthy, treacherous, and meddlesome."

Then there are the comments made by longtime Nevada senator Key Pittman. Testifying in Congress in 1913 against a wool tariff he felt would reward "alien" herders, he remarked, "As a general thing [the Basques] never associate with the other people of the state; they live among themselves; they can only speak a few words of the English language; they live in the lowest possible way for a human being to live; and they are nothing but sheepherders." When Nevada's many Basque supporters publicly took issue with his statements, Pittman responded not with a qualification or an apology but with an escalation, calling Basques "men of the lowest type and the most inferior intelligence." I'd like to think that today such rhetoric would result in immediate calls for resignation. At the time, though, Pittman's electability was ultimately unaffected by his remarks: he remained in office until his death in 1940.

The ranching-herding conflict was resolved in 1934, when the Taylor Grazing Act essentially outlawed itinerant sheepherding. Although it resulted in the departure of a number of Basque immigrants, the Taylor Act ultimately may have been a boon for those Basques who remained. Once Basque identity was uncoupled from itinerant herding, many of the negative stereotypes associated—however unfairly—with Basques and Basque culture began to fade away.

This process was hastened by decreased contact with the old country and increased association with the new. Immigration to the United States from Basque Country slowed during World War I before being cut off almost completely with the passage of the Emergency Quota Act in 1921 and the Immigration Act of 1924. The latter act allowed only 131 new immigrants from Spain to enter the United States each year.* Although there was an uptick in new arrivals after laws were passed to help lure back sheepherders in the 1940s and 1950s, Basque immigration would never again rise to its pre–World War I levels.

It was the rise of the sheepherding industry that brought the Basque to America, but in many ways it took the fall of the sheepherding industry for these Basques to become American. Not only did this push Basque Americans into industries where they would have more contact with and need more proficiency in English, but it also discouraged further immigration. Without a regular influx of native Basque-speakers, Basque American communities assimilated even more rapidly. Though the ancestors of Basque Americans may have gone for decades without learning English, today the overwhelming majority of Basque Americans speak only a few words of Basque—if, indeed, they speak any at all.

If you want to hear Basque in America, though, you can find it at a Basque festival. It will likely be nothing like the immersive fluency you would hear in another country. But you will at the very least notice the frequent use of Basque greetings. When I was there, festival-goers in Elko often greeted each other with *kaixo* (pronounced "KAI-sho") and parted with an affectionate *adio*. You'll probably also hear a lot of the specialized words that are still used to describe festival activities and events. Some festival-goers, for example, will refer to the woodcutting competition as *aizkolaritza* or the ribbon folk dances as the *zinta dantza*. Many men carry around a *zahato* (sometimes called a *zahako*)—a wine-

---

* The quotas in the act were calculated as a percentage of existing immigrant populations. For the sake of comparison, the quota for Great Britain and Northern Ireland was 34,007; for Germany it was 51,227.

skin traditionally used by shepherds—on their belts.* And almost everyone plays *pilota*, or handball.

The Basques were the first to use rubber from the Americas to add bounce to the *pilota*, a ball that previously had been made out of leather and string. This new and improved *pilota* was perfect for hurling or hitting against a wall, being both bouncy and painfully hard. Naturally, the combination of speed and danger proved a popular one, and soon *pilota* (or, more colloquially, *pelota*) was a common activity at Basque gatherings. Americans are more familiar with one particularly fast-paced version of the game that was given the name *jai alai*, from the Basque for "merry festival."†

(*Jai alai*, by the way, is typically pronounced "HIGH-lie." This may be old news to most, but I actually didn't realize the *j* wasn't pronounced the way it looks until I saw the third season of *Mad Men*.)

Basques also have a long tradition of so-called rural or country games (*herri kirolak*). These games are based on activities that were once part of everyday life in Basque Country, such as chopping wood, drilling holes, or lifting bales of hay. In order to maximize the entertainment value of these competitions, the games usually also incorporate some element of danger or absurdity. In Basque-style woodcutting competitions, for instance, competitors don't swing at the log from a secure position on the ground. Instead competitors are required to stand on top of the log they are cutting. If they want to maintain balance, then, they are forced to aim their axe at a point between their feet.

I saw more than a few of these *herri kirolak* on the first full day of the festival, which took place at the Elko County Fairgrounds. I arrived to find a healthy crowd milling about and taking their seats while concessions volunteers scurried around in T-shirts that read "Got Picon?" A

---

* In Elko a *ʒahato* was often also called a *bota* bag, which is the Spanish term for the container.

† In *A Basque History of the World*, Mark Kurlansky explains the origin of the *xistera*, the basket-like glove that jai alai players use to hurl the ball at maximum velocity: "In 1857, a young farm worker in St. Pée named Gantxiki Harotcha, scooping up potatoes into a basket, got the idea for killing the ball even faster with a long, scoop-shaped basket strapped to one hand."

few people lingered at nearby booths that were selling Basque parapher-
nalia such as berets and kerchiefs, but most attendees were interested in
catching up with old friends and watching the competitions that played
out in front of the grandstand over the course of the afternoon.

The afternoon featured a full program: in addition to the woodcutting, there was also weightlifting and weight carrying. In weightlifting
contests, each competitor would pick up a 225-pound cylinder, lift it up
to his shoulder, and then drop it to the ground, where it would land relatively gently on an old tire. Whoever lifted the cylinder the most times in
three minutes was declared the winner. Weight carrying was less a test of
pure strength than it was an endurance competition. Contestants each
had to carry two 52-pound weights back and forth between two cones
until they could go no farther. These weights, which look like small
boxes with handles, were laughingly referred to by the spectators as
"Basque suitcases."

I also watched a number of dance performances and two tug-of-war
contests featuring Elko high school students. The girls' tug-of-war pit-
ted the varsity cheerleaders against the junior varsity cheerleaders. Even
though I went to a school where the cheerleaders were actually not mean
or bitchy at all, I nevertheless felt a surge of instinctive animosity when
the varsity cheerleaders walked out. They looked smug, I thought, and
their hair was too pretty to be trusted. I cheered embarrassingly loudly
when the scrappy junior varsity team won.

There was also a sheepdog demonstration that was almost canceled
due to "technical difficulty with the sheep."

My favorite event of the day by far was the mixed relay, which combined weightlifting, weight carrying, wood chopping, and sprinting
to retrieve cans of beer. In the old country, I was told, the contestants
would have sprinted to retrieve ears of corn instead. This version, I decided, sounded much less fun.

I sat in the grandstand throughout the long afternoon, watching the
festival-goers nearly as much as I watched the festival itself. I saw young
families, teenagers, and garrulous twentysomethings. Scattered throughout the crowd were pockets of older men in matching Basque Club
button-down shirts. The Ariñak dancers had performed early in the
afternoon but had afterward dispersed throughout the bleachers, their

costumes looking less like costumes and more like clothes among the kerchiefs and berets.

Before I came to Elko I had read somewhere the suggestion that festivals were so prominent in Basque culture in part because the Basques lacked a vigorous literary tradition. I remember I circled the paragraph with a pencil and wrote "interesting" in the margin as if I knew what the author was talking about. It's an absurd suggestion, of course. The English have Shakespeare, but they also get together each year to watch a bunch of half-naked halfwits chase a wheel of cheese down a hill. People just like to get drunk together. It has nothing to do with whether or not they have things to read.

After a weekend in Elko, though, I can't deny the role the festivals seem to play in the preservation of Basque culture in America. Many of the attendees I met spent each summer going from festival to festival, checking in with various cousins and second cousins and in-laws, listening to Basque music and watching Basque sports, wearing Basque clothing and eating Basque food. Despite being (and despite having been for a long time) a significant cultural minority with a geographically dispersed population, the Basques in America have nevertheless managed to retain an impressive level of cultural cohesion. Lest we forget, this is a country where an immigrant group can assimilate so completely that the act of going to the gym, tanning salon, and Laundromat becomes a cultural touchstone.

For centuries language has been the primary mode of distinction between the Basques and their French and Spanish neighbors. As such, the Basque language is deeply entangled in issues relating to Basque identity, independence, and nationalism. It is not immaterial that *euskara*, the Basques' own word for their language, forms the basis of the name of their people (*euskaldunak*—literally, "ones who have Basque language") and their homeland (*euskal herria*—"land of the Basque language").

Like so many other minority languages throughout history, the Basque language has been regularly subjected to assimilatory pressures and repressive policies. Over the course of his thirty-six-year rule, Francisco Franco ruthlessly suppressed the Basque language, banning its use in public places and at official functions and forbidding its instruction in schools. At best, those who spoke Basque in public could, like fifteenth-century Moors, expect to be admonished to *hable usted en cristiano*, or "speak Christian." At worst, they could be arrested. Though restrictions on the language were not uniformly enforced for the duration of Franco's rule, the general policies remained largely the same. Prohibition of its use on TV and radio and in newspapers remained in place until Franco's death. Franco's focus on language policy, however, actually ensured that the preservation and, later, revival of the Basque language would become a key focus of the Basque nationalist movement.

One way the language was kept alive under Franco was through the establishment of underground Basque-language schools known as *ikastolak*. Today *ikastolak* operate openly and are a part of everyday life in much of Basque Country, but their mission remains the same. Educators are tasked with the promotion of multilingualism and multiculturalism, but their pedagogical emphasis is primarily on the promulgation of Basque language and culture.

Basque has also been safeguarded by the Euskaltzaindia, the Royal Academy of the Basque Language.* The academy was founded in 1919 to protect, preserve, and promote the Basque language, but its efforts came largely to a standstill under Franco. It wasn't until 1968 that the academy began to exert a substantive effect on the Basque language, laying out a number of systematic prescriptive rules for the language. While many of their guidelines were controversial, by focusing their efforts on a single version of Basque instead of on its many different dialects, language advocates have been better able to concentrate their resources.

These efforts have not been in vain. The number of Basque-speakers in Spain did drop precipitously under Franco, but the decline no doubt would have been even greater were it not for the *ikastolak*, the Euskaltzaindia, and other policies meant to encourage the use of Basque both in and outside the home. The campaign appears at the very least to have stanched the wound, and there are even signs that the language is actually

---

* *Euskaltzaindia* means, literally, "group of keepers of the Basque language." The "Royal" part of its English name is a nod to the Academy's patron, the Spanish monarchy. (The Academy is known in Spanish as *La Real Academia de la Lengua Vasca*.)

gaining ground. Over the past three decades, the proportion of bilingual Basque-speakers in Basque Country has actually risen substantially, from 21.6 percent in 1981 to 37.4 percent in 2006. In Gipuzkoa, meanwhile, the percentage of Basque-speakers ticked up to 51.5 percent in 2001, causing the Basque Statistics Office to trumpet the "first Province with a Basque-speaking majority."

Even so, policy makers in Basque Country are hardly able to rest on their laurels. The language still has fewer than a million speakers, and although it may be the majority language in isolated portions of Basque Country, it is by far the minority language in France and Spain. Though it may not yet qualify as an endangered language (along the lines of, say, any of the United States' indigenous languages), UNESCO's most recent *Atlas of the World's Languages in Danger* does classify Basque as "vulnerable."

Despite the strong support within Basque Country for the use and study of their traditional language, proficiency in Basque is no longer a reliable marker of the Basque people. There are Basque-speakers who are not Basque; there are Basques who are not Basque-speakers. The language itself reflects this new reality, and the use of *euskaldunak* is giving way to a host of new modes of identification, terms like *euskaldun zahar* ("old Basque," a native speaker), *euskaldun berri* ("new Basque," a Basque learner), and *euskotar* (ethnic Basque).

Meanwhile, in the United States the language is on its last legs. In the 2000 U.S. Census, 57,793 people identified themselves as "Basque." Only 2,513, however—a mere 4.3 percent of that number—reported speaking Basque at home. And only 355 of these Basque-speakers lived in Nevada, once the center of the Basque-dominated sheepherding industry; there were only 95 in Elko County. To be sure, the loss of a satellite language community is not the same as the loss of a core language community. Were Basque to disappear in the United States, it certainly would not be a cultural calamity on the scale of, say, the disappearance of Navajo or Gullah. Nevertheless—and perhaps because of the awareness engendered by the tyrannical policies of Franco—Basque Americans are more proactive than most immigrant groups in the promotion of their traditional language.

In the absence of continued immigration from Basque Country, the only realistic future for the Basque language in the United States is as a second language. And though festivals have managed to preserve personal and cultural ties among Basque Americans, they have been less than successful at encouraging the study of the Basque language. As anyone who has ever attended Hebrew school can tell you, language isn't something that can be learned on the weekend. Sure, you can pick up a few words here and there, but you'll probably never be proficient, and you'll certainly never be fluent.

This is a fact that Basque American cultural organizations are well aware of. In addition to hosting their yearly festivals, these groups also encourage exposure to the language by supporting programs at the University of Nevada–Reno and Boise State, by distributing language-learning software to local Basque clubs, and by promoting events such as the "Day of Basque." The motto of the North American Basque Organizations puts their mission most succinctly: *Ospatu + Heʒitu = Betikotu*, Celebrate + Educate = Perpetuate.

Of all such communities in the nation, the Basques in Boise have perhaps taken this most to heart. Since 1998, the city has been home to the Boiseko Ikastola, the country's only Basque immersion preschool. The school's first students are now in high school, and the majority of these students are still speaking Basque. One school, however, can have only a limited impact. It's not part of a larger network of *ikastolak*, nor does it have the backing of a federally funded language academy. And though it's true that Idaho was the only state in 2000 to report Basque-speaking children between the ages of five and seventeen, their number was only fifty-five.

Still, the best hopes for the Basque language in the United States seem to lie in the enviable linguistic acquisitiveness of children. In Elko I met a man from Boise who was in town to participate in the festival's handball tournament. Unlike the other festival-goers I spoke with, he knew more than a few token words of Basque, and he told me how he and his wife were working to pass the language on to their son. They were, he said, having some success—more, in fact, than they had bargained for. One day he asked his son, in Basque, how he was doing; his son answered in English. The boy's mother admonished him. "If you want to learn, you need to speak Basque with your father."

He replied matter-of-factly: "But Daddy doesn't speak Basque."

That Saturday night I found myself back at the fairgrounds for Fourth of July fireworks. I was feeling particularly irritable. After watching the competitions at the fairgrounds I had caught a *pilota* match before heading back to Stockmen's and the two-dollar blackjack table. There I had met two self-described cowboys named Will and Clint ("Like Eastwood," Clint told me, overenunciating in the way people do when they think you're very, very stupid). They had gone to a great deal of effort to let me know how despicable they thought New Yorkers were.

"You people think you know what's best for everyone. And I bet no one in New York even knows that we exist," Clint announced at one point, apropos of nothing.

"Know that you, personally, exist?"

"No," Will said. "That cowboys exist. That *real* cowboys exist, anyway. But that doesn't keep you from telling us what to do."

They went on like this for a while longer before I tried to change the subject by asking Will where he was from. "A little place called Katonah," he told me.

I just looked at him.

"What?" he asked.

"Katonah? In New York?"

"In New York state, yeah."

"Isn't that the place that got into a fight with Martha Stewart?"

"I wouldn't know about that."

"'Cause you're just a cowboy."

"Yes, ma'am."

"A real cowboy."

"That's right."

"A real-life cowboy." I took a breath, eyes narrowed. "From *Westchester.*"

I was still grumbling as I scavenged for a seat in the grandstand. I slid in next to a group of preteen girls who greeted me with warm smiles before returning to the serious business of scoping out new arrivals and outfitting themselves with glowing necklaces, bracelets, and headbands. I had no glow-in-the-dark jewelry, so I focused instead on lighting the candle I'd been given at the gates. It came in a flimsy paper holder I imagined was designed to collect stray wax. The way the breeze was blowing, I figured I'd be lucky if I made it through the night without setting my face on fire.

The crowd was larger than the one at the Basque games, but I saw many of the same faces, the same scattering of bright red kerchiefs. Off in the distance I recognized some of the *vascos* I'd met playing blackjack. From somewhere nearby I caught a fetid hint of *kalimotxo*, a foul concoction of red wine and Coca-Cola that was, inexplicably, wildly popular among locals. The speakers crackled to life with the sounds of country music, and the crowd surged to its feet, voices rising, pulling off baseball caps and berets and hoisting candles and lighters and neon-pink bracelets in the air. Amid the riotous swell of light and sound, I took off my own hat and joined the wild chorus.

CHAPTER SEVEN

North Dakota: Norwegian

O F ALL THE PLACES I visited throughout my travels, the destination I was the most excited about probably qualifies at the least exciting.

"I'm driving to North Dakota," I remember telling my father that fall.

I heard a bark of surprised laughter on the other end of the line. "You know when I used to go home to B.C. from grad school?" he asked.

"Yes," I said, knowing exactly where this was going.

"I'd leave Minneapolis in the late afternoon. That way I'd never have to look at North Dakota during the day." In a way, I understood where he was coming from. I'd driven through North Dakota myself.

For most people, North Dakota isn't a destination so much as a long stretch of highway. Many Americans, I suspect, view the landscape with the attitude of some sullen officer of the peace—*nothing to see here; move it along.* But this trip, I told myself, wasn't going to be like that, because this time I actually had a reason to be going to North Dakota.

For generations upon generations, most branches of my family were perfectly happy never to leave their chilly little northern European villages. But as soon as they decided to up and move to North America, they suddenly developed an inability to stay in any one city for more than a decade or two. So though there are only four places in Europe I can trace my relations to, there are dozens of cities throughout the United States and Canada that have some loose connection to my family, and few are able to inspire much more than a passing comment along the lines of "Oh, so this is where my great-aunt's brother-in-law used to live."

North Dakota, though, is different. Three generations of the Norwegian branch of my family lived just outside Grand Forks, and countless cousins still live there. What's more, I heard all about it growing up, my mother telling me all the stories she could remember about my grandfather's exploits as a kid. How he designed a heli-sled to help deliver the mail in winter. How he somehow managed to get a horse and cart onto the roof of his high school. How he once won a contest by knowing the greatest number of varieties of gladiola. I never got the chance to meet my grandfather, but I rather thought I'd like to meet his hometown.

So I would seek out my Norwegian American roots, I decided, and see what I'd missed out on. And just as in Nevada, I'd plan my visit around whatever looked to be the region's biggest party. All I had to do was find one.

My search led me to a modest little city about fifty miles south of the Canadian border. I was headed to a place called Minot.

Minot—pronounced "MY-not," as in "Why not Minot?"—was founded in 1886 when the men in charge of building the Great Northern Railroad decided to halt forward construction for the winter in order to build a bridge over a particularly inconvenient ravine. The company chose a location in the valley of the Souris River, named it after a friend of one of the railroad executives, and voilà: instant city. A tent city sprang up seemingly overnight, and within the first year of its creation, Minot's population had grown to 5,000. Ever since, the city has been known—to its own residents, at least—as the "Magic City."

In its early days Minot was known as a lawless, wild place, full of criminals and ne'er-do-wells. Later days weren't much better: during prohibition, for instance, Al Capone used the city to smuggle liquor. The *WPA Guide to North Dakota*, first published in 1938, reported, "Many pioneer residents of Minot still remember a certain railway passenger conductor who would call the name of the station, "MINOT, this is M-I-N-O-T, end of the line. Prepare to meet your God!" Today, in contrast, Minot is a staid and respectable sort of place, home to a major Air Force installation and yearly host to the North Dakota State Fair, an event that attracts upwards of a quarter of a million visitors.

It is also the location of Høstfest, North America's largest Scandinavian festival.

Although I'd planned my trip weeks in advance, Høstfest is such a popular event that hotel rooms in Minot proper were already fully booked by the time I called around. (The town's relatively small stock of hotel rooms is no major hindrance for festival attendees, many of whom travel by RV.) So I ended up staying in Bismarck, about 110 miles south of Minot. This initially seemed like a preposterous arrangement, but I soon discovered that 110 miles is next to nothing in North Dakota. It's just a flat, uneventful trip up US-83, one of those drives where a single stand of trees seems noteworthy. The landscape is so uniform you never have a gut sense of how far you've traveled. I felt a bit like Lawrence of Arabia, heading toward Aqaba: I could have been 10 miles away, I could have been 1,000 miles away. Eventually, though, the low clutch of streets and buildings that makes up Minot came into view.

My first stop in Minot was the Scandinavian Heritage Park, a somewhat idiosyncratic assortment of structures on a well-manicured patch of land just off the highway. I wandered around the park, passing statues I'd expected (Leif Ericson, Hans Christian Andersen), statues I hadn't expected (Sondre Norheim, the father of modern skiing), and statues I really hadn't expected (Casper Oimoen, Minot resident and member of the 1932 and 1936 U.S. Olympic ski teams). I snapped a few pictures of the replica thirteenth-century Norwegian church, the Danish windmill, the Finnish sauna, and the Swedish horse statue. (Apparently that's a thing.)

Then I stopped in front of a giant granite map of Scandinavia. It was shocking, really, how unfamiliar the shapes were. Somehow, despite an early education that was overwhelmingly focused on European history and culture, I had never learned very much about these particular countries. I hadn't even known that Denmark and Iceland were considered to be part of Scandinavia until a particularly humiliating loss at Trivial Pursuit; I hadn't known that Finland is often *not* considered to be part of

Scandinavia until about five minutes ago, when I read as much in the *Encyclopedia Britannica*. I was wholly unable, I realized, to identify in even the most approximate way the region my family came from.

I wondered, not for the first time, why I'd never felt compelled to learn about my heritage—or heritage language.

Norwegian is, all things considered, an extremely accessible language for English-speakers. For one thing, it's a Germanic language, which means that English and Norwegian share a number of lexical similarities. And the grammar of Norwegian is nothing scary. On a morphological level, Norwegian verbs are remarkably easy: the form of the verb doesn't change according to the subject. So instead of having verb forms like *I am*, *you are*, *he is*, and so on, Norwegian has something more like *I be*, *you be*, *he be*. This isn't a particularly unusual feature from a macro perspective, but for those used to struggling with French verbs it does cut down significantly on one's flash card time.

There are side benefits to learning Norwegian, too. For several hundred years, Norway was actually part of the same political entity as Denmark, and during that time government affairs were run out of Copenhagen and most official church and state documents were written in Danish. Over time, the political preeminence of written Danish had an impact on spoken Norwegian. Though the speech of rural Norway remained relatively unaffected by these developments, by the nineteenth century the educated urban classes had begun to use a Danish-Norwegian hybrid.* The modern form of Norwegian generally taught to foreigners is closer to this latter language, which means that if you learn Norwegian, you'll have little trouble reading Danish. As an added bonus, Norwegian-speakers are typically also able to understand a great deal of Swedish.† Normally this sort of low-cost, high-benefit language would

---

* As a result of this schism, Norway today actually has two official written languages: *bokmål* ("book language"), a form based largely on Dano-Norwegian, and *nynorsk* ("New Norwegian"), a form based on rural Norwegian dialects.

† Lest you get the impression that Scandinavian languages are a complete package deal, I should point out that Norwegians cannot typically understand spoken Danish. In fact, conventional wisdom holds that no one can understand spoken Danish—

be tremendously appealing to me, but I'd never managed to get past even the first chapter of *Teach Yourself Norwegian*.

One of the reasons I'd decided to visit North Dakota was to learn why that was. After all, I of all people should have been beating down the library doors to learn my ancestral language. (Well, one of my ancestral languages.) And yet I'd never felt any particular urgency or need to learn Norwegian. Scottish Gaelic, maybe. Polish, certainly. But not Norwegian.

This was at least partially a result of growing up in St. Louis, a city not particularly known for its Nordic culture. Had I not been separated from my extended Norwegian family, surely I would have developed a stronger connection to the culture. But I suspected there were other forces at work, too. I had a feeling that, in sharp contrast to the attitudes of Basque Americans, the Norwegian American community had decided to stop fighting the loss of their language.

Or maybe I was projecting. Either way, I'd soon find out. With a last, wistful glance at the Finnish sauna, I packed up my camera and headed off to spend the rest of my day in the company of Vikings, trolls, and lutefisk. It was time to check out Høstfest.

The first Høstfest—in Norwegian, "fall festival"—was held in Minot in 1978. Compared to the spectacle organizers are able to wrangle today, this first festival was something of a slapdash affair, put together from start to finish in just under two months. Even so, it drew more than 5,000 people, and the crowds have been growing ever since. While Minot might not be the most Norwegian city in the state, it is home to something far more important: the state fairgrounds. As such, Minot is uniquely suited to accommodate the tens of thousands of tourists who attend the festival each year.

Høstfest is just one of a number of Norwegian and Scandinavian festivals throughout the United States, in both small, heavily Norwegian towns such as Decorah, Iowa, or Spring Grove, Minnesota, and diverse

---

not even the Danes. A surprisingly common description of Danish pronunciation is that it sounds as if its speakers are trying to talk with a hot potato in their mouths. I gather this is all very funny to Scandinavians.

urban metropolises like Chicago or Seattle. But nothing else comes close to Høstfest—or, as it is billed, "North America's Largest Scandinavian Festival." The year I attended, the festival had booked acts including the Beach Boys, Kenny Rogers, and Randy Travis, and attendance was expected to be upward of 80,000.

With such large crowds you might expect a certain amount of chaos—particularly if the town only has a population of 40,000—but when I arrived on the fairgrounds, festival organizers had crowd control and parking down to a science. I was skillfully directed into a lot by a seemingly unending line of teenagers in reflective vests, and in no time at all I found myself on a shuttle that would take me to the main complex that housed the festival.

On the shuttle I sat behind a middle-aged couple. The man was literally rubbing his hands together in anticipation.

"I cannot wait for the lutefisk," he said to his wife.

At this point I hadn't yet eaten lutefisk, so I was willing to give him the benefit of the doubt. I found it difficult, however, to imagine that any whitefish-based dish could be good enough to merit the gleeful trot the man adopted as he leapt off the shuttle and hurried inside. I proceeded somewhat more cautiously, giving a wide berth to a man dressed as a troll and balanced precariously on a pair of stilts.

I bought a ticket and a map and took a minute to orient myself before heading to the main exhibition hall. I found what I thought was the right door, presented my ticket, and proceeded to stop dead in my tracks. I was confronted not just with a churning mass of people but also with a vast sea of Scandinavian tchotchkes. Admittedly, I shouldn't have been surprised. If you're going to attract 80,000 people to your festival, you probably have to offer some combination of the classic tourist trifecta of shows, shopping, and sustenance. But the festival brochure had focused heavily on the friendship and hospitality that was to be found at Høstfest. I'd read all about how polite and welcoming Norwegians were, greeting each other with *tak for sidst*—"thanks for the last time I saw you." There was even a monetary incentive to be nice: you could get $100 if the person you introduced yourself to happened to be the "Mystery Viking."

And to be fair, the atmosphere at Høstfest was exceptionally congenial. But the bulk of the festival in terms of both space and energy was dedicated to sales. Most stalls dealt in traditional Scandinavian arts and crafts. Hand-knit sweaters were popular items, as was anything decorated with the traditional Norwegian flower painting known as *rosemåling*. Also available was a wide range of books about Norway or by Norwegians, and I saw more than one travel agency advertising package tours to Scandinavia. Then there were the items of more general interest. One stall I walked past sold winter-weather gear. A yellow sign proclaimed "Diabetics Love Our Socks!"

The entertainment was similarly split. There were Scandinavian acts such as Norwegian country singer Bjøro Håland and Ole Olsson's Old-time Orkestra, but the lineup was dominated by non-Norwegian acts, perhaps most discordantly the Peking Acrobats. I squeezed into a packed room to hear part of a routine by Bruce Williams and Terry Ree, two comics who play Høstfest so frequently there's a wood carving of the men on display in the fair center lobby. They were old hands, gauging the audience in nanoseconds, and they killed. (Granted, the large group from the capital of Saskatchewan ensured they would never have to reach too far for a joke.) No one seemed remotely disappointed that they didn't have anything to do with Norway.

Luckily, there were so many exhibitors that though only 50 percent or so seemed to be even remotely relevant to the festival at hand, there was still plenty of Norwegian culture to be found or purchased. There were even a few bits of Norwegian language scattered here and there.

There are, as I mentioned before, a great many words that English and Norwegian have in common thanks to their shared Germanic origins, but English has borrowed very few of these directly from Norwegian. The most well known are those relating to Nordic sport (*ski* and *slalom*) or the peculiarities of Norwegian geography (*fjord*). But there are a few others, too. A kraken, for instance, was originally a mythological Norwegian sea monster. And the word *quisling*, a somewhat uncommon term for a traitor, acquired its meaning when a Norwegian named Vidkun Quisling collaborated with the Nazis during World War II.

Of course, these are words that you can encounter in any part of the country. The Norwegian you encounter in Scandinavian communities in the United States is more distinctive. The most common Norwegian you'll hear is *uff da*. This phrase is one of those interjections that never seems to have a truly satisfactory dictionary definition, but a good general rule of thumb is this: if you know when to use *oy vey*, you know when to use *uff da*.

As with *oy vey*, the use of *uff da* is also a kind of cultural signal, and it's the only Norwegian many Norwegian Americans know. So not only will you hear it fairly frequently when traveling throughout historically Scandinavian areas in the United States, you'll also see the phrase emblazoned on mugs, T-shirts, and other mementos. It's essentially the Norwegian American equivalent of I♥NY. In Iowa I once bought a dish for my cats that had, on the bottom of the bowl, a picture of a cat gazing woefully at the skeleton of a fish. *Uff da*, thinks the cat.

In fact, an entire genre of Norwegian American jokes revolves around *uff da* and the best time to say it (typical example: "seeing Swedish meatballs at a lutefisk dinner"). There's only one joke template you'll hear more often from Norwegian Americans, and that's the Ole and Lena gag. In an Ole and Lena joke (sometimes their friend Per also makes an appearance), the punch line inevitably exposes the innocent stupidity of one or all of the characters involved. For instance, Ole and Lena go to the ballet. At intermission Ole turns to Lena and says, "I don't understand why they're all standing on their toes. Couldn't they get taller dancers?"

Or: Ole and Lena finally get married. As they're driving to Niagara Falls for their honeymoon, Ole puts his hand on Lena's knee. She giggles. "We're married now, Ole. You can go a bit farther than that." So he drives to Syracuse.

You get the idea. If you don't, there are about a dozen Ole and Lena joke collections you can buy.

The vast majority of the Norwegian I heard at Høstfest, however, was culinary Norwegian. I could hardly walk two feet without seeing meatballs, dumplings, and potato sides. People couldn't get enough of it. Almost every food stall sold some kind of *lefse*, one of the most characteristic Norwegian dishes and something you'll find at grocery stores throughout North Dakota and the Upper Midwest. Typically made with potato and flour, lefse is called flatbread, but the emphasis should be on the flat rather than the bread. It's really more of a tortilla, just without quite so much flavor. It can be used to roll up meat or fish, but often it's just eaten on its own with butter or sugar to taste. I saw more than one person at Høstfest dumping whole packetfuls of Sweet'N Low on their lefse.

Then there's lutefisk. There is no more capital-*N* Norwegian dish than lutefisk, which is really unfortunate for all the other Norwegian dishes hoping to make a good impression on the world. Here's how you make lutefisk: first you take some fish, usually cod or a relative of cod called ling. Then you dump that fish into cold water for about a week. Next you add lye—as in the corrosive alkali used to make soap, clean ovens, and clear drains. As in the stuff Brad Pitt dumped on Ed Norton's hand in *Fight Club*. Lye.

Finally, you soak the fish some more (on account of all that lye having made it caustic), cook it, and eat it.

Lutefisk, like lefse and *uff da*, is a cultural touchstone for Norwegian America. Anytime a group of Norwegian Americans come together, you're going to find lutefisk, whether it's at the event itself or part of a nearby church function. Madison, Minnesota, has even gone so far as to declare itself "Lutefisk Capital USA." Lutefisk is to this vast stretch of farmland what barbeque is to Kansas City or Memphis, what gumbo is to New Orleans—if barbeque and gumbo were incredibly disgusting.

I can say this because I lined up with the rest of the crowd to get my own hunk of lutefisk, lovingly prepared by members of Minot's Bethany Lutheran Church.

I sat down at a picnic table with three chatty festival-goers, one who lived in Minot, two who used to live in Minot. As they wondered aloud to each other whether Sarah Palin's frequent use of "yah, you betcha" would lead people to believe she was Norwegian—and whether such a thing was desirable—they scarfed down their food. I just stared at my tray: a scoop of sweet corn, equal parts mashed potato and gravy, two meatballs, two rolls of lefse, and two huge, shiny pieces of lutefisk. My tablemates asked me if everything was all right.

"Of course!" I said brightly. And then I tucked in to my meal.

If you haven't eaten lutefisk, allow me to describe it for you. As the fish soaks in the lye it swells and acquires a characteristic gelatinous consistency. So what you get is basically a thick, fishy Jell-O. The flavor of mine was fairly insipid, and I understand that this lack of flavor is actually a hallmark of a well-made lutefisk. If only the texture were so unobjectionable. The only way I can describe the feel of it is to say that it seemed a little bit like something was decomposing in my mouth. Like it had died on the side of the road and swelled in the sun and then I'd decided to have it for dinner. That's about how it felt.

Of course, it did once make some sense to prepare the dish this way. Back in the day fish was salted so it would keep longer, and the lye treatment leached some of the salt from the fish, making it more palatable. I have yet, however, to hear a satisfactory explanation for the continued existence of lutefisk given modern methods of refrigeration and food preparation.

As much as I relished the opportunity to learn a few words of Norwegian, my time in the Høstfest food hall was, from a linguistic standpoint, mildly depressing. I didn't need a sociolinguist to tell me why I'd never tried lutefisk or learned of lefse before. I was pretty sure, in fact, that the reason I'd never heard any Norwegian food terms before was because Norwegian food sucks. For every *kransekake* (a pyramid-shaped cake made with almonds and egg whites), there's something like *rømmegrøt* (a sour-cream dinner porridge occasionally topped with bits of meat or hard-boiled egg), which is said by Norwegians to be delicious. After my experience with lutefisk I think I'll just take their word on that.

Throughout my trip I was thinking, always, about models of cultural change, weighing variables and gauging effects, trying to figure out in my own anecdotal way the mechanics of the melting pot. I thought about geographical isolation and demographic concentration. I wondered about the differences between agriculture, manufacturing, and service-based industries. I cataloged institutional pressures and social compulsions. It wasn't until I went to Høstfest that I began to think about the marketability of culture and ethnicity and how that might affect the rate and scope of assimilation.

I kept thinking about a particular turn of phrase I had come across recently in a book by historian Odd Lovoll, an examination of Norwegian American towns in western Minnesota in which he discusses the idea of "chamber of commerce ethnicity." I had grasped his intended meaning almost immediately, recalling with an end–of–*The Usual Suspects*–like parade of images all the towns and cities I had been dragged through on road trips as a kid in order to take in an "ethnic," "historic," or otherwise country-specific "Guinness World Record–holding" sight. Towns that were otherwise almost impossibly generic would dig up a few dimly remembered traditions from the old country, print up a brochure, and hope the tourists would come.

Here, for once, was an economic incentive that favored the retention of distinctive cultural practices. Naturally, of course, this would particularly incentivize the preservation of marketable traditions such as food, drink, and ridiculous dances. Even speaking as someone with an unfussy and irrepressible interest in all things linguistic, I don't see any way that language might be used to drum up tourism.

As I struggled not to gag over the mucilaginous lumps of flesh I was gamely shoveling into my mouth, I realized with some horror that in the business of ethnicity, language was no match for lutefisk.

After two days wandering the stalls and booths of Høstfest, I decided I needed a change of scene. I couldn't think of anything more Norwegian than lefse and lutefisk, and I couldn't think of anything more American than an exhibition hall full of small businesses, but I wasn't getting a particular sense of what it actually meant to be Norwegian American. I was mostly learning what it was like to be a tourist from Manitoba. Something about the festival rang false.

It wasn't just that Høstfest was a clusterfuck of commerce. It was that Høstfest was a clusterfuck, period. North Dakota is a state with a population density of 9.3 people per square mile. If you're palling about with 80,000 of your closest friends, you're probably not getting the most accurate impression of the state. North Dakota isn't defined by its cities; it lives and breathes in its negative space.

So I spent a few days driving. Sometimes I had specific destinations in mind—the scenic drive through Killdeer, maybe, or the tiny downtown of Devil's Lake—but more often than not I would just follow a meandering, impromptu route down dusty two-lane highways and unmarked county roads. I rarely encountered other cars (much less other people), and I made frequent stops along the side of the road to take pictures or, sometimes, just to look. It was late fall when I was there, and so I missed what many would probably consider to be the state's best season, the time of amber waves of grain and whatnot. But I think I preferred the fields the way they were, preparing for the winter, lying in wait.

Already I could smell the frost on the air. It is so remote up there and so sparsely populated, yet nearly every acre of land is planted, tilled, cared for. The sheer amount of physical work represented by the bales of hay, the miles of barbed-wire fence, and the first fledgling stalks of winter wheat is incredible to me. Even when I take into account modern machinery, it still seems an impossible feat. It must have been brutal, I thought, to have lived here in the nineteenth century. It must have been brutal to have lived here in the early twentieth century. I began to suspect that my grandfather had given us a slightly unrealistically rosy view of rural life in North Dakota.

Norwegian immigration to the United States is traditionally dated to July 4, 1825, when a ship called the *Restauration* left for New York from Stavanger, a city on the southwest coast of Norway. These first immigrants initially settled in Kendall, a small town on Lake Ontario, but many of them eventually made their way west to Illinois. For the next forty years a slow influx of Norwegians dispersed from here throughout the American Midwest, settling primarily in Wisconsin, Minnesota, and Iowa. Some years would see only a thousand or so new arrivals from Norway; other years—1849 and 1850, for example—the number would rise as high as 8,000. But even in these boom years, immigration from Norway was still fairly limited. By the end of the 1860s, out of almost 40 million total Americans there were only about 77,000 thousand Norwegians living in the United States.

The decades to follow would tell another story. Between the 1860s and the 1920s, more than 770,000 Norwegians came to the United States, and by 1920, the Norwegian population in the country had risen to 1.2 million. This massive demographic shift was the result not only of economic stagnation in Norway but also of increasing economic opportunities in the United States—opportunities that were largely concentrated in agriculturally driven pioneer states such as North Dakota. So even though Stoughton, Wisconsin, claims to be the "most Norwegian city in America" and even though Bay Ridge, Brooklyn, used to have more

Norwegians than Oslo, North Dakota is today the state with the highest percentage of residents with Norwegian ancestry.

North Dakota is the nineteenth-largest state in the United States and has the third-smallest population. In the west are the Badlands and the Missouri River, to the east is the Red River of the North, and there's a heck of a lot of sparsely populated farmland in between. Most of present-day North Dakota was acquired from the French as part of the Louisiana Purchase in 1803; the rest was handed over fifteen years later by the United Kingdom under the terms of the Treaty of 1818. But it would be another forty-two years before the area was incorporated into the Dakota Territory and thirty-eight years after that before North Dakota became the thirty-ninth state in the Union.*

There just wasn't an urgent need to make North Dakota a state—it wasn't a particularly popular place to live in the nineteenth century, either. In fact, the government actually had to find ways to encourage settlement of the area. The first of these was the Preemption Act of 1841, which gave heads of households on government land the opportunity to buy up to 160 acres for $1.25 an acre. But apparently even this price was too high, because in 1862 President Lincoln signed the Homestead Act, which reduced the price of federal land in the Dakotas to next to nothing: all you had to do was be twenty-one or older, pay an $18 filing fee, and live on the land for five years. If the land was undeveloped, you had to build a house larger than ten by twelve feet and cultivate at least ten acres of land. Additionally, if you were an immigrant, you had to become a U.S. citizen.

The institution of the Homestead Act coincided with a period of economic and agricultural decline in Norway, creating the perfect conditions for a population transfer between the two countries. But even

---

* Well, kind of. When North and South Dakota were admitted to the United States in 1889, then secretary of state James Blaine shuffled up the papers before signing them in order to appease parties from both states, each of which wanted to be admitted first. It's possible, then, that North Dakota is actually *officially* the fortieth state. Unfortunately for South Dakota, no amount of diplomatic maneuvering can make *S* come before *N* in the alphabet, and so North Dakota usually comes first in the list anyway.

so, many in Norway were reluctant to leave. They simply had difficulty believing the stories were true. What kind of country gave away land for free? In 1869, a Norwegian journalist named Paul Hjelm-Hansen visited the Red River Valley and sent back to Norway not only reports of the quality of the land but also verification that it could be had for free. The subsequent surge in immigration was further enabled by the construction of the Great Northern Railroad and the development of new milling technology that increased demand for the hard spring wheat that grew so well in the area. Between 1878 and 1890, the population of North Dakota increased from 16,000 to 191,000. And of those 191,000, more than 25,000 had come from Norway.

Even with the construction of the railroads and the late-nineteenth-century population boom, North Dakota continued to consist of widely scattered and largely isolated settlements. As a result, the state's Norwegian population was relatively insulated from the type of cultural and economic interactions that might speed up assimilation. This high level of cultural adhesion was particularly reinforced by the impressive size and scope of the Norwegian-language press in nineteenth- and early-twentieth-century America.

The first Norwegian-language paper was *Nordlyset* (The Northern Light), founded in 1847 by three Norwegians living near Muskego, Wisconsin. It survived only briefly, but it paved the way for the creation of dozens of other papers, including the Minneapolis *Tidende*, the Brooklyn *Nordisk Tidende*, and the Seattle *Washington-Posten*. According to Ingrid Semmingsen, a historian at the University of Oslo, from 1865 to 1914 at least 565 Norwegian-language newspapers and periodicals were founded. And although many failed soon after their debut, quite a few went on to develop a dedicated readership. The sixty-two newspapers that still existed in 1915 had a combined circulation of 490,000.

Although a secondary effect of the papers was surely an increase in Norwegian literacy rates, their primary purpose was political. *Normanden* (The Norseman), widely considered to be the most influential Norwegian paper in North Dakota, was published from 1887 to 1954, during which time the paper agitated against expansion of the railroads and for regulation of the wheat market. *Fram* (Forward), a major paper published out of Fargo, became known in the early 1900s as an avid supporter of the temperance movement. As Odd Lovoll points out, however, *Fram*'s circulation soon declined. "Many readers tired," he writes, "of *Fram*'s endless preoccupation with people's drinking habits."

Some papers, of course, served more practical purposes, providing a forum for the discussion of agricultural practices and relaying news from Norway. But for political parties, candidates, and interest groups, the allure of a direct link to large Norwegian immigrant populations was irresistible, particularly in North Dakota and Minnesota. And so it is not inconceivable that the Norwegian-language media—and, therefore, the Norwegian language itself—was buoyed if not outright subsidized on account of the political utility of Norwegian Americans.

Neither isolation nor insulation, however, could fully protect the Norwegian language from the pervasive influence of English. It began as it so often does, with the marginal appropriation of English words to describe items, activities, and conditions immigrants were encountering for the first time—words such as *prairie*, which describes a type of landscape unknown in Norway. Einar Haugen, who during his career served on the faculties of the University of Wisconsin and Harvard and is perhaps the most prominent linguist to have studied the Norwegian language in America, wrote extensively on the specifics of the English that wormed its way into Norwegian, identifying words and phrases that were coined by homesteaders coming into contact for the first time with American-style bureaucracy. As Haugen writes, "By filing a *kleim* [settlers] were entitled to a *homstedd* if they would *settla* on the land for a prescribed period and till it. The *settlar* then acquired a *did* 'deed' to the homestead, which became the *heimfarm* or *heimplass* 'home place' because it had been *dida* 'deeded' to the owner by *gåvvemente* 'the government.' "

When English words were borrowed, however, they had to be adapted to work with Norwegian pronunciation. In his 1921 survey of the American language, H. L. Mencken lists a number of these words, including *bir* (beer), *inschurings* (insurance), and *kjokfuldt* (chock-full). He also references the work of one Dr. Nils Flaten of Northfield, Minnesota, who describes this borrowed vocabulary as being "mutilated beyond recognition." Certainly such words would not have been understood in Norway.

The loan words also had to be adjusted to work with Norwegian inflection patterns. Although modern Norwegian has largely done away with noun case, many of the rural dialects that made their way to America were not so simplified. So an English borrowing first would be made to fit Norwegian pronunciation and then would be slotted into the usual grammatical paradigms. In another example cited by Mencken, Dr. Flaten provides a demonstration of this—as well as what I can only imagine is his subtle editorial on Norwegian American relations—in the Norwegian borrowing of the word *swindler*. The first changes are simple: there's no *w* in Norwegian, so *swindler* becomes *svindler*. Then, because the *-er* function in English is expressed with an *-ar* in Norwegian, the word becomes *svindlar*. Once these changes were made, any Norwegian speaker could infer a regular declension:

Singular	Indefinite	Definite
Nom.	*ein svindlar*	*svindlarn*
Gen.	*aat svindlar*	*aat svindlaré*
Dat.	*(te) ein svindlar*	*(te) svindlaré*
Acc.	*ein svindlar*	*svindlarn*

Plural		
Nom.	*noko svindlara*	*svindlaradn*
Gen.	*aat noko svindlara*	*aat svindlaro*
Dat.	*(te) noko svindlara*	*(te) svindlaro*
Acc.	*noko svindlara*	*svindlaradn*

For some, these loan words were an ominous sign of things to come. Ingrid Semmingsen relates the frustration of a Norwegian reverend, as expressed in an 1850s letter: "We never heard words like *hvetemel*, but instead 'flour'; never *gjerde*, but 'fence'; never *lade*, but 'barn'; never *stall*, but 'stable'; if a horse is *gardsprungen*, they say that it 'jomper fence.'"

English soon began to influence naming practices as well. Patronyms were abandoned in favor of consistent surnames, and American first names became more and more popular. Children were less frequently named after their grandparents, their parents instead choosing American names that began with the same letter. Older immigrants and linguistic purists were horrified by these developments. Einar Haugen even lamented the Americanization of livestock names: "In early years the cows had their proper names, rich and melodious descriptions such as Lauvlin, Snøgås, Dagros, Flekkrei, Storigo, Gullsi; but time passed, and names were forgotten as the herds grew larger and the urge to distinguish each cow as a personality was lost."

Judging by the letters of Norwegian immigrants, young parents frequently took a more pragmatic view. Berta Serina, who emigrated from the island of Finnøy to Illinois in 1886, wrote to her sister of her new baby: "His name was Gunder, and we will call the baby Grant. You probably think that is a strange name, but it is much used in this country, and usually if we call them by Norwegian names, they just twist them around to English when they get big."

Many parents were equally no-nonsense about language instruction. Gunnar Høst, living in Grand Forks, wrote to his sisters Agnes and Malla in 1899 about his views on Norwegian:

> Pastor H. thinks I am taking a great responsibility upon myself by sending my children to the American Sunday School instead of the Norwegian, but since my children don't understand a word of Norwegian and there is never a word of Norwegian spoken in my home, then I certainly don't understand why they should have their religious instruction in Norwegian. Of course my children will learn Norwegian, but first and foremost they are Americans and shall be brought up as American citizens. And as far as religion is concerned, I am quite certain that Our Lord understands English as well as Norwegian, even though one of our honorable pastors up here assures me to the contrary!

Like many other languages, Norwegian was also subject to occasional legal challenges. The status of Norwegian was most seriously threatened with the onset of World War I and the rampant anti-German and anti-foreign sentiment that attended it. In Iowa, a state with a sizable Norwegian population, Governor William Harding issued a "Babel Proclamation," banning the use of all languages other than English. This was a measure largely aimed at curbing the use of German—among those arrested under the proclamation were five farmwives in LeClaire who were caught speaking German on a party line—but Harding considered all foreign-language use to be a security risk. Iowa was home to a wide range of immigrant communities, nearly all of which took umbrage at Harding's proclamation, and so even though German interest groups were at this time certainly not flush with political capital, the combined might of the state's immigrant groups meant they were able to organize efforts against the ban. The Babel Proclamation was repealed in December 1918, not even seven months after it had been put into effect.

But the decline of Norwegian largely originated in the Norwegian community itself, as historically Norwegians have been subject to little of the discrimination and threatening legislation faced by speakers of other languages such as African-influenced creoles or indigenous languages. And it is no doubt not unrelated that the use of Norwegian in the United States tapered off relatively slowly, with the language being taught not only to the second but also to the third generations of immigrants. Linguist Joshua Fishman estimates that between 1940 and 1960, nearly half of second-generation Norwegian Americans were still using the language, as were as many as 40,000 from the third generation.

Nevertheless, this slow decline has been a steady one. Though in the 1910 U.S. Census 402,587 residents reported Norwegian as their mother tongue, by 1970 that number had fallen to 94,365. The latest estimates, from 2000, indicate a Norwegian-speaking population of just 55,311. More than 20,000 of these speakers are sixty-five or older.

I eventually ended up on the east side of the state, in a little town called Northwood, about thirty miles southwest of Grand Forks. With more than half of its population reporting Norwegian ancestry, Northwood is one of the most heavily Norwegian cities in the country. Fewer than a thousand people live here, in the houses and on the farms that radiate out from the massive grain elevator that dominates the horizon. In 2007, Northwood made the national news when it was hit by a tornado that killed one man and destroyed large parts of the town. If you missed this story, though, it's likely that you've never heard of Northwood. The only reason I've heard of it is because that's where my family is from.

In March 1884, Edvard Nikolai Olsen Knain, his wife, Mina, and his son Emil left their hometown of Hurdal and traveled forty or so miles south to Oslo, where they booked passage on a ship first to England and then on to New York. From there, they took the Great Northern Railroad to its terminus in Portland, North Dakota. Then they made their way to Northwood, twenty miles away, finally arriving on July 12, four months after their journey started.

For the first few years, the Knains lived on a farm owned by a man named Ole Hagen. In Norway, Edvard had been a member of the militia and had served as the assistant to the sheriff in Hurdal, but he came to America to work as a farmhand. He cut hay with a hand scythe, tied up and stacked bundles of wheat, and used a horse-powered threshing machine. Mina, meanwhile, raised Emil and gave birth to three more children.

In 1891 Edvard bought 160 acres of land seven miles west of Northwood and established his own farm, breaking sod, clearing the land, moving existing buildings, and building new ones. He started out with just his two hands and his two oxen, but he later added a quartet of horses—Jim, Nellie, Dick, and Gray Dick—to his team. He and Mina had another four children and worked the farm until they died.

Emil eventually married a second-generation Norwegian American named Annie Onsager, and they settled down in Northwood proper. Their youngest son, Wendell, was my grandfather.

By the time I was born, my grandfather had already passed away, and my mother had fallen out of touch with our relatives in North Dakota. We never visited Northwood when I was a child, and certainly no one from Northwood ever came to visit us. There is still a scattering of Knains in and around Northwood and Grand Forks, and the surname is rare enough that I can be almost certain we're reasonably closely related, but I'm too shy to call up unannounced.

This is why, when I finally found myself exploring Northwood at the tail end of my time in North Dakota, it wasn't to visit the living.

I knew my destination by three words: Bethania Lutheran Church. I didn't have an address or a map or directions. I just had the name of the village where Jesus raised Lazarus from the dead and a general idea that the church had to be somewhere near Northwood.

Bethania Lutheran Church was originally founded because the families who lived on Northwood's outskirts found it too difficult to drive the five to eight miles into town, particularly in North Dakota's brutal winters. At first they asked the pastor from the Northwood church to come once a week to one of their homes, where they would all gather for services. But eventually the group decided to raise money for the construction of their own church. It was completed in 1900.

Six months later it was struck by lightning and burned to the ground. Not, apparently, being a superstitious bunch, they raised some more money and built another church on the same lot.

The history of the Norwegian Lutheran Church is complicated to say the least, full of controversies and schisms both large and small. But one thing the various branches of the church did agree on was the importance of the preservation of Norwegian language and culture and the threat to that language and culture posed by public schools. In an article in *Norwegian-American Studies*, education professor Frank C. Nelsen describes the attitude of the Norwegian Lutheran church at a meeting on the question of public schools. "The Synod spent considerable time," he writes, "discussing the most appropriate adjective to describe the American school. The pastors debated whether it should be called 'heathen' or 'religionless.'"

So in 1866 the Church put forth its plan to build a parochial school system. In some Lutheran communities, the church allowed for public school attendance but recommended a strategy of infiltration to ensure that Norwegian Lutherans were hired as public school teachers. Many laymen, however, believed that Norwegian and American cultures could—and, indeed, should—coexist. They felt strongly that public schools were key to the future success of the Norwegian American community. The controversy over public schools raged for more than ten years, but ultimately the church lost. Although there were a number of private Norwegian-language schools successfully established, Norwegian Americans overwhelmingly elected to send their children to public schools.

And the linguistic preferences of the community ultimately dictated those of their church. As late as 1925 the Norwegian Lutheran Church of America was offering an equal number of services in English and Norwegian—though Odd Lovoll notes that the Norwegian services almost certainly drew fewer parishioners. In the following years, however, the use of Norwegian in the church continued to decline: more services and classes were offered in English and fewer pastors were trained in Norwegian. By the mid-1940s, less than 7 percent of services were conducted in Norwegian. In 1946, the word *Norwegian* was dropped from the name of the church entirely. There are today in the United States only two churches still conducting services in Norwegian: the Norwegian Lutheran Memorial Church of Minneapolis and the Norwegian Lutheran Memorial Church in Logan Square, Chicago.

This is really just an aside, though, because I wasn't looking for Bethania Lutheran in an effort to research the ecclesiastic effects on the Norwegian language. The church itself wasn't even there anymore. Bethania Lutheran was disbanded in 1988, and in 1992 the entire structure was moved to the Vesterheim Norwegian-American Museum in Decorah, Iowa. You can see it there today, on a quiet street amid a hodgepodge of other relocated bits of Norwegian Americana. Its cemetery, however, had not been moved. And unless I was very much mistaken, it was there I would find my great-great-grandparents.

I haven't been able to re-create the search string since, but the gods of Google were clearly behind me at the time, because I somehow came up with a plausible location. The Internet didn't give me a street or number, but it did give me latitude and longitude. And my off-brand GPS was just barely not-shitty enough that it was able to tell me what those numbers meant.

So I entered the coordinates into the machine, sent a quick hey-how're-you-doing to St. Christopher, and headed out.

Until then I'd thought that the back roads of North Dakota were just so quaint and beautiful, but I radically reconsidered this notion as I drove down ever dustier roads, each bumpier and more confusing than the last. I eventually found myself driving through a dairy farm, cows to either side, convinced that I was somehow trespassing. (I probably was.) As I adjusted to the mouth-only breathing essential in the presence of livestock, I thought, in quick succession: *This was a terrible idea. I can't possibly be in the right place. Fuck this fucking GPS.*

Fully lost now in a maze of cow paths, I came to a kind of crossroads and just took a guess, turning right toward a small cluster of trees. That's when I saw a church bell, which had been mounted on a low pillar set just off the side of the road. I pulled off onto the grass and got out to investigate. There was a small sign beneath the bell that read "Former site of Bethania Lutheran Church 1883–1989." I read it twice just to be sure. I couldn't quite believe I'd come to the right place. But there behind the bell was a small clearing surrounded by a fence, and in that clearing was the cemetery.

When I walked up to the fence I discovered that the gate was locked, and for a moment I actually considered leaving. But I strongly doubted I'd ever be able to find this place again, so after taking a quick glance around on the extremely off chance that one of North Dakota's eight police officers happened to be in the area, I threw a leg over the fence and climbed over, giving a quick prayer of thanks for my Norwegian gangliness as I did so.

I don't think I had really expected to find anything at the cemetery. My relationship with my Norwegian relatives had always been second-hand, just a meager handful of stories passed along at family gatherings. If I hadn't been so keenly aware that my existence was predicated on theirs, my grandfather and his family might as well have been characters in a fairy tale.

So it was something of a shock, then, to find almost without trying the two small stones marked Edvard and Mina Knain.

The only reason I know anything about Bethania, Northwood, and Edvard and Mina is that I stole my mother's moldy old copy of our family tree. It's more than a family tree, really—it's a collection of stories and genealogical information prepared by distant cousins in Cedar Rapids and Winter Park, painstakingly typed out, and then distributed to the family on forty-four mimeographed pages. But on the cover someone drew a picture of a tree and inscribed the words "Our Family Tree," so that's what I call it.

When the family tree is informative, it is very informative. But when it is not, it is maddening. It offers only a few terse sentences about Ole Ronneby, the seventeenth-century family patriarch. For my great-grandfather it reads simply, "Emil was a plumber, sheet-metal worker, and furnace man for many years." And my grandfather's entry, arguably the one that interests me most, is the very least informative: "Wendell

Knain. Born Dec. 11, 1916. Married Regina Lupka of Schenectady, NY, August 24, 1941. Graduated from University of ND in 1937."

The day after I went to Northwood I called my mother to see if she remembered anything else. "Oh, only bits and pieces," she responded. She told me that Emil was also an embalmer—"Which makes sense, you know, because it's probably a lot like plumbing"—and that his wife, Annie, had gone to teacher's college. On one trip they had gone out to visit the farm, and my mother remembered milking cows and jumping out of the second-story barn door into bales of hay. They had gone to see my great-uncle Henry, who lived alone on his potato farm.

"Did Grandpa speak Norwegian?" I asked.

She paused for a moment. "I think that when Daddy was growing up, they spoke some Norwegian, but I think that didn't last for too long—he went away to college when he was only sixteen. And he certainly forgot what he knew. But I know *my* grandfather grew up speaking it."

"So Grandpa didn't speak any Norwegian? Not even a word or two here and there?"

"There was one phrase. And he used it all the time. He liked to tell your grandma *jeg elsker deg*."

"What does that mean?"

"Well," she said, "it means 'I love you.'"

I smiled. It seemed my family had—in an utterly uncharacteristic fit of sentimentality—left me some Norwegian after all.

CHAPTER EIGHT

Florida: Haitian Creole

T HE PATTERNS OF LATE-NINETEENTH- and early-twentieth-century American immigration shifted abruptly and radically with the passage of the Emergency Quota Act in 1921 and the Immigration Act of 1924. With the adoption of quota systems such as the national origins formula, the rate of immigration to the United States was drastically reduced, with numbers of new arrivals from countries in eastern and southern Europe falling most precipitously. The quota system remained in place until 1965, when it was replaced with a new system based on professional qualifications and family ties. With the passage of this new legislation, rates of immigration began to increase once again. This time, however, immigrants weren't just coming from Europe. They were also coming, in ever-increasing numbers, from Africa, the Middle East, and Asia.

But most of all they were coming from the Americas. And though many of these new immigrants spoke languages such as Portuguese, Caribbean creoles, or even English, the vast majority were speakers of Spanish. This is a trend that continues today, with the nation's Hispanic/ Latino population acting as the driving force behind the country's overall population growth. Though Hispanic/Latino heritage does not necessarily imply Spanish-language proficiency, Spanish is nevertheless now the second-most-spoken language in the United States. Current population estimates suggest that speakers of Spanish and Spanish creoles number nearly 35 million. Taken in total, without even accounting for undocumented speakers, the Spanish-speaking population in the United States is, after Mexico's, the second-largest in the world. By 2050 it could be the largest.

The growing influence of the Spanish language is hard to miss, whether you live in New York or New Trier. It can be seen on TV and billboards, in grocery stores and newspapers. It seems, on balance, as if it would be harder to find a city where you can't hear Spanish than to find one where you can. At the national level English is still the majority language by a wide margin—as of 2005 the ratio of English-speakers to Spanish-speakers was just slightly less than 7 to 1. In a few exceptional areas, however, Spanish is now the dominant language.

Though Spanish-language communities were nothing new to me after five years in New York, I had no intention of overlooking them on my travels. And so I planned one last long-distance drive, from the historic Spanish-speaking settlements in New Mexico to the most heavily Spanish-speaking city in Texas. But before I did that I needed first to make a stop in Florida to see a city I'd been avoiding for years. It was time for me to go to Miami.

There really is no other city in the country whose public image is less compatible with my private reality. Miami always seemed to me to be the Regina George of America: a little too pretty, a little too flashy, and a lot too bitchy. Everyone had to look gorgeous; everyone had to wear heels. It was a city of rappers and reality stars, rappers who were reality stars, and—most terrifying—reality stars who were rappers. Even its crime scene investigators were too cool for school. I was a little worried that I'd be stopped on my way into town as part of an effort to ensure that no one in the city had ever not been asked to prom.

Fortunately for me, Miami's nothing like this.

Oh, don't get me wrong. Miami Beach is *definitely* like this. I spent a half a day in South Beach and it was like I'd looked into the gaping maw of a mythical beast composed of eight hundred disapproving beauty editors. But Miami Beach is not, as it turns out, the same thing as Miami.

Miami Beach is actually a barrier island just across the Bay of Biscayne from the rest of the city, a fact that gave me no small measure of comfort. I was good at ignoring islands. I'd done it with Staten Island for years.

The Miami I was in town to see was on the other side of the bridge. This is the Miami that has the highest proportion of foreign-born residents of any major city in the United States. Here in Miami and its surrounding metropolitan areas you will find the nation's largest Cuban community, its largest Nicaraguan community, and its largest Venezuelan community. And these aren't just isolated or marginal ethnic neighborhoods. These communities are large, influential, and very much a part of mainstream Miami. According to the 2010 Census, Miami-Dade County was fully 65 percent Hispanic/Latino, a 5 percent increase from 2000, when the country was already home to nearly two times as many Spanish-speakers as English-speakers.

But though I ultimately came to Miami because of its large Spanish-speaking population, I was primarily interested in investigating a language other than Spanish, which is why I didn't head straight out to Hialeah or Sweetwater. Instead I drove up to the area between 54th and 86th streets, between I-95 and the Florida East Coast Railroad. Once called Lemon City, this part of town is now known as Little Haiti. And I was going here to find Haitian Creole.*

Two things drew me to Haitian Creole. First of all, I was just plain curious about the language. I had looked at creoles in Louisiana and South Carolina, but this creole was different. According to the linguist and creole specialist John Holm, the first seeds for the development of Haitian Creole were sown in the seventeenth century, when the area was frequented by buccaneers from France, England, and Africa. Some of these men married French women and established plantations, and soon enough they were importing slaves from nearby colonies and from Africa. On one very small island, then, you had speakers of French, Spanish, English, Caribbean creoles, and a diverse set of African languages in a

---

* In its own language, Haitian Creole is called *Kreyòl*, and this term is being used more and more in English-language texts. However, were I to use *Kreyòl*, then I would feel compelled to consistently use endonymic language names, which might cause some confusion, as Louisiana Creole is called *Kréyol*. So "Haitian Creole" it is.

colonial context that required the rapid development of a shared means of communication. By the end of the eighteenth century both slaves and slave owners were speaking a form of Haitian Creole.

None of this is substantially different from the story of Louisiana Creole or Gullah. (In fact, linguistically there are so many similarities between Louisiana Creole and Haitian Creole that experts continue to debate whether they developed independently.) What is different about Haitian Creole, however, is that it is today an official language. And for a creole that's a relatively unusual thing, because given the circumstances of creole formation, creole-speaking populations typically have little political, social, or economic power.

I wondered, then, how Haitian Creole had become an official language and what, if anything, that meant to the Haitian diaspora and their attitudes toward language retention.

More important, though, I wanted to visit a non-Spanish-language community in a Spanish-language town. In every other language community I'd visited I'd gotten the impression that the pull of English was so strong as to be inescapable. I wanted to know if that was still true in a city where the majority of the population spoke Spanish. If it wasn't, if speakers of Haitian Creole were choosing to learn Spanish or choosing not to learn a new language at all, then that would seem to play into the idea that Spanish-language enclaves were a growing threat to the primacy of English. If it was, though, then that would be an indication that language prestige in the United States was determined by something other than population and proximity.

Because Miami was from the start an unexpected sort of place, it gave me the chance to think about all this and more.

The first Europeans to land in Miami were part of an expedition led by Pedro Menéndez de Avilés, the same explorer who happened to found St. Augustine, the oldest continuously occupied European settlement in the continental United States. He apparently didn't take to Miami the same way, because the Spanish only bothered to establish a single mission, and they abandoned it after a year.

For the next three centuries the area was only sparsely and sporadically populated by Europeans. In the winter of 1894–95, however, the region suddenly began to attract speculative attention when most of Florida's citrus crop was lost to a spate of unusually cold weather in the northern part of the state. Only one citrus crop survived: that of Mrs. Julia Tuttle, from the town of Miami. She sent a railroad executive word of Miami's frost-free winter, and before long there were plans for a railroad extension and a resort hotel. The first railroad tracks reached Miami in 1896; the city of Miami was incorporated soon thereafter. Its rapid growth into the major metropolis it is today earned it the nickname "Magic City." This is probably the one and only thing Miami has in common with Minot.

The first major wave of Haitian immigration to the United States, meanwhile, began with the rise to power of François Duvalier, the repressive leader known as Papa Doc. Most of these early transplants went to New York City, and to this day the city has a substantial Haitian population. By the 1970s, however, south Florida was on its way to becoming the preferred port of entry, attracting increasing numbers of Haiti's rural poor and urban working class. Soon Haitians from other parts of the United States and Canada, having realized as all sensible people inevitably do that winters in the Northeast are the pits, began relocating to Miami, bolstering the community's economic base.

New arrivals to Miami are concentrated in Little Haiti, where the cost of living is low and access to support networks is high. Those immigrants who are able to attain some measure of economic stability then move to relatively more affluent neighborhoods, a pattern of relocation familiar to anyone who has ever watched the ebb and flow of an immigrant neighborhood. For the Haitian population, these satellite neighborhoods are located to the north of the city, in places such as El Portal, Opa-Locka, and North Miami. Community groups such as Sant La, a non-profit based out of Little Haiti, estimate that more than 400,000 Haitians and Haitian Americans live in the vicinity of Miami. It is the country's largest Haitian population.

If I had been just a regular, everyday tourist in Miami, I probably never would have set foot in Little Haiti. I've read more than my fair share of travel guides, and I can't think of a single place I've ever seen depicted as ominously as Little Haiti. Travelers are admonished not to go at night, not to carry cash (not to carry anything of value, actually), and not to talk to anyone. Maybe, for that matter, you should just not go at all. The warnings felt not dissimilar to some I'd written myself for a travel guide—about the importance of steering clear of the North Korean border.

To be fair, those few guidebooks not in the business of scaring visitors away from Little Haiti aren't much better, waxing rhapsodically about the exotic rhythms of Kreyòl and the pounding beats of kompa music and generally patting themselves on the back for being so forward-thinking as to set foot into the area.

Nevertheless, when I got my first look at Little Haiti, I was prepared for the worst. Now, I'm not going to sugarcoat it. With 26.3 percent of its population living below the poverty line, according to Census Bureau estimates, Miami is the poorest large city in the United States. And Little Haiti is even poorer, an economically distressed neighborhood in an economically distressed city. You can see evidence of this wherever you look. The yards are patchy and strewn with assorted possessions and debris. Many of the chain-link fences have holes in them. Windows are barred, and barbed wire is everywhere.

The commercial thoroughfares are more welcoming, though, successions of painted storefronts and open doors and small clusters of residents chatting in the shade. And though there are botanicas promising spiritual guidance and restaurants serving *griot* and *diri ak pwa*, most of the stores just sell the same sorts of goods and services you could find in any part of town—or any part of the country. At the corner of NE 54th Street and NE 2nd Avenue, the neighborhood's main commercial stretch is anchored now by a Walgreens. For better or for worse, it is a neighborhood in transition.

Across the street from that Walgreen's is a place called Churchill's, one of Miami's more distinctive bars and music venues. Despite being in the heart of Little Haiti, Churchill's is a full-on English pub, with a Union Jack painted on the side of the building, rusting double-decker buses in the parking lot, and, over the entrance, a giant portrait of Winnie himself. As soon as I saw it I knew I had to go inside, if only to prove to myself that it was real.

It was around noon on a Friday when I pulled open the door and peered inside. There weren't any customers at that time of day, and the employees were all hustling to prepare for the evening's performances. So I had a good five minutes to stand there and just sort of take everything in. Now, everything about the place screamed "dive bar." It's the kind of place that would refuse to clean its bathrooms just to make a point. But when I walked in that day, the first thing I saw was Martha Stewart on the TV. This was, I have to admit, not how I imagined the bar best known for breaking bands such as Marilyn Manson and the Spooky Kids.

Eventually someone took notice of the weird girl watching the segment on how to fold fitted sheets, and I soon found myself talking to longtime employee Barbara Eisenhower. She loves the place, and despite obviously having a great deal of work to do, she sat down to talk to me about the clientele, the music, and the neighborhood. I asked her if the Haitians who live in the area come in a lot. "They don't really drink," she said. "They're not a bar culture, really." I learned later that many of the bars that had been in the area when it was still known as Lemon City were converted to churches after the Haitians moved in.

I asked Barbara if she felt safe here, and she said yes—mostly. Granted, she wouldn't necessarily want to walk alone three blocks that way or three blocks this way, but she felt fine on the major thoroughfares. "There's good and bad, like everywhere," she told me. Then, almost offhandedly, she mentioned that most of the crime had moved to the north of Miami, something I would hear over and over again while I was in Little Haiti, with various degrees of verisimilitude.

At this point we were joined by the owner of Churchill's, a man named David Barry Daniels, who looked far more like an English professor than a publican. He had caught the tail end of our conversation, and as I introduced myself I detected in his expression a hint of exasperation. I assured him I wasn't writing a story about the dangers of Little Haiti, and he relaxed and sat down heavily. Why was it, he wondered aloud, that so many journalists thought the secrets to Little Haiti could be found in a bar? He told me of the reporters—many from the United Kingdom—who came to Churchill's to try to get the lowdown on the area's Haitian gangs. "But there's no scoop here," he assured me, "because there's no real gang violence." My skepticism must have shown on my face, because he hastened to add, "Well, no real gang violence *here*, anyway. It's all moved north of the city."

In the end, I decided I wasn't overly concerned about daytime safety, but my first visits to the area had revealed that the extent of the neighborhood was rather larger than I had expected, and so I thought it prudent to hire the services of a guide to help me get the lay of the land. So it was that I spent my first day in Little Haiti in the company of David Brown, a tour guide who specializes in the Haitian and Cuban communities. Originally from New Britain, Connecticut, Mr. Brown got his start as an educator, and his current work is actually very similar, except now his students are the tourists and journalists and academics who are looking for an introduction to Haitian life in Miami. His style, accordingly, was more professorial than that of many other tour guides I've used, and this was something I appreciated as I began to realize just how much there was to learn about the community.

We spent several hours exploring Little Haiti as Mr. Brown delivered his lectures and patiently answered any questions I had. We drove by the elementary school whose cafeteria had been converted into the first Haitian church back in the 1980s. We wandered through the Little Haiti Cultural Center, a sleek, modern building that serves as a performance, gathering, and exhibition space. We stopped to examine a portrait of Father Gérard Jean-Juste, the first Haitian minister to be ordained in the United States and a longtime advocate for the rights of Haitian immigrants. He had passed away less than a month earlier. Mr. Brown told me that more than 3,000 people had attended his funeral.

And along the way I collected fragments of information that I tried to fit together to form a reasonably comprehensive whole. Such as the fact that there is, apparently, little interaction between the Haitian, Cuban, African American, and Anglo communities in Miami. Or that many Haitian immigrants work in hospitality or health care. I discovered that the Haitian population of North Miami was growing in both size and stature, and that the city's current mayor, Andre Pierre, is of Haitian descent.

I also learned that many of the area's residents still get their news from radio stations based in Port-au-Prince. This is just one way in which Haitians in Miami stay in touch with their home country. The groups are also closely linked economically, with the struggling Haitian economy dependent on remittances from the diaspora, which make up as much as

30 percent of Haiti's GDP. It is clear that strong emotional ties still exist. Mr. Brown put it in stark terms: "When Haiti is hurting, Miami is hurting." I would remember this most vividly six months later, when I watched coverage of the island's devastating earthquake.

But, as usual, most of the time I was in Little Haiti I was thinking about language. Upon hearing about my general field of interest, Mr. Brown had laughed and said that languages were no skill of his. For this he had his assistant, a young Haitian woman named Archemine. Archemine spoke French, Haitian Creole, and *un poquito* of Spanish, and she proved to be an essential part of the tour, adding personal detail to Mr. Brown's academic overview. But, even more important, she also acted as an occasional translator. Though most residents I talked to were able to speak some English if they needed to, on both this and my later visits to Little Haiti I heard very little English on the streets and in the stores. So when Mr. Brown's friendly but rudimentary Spanish or Haitian Creole failed him, Archemine was able to step in and handle things.

For this reason I ended up watching her as much as anything. I had thought that I was going to have a linguistic advantage in Little Haiti given that I speak both French and Spanish. Moreover, I'd spent a few hours the night before cramming some Haitian Creole into my brain. I was fairly certain I'd mispronounce it, but I thought it would do in a pinch. What I noticed while watching Archemine work, however, was that navigating the streets and stores of Little Haiti required more than knowledge of the languages themselves. You also needed to have a sense of which language to speak to whom.

"Some people speak French," she told me when I asked. "But more can only understand it." Then there were those—not Haitians, she assured me—who only spoke Spanish. Most people in the neighborhood spoke Haitian Creole. Some spoke English as well; most of those who didn't were in the process of learning it.

I began to get a better sense for the complications of this kind of linguistic environment later that afternoon. The three of us stopped to get a bite to eat at Lakay Tropical Ice Cream and Bakery (*lakay*, I later found out, is Haitian Creole for "home"). Mr. Brown walked right in and happily called out, *"Bonsoir!"* The woman behind the counter smiled. *"Bonju,"* she replied. They exchanged a few more words, and before too long we were holding in our hands piping hot meat pies called *pate*. Never one to pass up an opportunity to try a mysterious pastry, I bit into the buttery, flaky crust. It was filled with fish paste. It was delicious, but it was still fish paste, and I had been expecting something else. I took a minute to adjust my expectations and then inhaled the rest of the pie. Archemine handed hers to me. "I don't eat fish," she said, a bit regretfully.

Suddenly realizing that he'd purchased three fish pies when he'd meant to buy an assortment, Mr. Brown turned back to the proprietress to explain his mistake and request an exchange. Their respective language skills, though perfectly able to handle a routine transaction, were not up to the task of this particular negotiation. Mr. Brown was getting frustrated; the proprietress began to get annoyed. Archemine stepped in and smoothed things over. I, meanwhile, ate the extra fish pie.

Our next stop was just across the street, a botanica whose painted sign promised "Religious Articles—Reading—Treatments—Any Prob." Mr. Brown was going on about the history of Vodou as he walked through the door, but I was only half listening as I followed hesitantly behind. Not because I was scared, mind you, but rather because I was raised not as a Roman Catholic so much as a Bad Catholic. And to this day I can't help but feel a low level of anxiety whenever I am in or near houses of worship, as if the priest from Our Lady of Lourdes in University City is going to jump out and ask where I've been all this time.

Once inside, I tried to blend into the background as Mr. Brown pointed out the various candles and statuary. My nervousness must have shown on my face, because the woman in charge of the store gave me a curious look. *It's not because of the Vodou!* I wanted to tell her, *I'm just always like this!*

The botanica wasn't like any Vodou shops I'd seen in movies or on TV. It was spacious and well organized, not a dead animal in sight. It was also filled with Catholic iconography. It was explained to me that when Haitian slaves were obliged to convert to Catholicism, they used Christian saints as proxies for *loa*, or Vodou spirits. I was easy to see how this would have been an effective strategy. This room of the botanica looked like it did little more than supply devout Catholics with the necessary implements for prayer.

Soon enough, my anxiety was replaced by curiosity. I had read of the city's so-called Voodoo Squad, a courthouse janitorial crew that was kept busy cleaning up the offerings made in support of defendants. Miami, I was told, was practically Vodou central. Everyone practiced it. But from what I could see in the botanica, that practice must consist solely of lighting candles. Where was the rest of it? I wondered.

"So now we'll go see the temple."

I turned to look at Mr. Brown, who was heading purposefully toward a back room, seemingly having guessed precisely where my thoughts had been wandering. The shopkeeper held up her hands. "You cannot go there," she said with a thick Spanish accent.

Mr. Brown shook his head. "Oh no, I'm a friend of Mamita—*yo soy un amigo de Mamita*. She said I could take visitors to the temple."

I edged toward the entrance. I wanted to see this temple, sure, but not enough to cause a scene. "Please don't go to any trouble on my account," I murmured.

The fractured conversation that ensued lasted for nearly ten minutes as Mr. Brown tried to explain his relationship with Mamita and the woman tried to explain that she didn't know us, that she was alone in the shop, and that she couldn't possibly watch both us and it at the same time. We would have to come back another time. Neither understood the other. I interceded, reluctantly.

"*Si prometemos tener cuidado de no tocar nada . . . ?*"

She glared at me.

I said the words again in my mind, checking to make sure I hadn't said something mortally offensive.

"*No. No soy el jefe,*" she said, brooking no argument.

And that was that. I never found out what was in that room.

I came back to Little Haiti later that week to spend some time getting to know the area on my own terms. I was, I must admit, finding it hard to figure out Miami. Not only did I not feel like I fit in there, but I also couldn't really treat it the same way I had many of my other destinations. I didn't have any festivals to attend or museums to visit. For the first time I was exploring contemporary issues, and all it was doing was making me miss my books.

As luck would have it, though, one of the most interesting people in Little Haiti happens to run a bookstore.

Libreri Mapou is, some say, home to the world's largest collection of Haitian Creole books. It's located in a cheerful pink and white cupcake of a building up on NE 2nd Avenue, a few blocks north of Churchill's. The first time I visited I was just there to browse, but no matter how much I tried to remind myself that I couldn't actually read Haitian Creole, I just couldn't help myself. When the cashier rang me up, she was hiding her smile quite badly. "Are you studying Kreyòl?" she asked.

"A little," I replied, somewhat distracted by the shiny new dictionary I had just purchased.

"The *Herald* or the AP?"

I looked up from my book. "I beg your pardon?"

"Do you work for the *Herald* or the AP?"

"Oh," I said. "Neither. Why?"

"This is where they send all their reporters to learn Kreyòl." She said this with a little shrug I found hard to interpret. I chose to believe it was approval.

The second time I visited the bookstore I was there to meet its owner.

Libreri Mapou's owner is a man named Jean-Marie Willer Denis. He is known in Little Haiti, however, as Jan Mapou, and as far as I can tell, he is the community's unofficial cultural ambassador. When I sat down with him one morning, I could tell immediately that he made a regular habit of talking to strange writers. I felt for one disorienting moment like a participant in a press junket. But then he began to speak, and I realized that there was a good reason so many people had come to interview Mr. Mapou. His story is fascinating.

Born in 1941 in a small town in southwest Haiti, Mr. Mapou was involved in language politics from an early age, working with the Haitian Creole Movement to promote the official use of the language. For a short time he hosted a radio show dedicated to the celebration of Haitian Creole, but Duvalier's French-speaking government was less than receptive, and in 1969 Mr. Mapou was arrested and sent to Fort Dimanche prison. Upon his release, he immediately began planning to leave the country. He arrived in New York in 1971 and moved to Miami in 1984.

During the day he manages the parking facilities at Miami International Airport. But at night and on the weekends he continues to advocate for Haitian culture and language through his bookstore and Sosyete Koukouy (Society of Fireflies), the repertory company of writers, artists, and performers Mr. Mapou founded in 1985. The *sosyete* stages cultural exhibitions throughout the city with the express intent of enriching the community's relationship with Haitian Creole. Their motto is *n'ap klere nan fenwa*—"We illuminate the darkness."

Though Mr. Mapou has dedicated decades of his life to the defense of the Haitian language, there was no sign that his fervor has dimmed or that his will has faltered. When we spoke he got visibly emotional as he told me of the difficulties Haitian children still face in French-language schools. "How can you ask questions if you don't know the language?" he asked. "How can you learn if you can't ask questions?" It was clear to me that Mr. Mapou did not value language for its cultural content alone. He also saw it as a means to an end. The use of Haitian Creole in Haiti's government and schools would open new worlds of opportunity to the country's struggling population, the vast majority of whom are monolingual in Haitian Creole.

He is, in other words, both passionate and pragmatic. Unsurprisingly, then, he is also no blind enemy of English. There were two things that Haitian immigrants in the United States wanted, he said: "Number one, we want to learn; number two, we want to work." Neither of these was possible without English. But he was understandably wary of the rapidity with which English could take over. While he was living in New York City he first began to notice how quickly Haitians could lose touch with their native language. It was this that served as the impetus for the creation of the first chapter of Sosyete Koukouy.

Mr. Mapou held out hope, however, that soon the language would not need so much help. He told me that two of his daughters, both doctors in New York City, call him regularly to ask for help with Haitian Creole. "How do I say this?" they ask. And every time he laughs and says they should have listened when he was trying to teach them as children. Then he made an interesting observation. As the Haitian community in the United States becomes ever larger and more influential, many Haitians who abandoned the language in the past now have reason to return to it. Mr. Mapou called this phenomenon "slow-cooking the language."

Many months later, a friend of mine asked me if creole languages had ever been able to successfully combat the perception that they are corrupt or less sophisticated versions of the superstratum. The first language that came to mind was Haitian Creole, a language that is supported by a lengthy literary tradition and a language that has managed to acquire a measure of political consequence. In 1987, due in no small part to efforts of men and women like Jan Mapou, Haitian Creole was made an official language of Haiti, the first time a creole language in the Caribbean was granted such status.

However, this has not changed the fact that French continues to be the language of Haiti's political, economic, and social elite. This serves as a reminder that majority rule is not the sole determinant of linguistic prestige. Only 7 percent of the country's population is bilingual in French, and yet throughout the island nation there is still the idea that Haitian Creole is a coarse, simple tongue. As New York University's Bambi B. Schieffelin and Rachelle Charlier Doucet write, "Many educated middle-class Haitians, members of the petite-bourgeoisie, as well as Haitian elites, view [Haitian Creole] as a simplified form of French at best. Many claim it is not a real language at all, but a mixture of languages without a grammar." Numerical force is, ultimately, no match for political and economic power. These, more so than demographics, are the determinants of perception and prestige.

This observation may be of theoretical use, but as I continued to explore Miami I found it to be of limited practical value. Though I was convinced that the same rules that applied in Haiti should also apply in the United States—and, indeed, the history of Gullah seemed to support that contention—I found Miami's linguistic and political environment to be almost impossibly complicated. There were so many opposing forces that I found myself hopelessly confused about what "power" would even look like here. I was reminded of my brief stint in graduate school, when I struggled to find ways to operationalize the variables I was most interested in, and my professors informed me archly that history is just "a mediocre data source." People so rarely operate according to the neat little equations I would like them to.

Miami itself is a recalcitrant beast of a city, a place more suited to those looking for questions than those looking for answers. It reminded me, unrelentingly, of all the things I didn't know. From the moment I got there I was overwhelmed with facts and issues that I'd somehow managed to be blind to. Some of this was trivial, mind you—such as the fact that Miami Beach is actually an island on the other side of Biscayne Bay. But most of it wasn't.

Particularly significant were the things I learned about U.S. immigration policy.

Given Miami's geographical location, it is in addition to being a major center of trade also a frequent port of entry and final destination for immigrants from Central and South America and the Caribbean. It would be easy to characterize Miami's immigrant population in broad terms, as largely "Latinos" or "Hispanics" or "Spanish-speakers," but there are considerable differences between the city's immigrant communities, something I discovered firsthand when I visited Little Havana.

Of all the city's immigrant groups—and given that half of Miami-Dade County's 2.5 million residents are foreign-born, there are more than a few—arguably the most influential is the Cuban community. Cuban immigration to the United States began in the nineteenth century, when cigar makers went to work in factories in Key West. Later immigration was driven not only by economic opportunity but also by political instability, with nearly one tenth of the Cuban population immigrating to the United States during the decades of struggle for independence from Spain. By the end of the nineteenth century there were approximately 100,000 Cubans living in the United States. After the Cuban Revolution of 1959, rates of Cuban immigration skyrocketed, and Miami soon became the primary center of the U.S. Cuban community.

Though the Cuban population has dispersed throughout the county over the years—there are particularly large Cuban and Cuban American populations in and around Hialeah—the spiritual heart of the community is still Calle Ocho in Little Havana.

There was something about Little Havana I couldn't quite figure out. I knew it was a heavily touristed area, but though there was some measure of commercial rapacity to be found, it didn't feel nearly as performative as Times Square or Hollywood Boulevard. Or maybe it was and I didn't know enough to recognize it. Even more disorienting, Little Havana didn't feel like any of the other "ethnic" neighborhoods I'd been to.

While I was there, I met a man who was the fifth-generation scion of a cigar-rolling company and a gallery owner. He had traveled to the United States by boat and been picked up by the Coast Guard after three days at sea, with no food and no water but an entire intact art collection. I also spent some time talking to an artist named Molina. (I will never forget him, because when I met him I burst out with "You have the same name as my favorite baseball player!") It was Molina who pinpointed what was bothering me about Little Havana. Molina was born in Cuba, but he lived in Manhattan before moving to Miami. When I asked him which he liked better, he just shook his head. "New York is a great city—I lived there for twenty years. But Miami . . . Miami is like being in Cuba."

That was it. It wasn't that Little Havana hadn't sacrificed authenticity for commercial appeal. Authenticity wasn't the issue at all. What I was seeing was a community that had fended off assimilation. But in my experience that isn't something that can be achieved by sheer force of will. Rather, it requires some combination of economic resources, political clout, and cultural vitality—which is to say it requires a kind of power. Little Havana, I realized, has it; Little Haiti does not.

One way in which this is glaringly apparent is in the disparate U.S. government policies toward Cuban and Haitian refugees.

As presumed political refugees from an antagonistic, Communist state, Cuban refugees have long been granted preferential treatment by the United States. Repatriation in any form was a relatively rare occurrence until 1996, when the U.S. government adopted its "wet foot, dry foot" policy. Under this policy, if the Coast Guard intercepts a Cuban refugee in the water, he is sent back to Cuba or to a third country. If the refugee makes it to land, however, he will be given the opportunity to stay and—thanks to the Cuban Adjustment Act—to apply for permanent residency after a year. It is, relatively speaking, an incredibly lenient policy. It also, from what I understand, is not without its popular appeal. While I was in Miami I heard more than once of beach-goers cheering on Cuban refugees as they tried to make it to land before being caught by the Coast Guard.

Things are not as easy for Haitian refugees. Since the Mariel boatlift of 1980 the U.S. Coast Guard has patrolled the waters between Cuba, Haiti, and South Florida in an attempt to discourage so-called boat people from making the journey to Miami. Though it is Coast Guard policy to interview refugees and determine whether they might face real danger in their home country, Haitians are overwhelmingly dismissed as "economic refugees." Between 1981 and 1991, out of 25,000 intercepted Haitian refugees, only twenty-eight were granted political asylum.

These divergent practices are certainly influenced by the government's persistent and reflexive anti-Communism, but there is a strong sense—both in the Haitian community and outside it—that these policies and their outcomes are born of racism and discrimination. I certainly heard anecdotal evidence to support this, stories of the disproportionately low success of Haitian asylum requests and of sting operations designed to catch Haitian illegals. On several occasions I was even told about individual Haitians who were in the process of being deported. One was a friend of Mr. Mapou's who had been in Miami for ten years. His family in Haiti had all left or passed away; he was being sent back to nothing. Another was a mother whose children had been born in the United States; she was being sent back without them.

Indeed, when you look at the two neighborhoods, one relatively affluent and one deeply impoverished, one relatively light-skinned and one relatively dark, it is hard not to imagine there are other calculations at work. The more time I spent in Little Havana and Little Haiti, the more I began to think that the only minority languages or cultures that could survive the assimilative might of American society were those of communities with their own inherent political and economic resources. The Cuban population, I thought, had managed not to blend in because they were able to opt out.

The Haitian Creole I remember best from my time in Miami is a proverb I learned while I was in Little Haiti. It comes from Georges Sylvain's book *Cric? Crac!*, a volume of fables based on the work of Jean de La Fontaine and arguably the first major literary work to be written in Haitian

Creole. The third fable in the collection tells the well-known story of the ant and the grasshopper, in which the grasshopper, faint with hunger after whiling away the summer instead of storing food for winter, is forced to beg for sustenance from the hardworking ant.

In the United States the fable is probably most familiar to those of us who were raised on Walt Disney Silly Symphonies. In this version, the grasshopper is an affable performer who would rather sing and dance ("The world owes me a living!") while a parade of ants harvest food under the supervision of their imperious queen. That winter, when the grasshopper stumbles into the ants' warm and cozy colony, the queen is at first less than hospitable. "With ants, just those who work may stay," she informs the ailing grasshopper. "So take your fiddle . . . and play!"

Sylvain's version is no less pointed:

> Vouésin millò passé fanmill'!
> Cé con ça moun' longtemps té dit;
> Main, temps passé pas temps joki:
> A lhè qui lé,—pas palé ça!—
> Toutt coucouill' cléré pou gé yo.
> Moin pas méprisé sièq' ça-là:
> Main, dit-moin quil-ess' ou pito?*
>
> Voisin vaut mieux que parent!
> Ainsi disaient les gens d'autrefois;
> Mais le temps jadis n'est pas celui d'aujourd'hui.
> A present,—ne m'en parlez pas—
> C'est pour ses yeux que toute luciole luit.
> Je ne méprise pas ce siècle-ci,
> Mais dites-moi lequel vous préférez!
>
> Neighbors better than family!
> That's what everyone used to say.

---

* The orthography of Haitian Creole wasn't standardized until 1979. This passage, however, dates back to 1929, and so it may look very different from other Haitian Creole you might have seen.

But time past is not today.
These days—don't speak of them!—
Fireflies glow for their own eyes.
I don't despise this century:
But, tell me, which do you prefer!

The line that spawned the proverb I remember is the antepenultimate: *Toutt coucouill' cléré pou gé yo*—or, in modern spelling, *Tout koukouy klere pou je yo*. It means "Fireflies glow for their own eyes."

The fable is immensely clever in that it can be interpreted or reimagined in any number of ways depending on whose side you take. I've often thought that zombies are a perfect allegorical monster in that they can stand in for just about anything you'd like them to; similarly, the story of the grasshopper and the ant could be used to criticize the rich, the poor, the powerful, or the subjugated. The Disney cartoon alone is the stuff master's theses are made of.

As such, there would seem to be any number of possible readings of *tout koukouy klere pou je yo*. Is it a celebration of self-sufficiency or a condemnation of uncharitableness? An ode to the workingman or an artist's lament? Even the simplest and most common interpretation, which is something like "every man for himself," has a wealth of potential implications—an ambiguity that Sylvain himself seems to acknowledge with his closing line.

I remember this proverb in particular because these are the *koukouy* of Mr. Mapou's *sosyete*. They do not merely illuminate the darkness; they glow for their own eyes. For me, this is an eloquent articulation of the purpose of and challenges faced by language activists. In Haiti and in Miami, Haitian Creole cannot expect either active support from outside the community or passive support in the form of political, economic, or social incentives, a reality that appears to be readily accepted if not necessarily celebrated by the Haitian community. Even those who are dedicated to the celebration of Haitian Creole do not try to underplay the fact that English proficiency is essential if Haitians in Miami wish to better their circumstances. It's telling, too, that Haitians in Miami are learning Spanish in addition to English—and that Spanish-speakers in Miami are *not* learning Haitian Creole.

A person's language is necessarily a reflection of his or her political environment, of the social and economic forces that influence survival and success. The languages of prestige are the languages of power. The preservation and promotion of heritage languages, then, is something of a radical act, a pinpoint of opposition amid the glare of the status quo. *Tout koukouy klere pou je yo* is no mere acknowledgment of self-interest; it is a celebration of self-determination.

That's how I read it, anyway.

But then, maybe I too am just seeing what I want to see.

CHAPTER NINE

New Mexico: Spanish

And so it was, finally, that I came to Spanish: not as an after-thought but as a culmination. I had traveled through the deserts of Nevada and the bayous of Louisiana, through the rain forests of Washington state and the tranquil prairies of North Dakota. And in many of these places I'd heard more Spanish than the language I had actually set out to find. It was in Elko, creeping into Basque American vernacular, and it was in South Carolina, tripping from the lips of southern belles. Always it was in Queens as I went about my daily life. Even were it not my favorite and most fluent acquired language, Spanish was hardly something I could ignore.

The majority of America's Latino population lives in the southwestern states of New Mexico, Texas, California, Arizona, and Colorado, in cities such as L.A., Houston, San Antonio, and El Paso. This is not a new development. The Spanish were the first European settlers to come to the area, moving into New Mexico by 1598 and Texas by 1659. The first explorers ventured into Arizona in the 1530s; the first Spanish mission in California was founded in 1769. By the time Mexico ceded the bulk of its territories north of the Rio Grande to the United States, Spanish had for several generations been established as the local prestige language. Though the demographics of the region changed with the advent of statehood and other economic developments, New Mexico, home to the earliest Spanish settlements in the country, remains the most heavily Latino state in the nation. According to the most recent estimates, more than 45 percent of its population is Latino.

The terms *Latino* and *Hispanic* do little to reveal the differences, both subtle and conspicuous, between various Spanish-speaking immigrant groups. (This is particularly true with regard to Census data, which leaves it up to the respondent to decide how to self-identify.) For a variety of reasons, not the least of which is geographical proximity, the largest of these groups is of Mexican origin. Next are Spanish-speakers from Puerto Rico, who are largely concentrated in the Northeast. Today there are approximately 750,000 Puerto Ricans in New York City, 33 percent of the city's total Latino population, and the annual Puerto Rican Day Parade is one of city's largest public celebrations—something I would invariably forget each year until I found myself once again stuck in unrelenting pedestrian traffic on the Upper East Side.

Then there are groups from the Caribbean and Central America, including Cubans, nearly half of whom live in and around Miami, and Dominicans, nearly half of whom live in New York. As I have mentioned, Miami also has the country's largest Nicaraguan population, and there are major Salvadorean communities in Houston, Chicago, and L.A. These numbers are rounded out by arrivals from South American countries (particularly Colombia, Ecuador, and Peru). And then, with a couple of thousand new arrivals each year, there are the immigrants from Spain. A sign of how much things have changed in the United States since the days of the Spanish Empire is that Spaniards don't even get their own subcategory in most Census tables, being relegated instead to "All other Hispanic."

As you might expect, this diversity also extends to the Spanish language. Most high-school students who study Spanish are well aware of the differences between European and Latin American Spanish, but there are, of course, also substantial differences among Latin American dialects. These differences are so strong that, at times, mutual intelligibility is not at all a given. When I went to Miami, for instance, I had relatively recently spent three weeks in Mexico, and I was feeling fairly confident about my Spanish-language skills. In Little Havana, however, I was confronted with a Spanish that was spoken so rapidly and so differently that I had to struggle to keep up with simple conversations.

So though the last leg of my journey was, on the whole, devoted to the Spanish language, it would be misleading to say that it was devoted to a single kind of Spanish language. I started with the Spanish of the past, traveling to the oldest community of European-language-speakers in the United States. And I finished with the Spanish of the future, traveling to a border town to try to understand how Spanish and English might begin to interact as their relative status changes—if, indeed, their relative status is allowed to change.

If Santa Fe is your kind of thing, it's probably your favorite place in the world. For a woman of a certain age and a certain artistic inclination, no city in the country—not New York, not San Francisco, and certainly not Las Vegas—can hold a candle to Santa Fe. It is a city of art and music and the kinds of cultural events you hear advertised on NPR, a riot of turquoise jewelry, Georgia O'Keefe, and moderately priced white wine. Whenever I've visited—and, strangely, I've been there a lot—I've felt like I've just walked in on someone else's slumber party. I was out of place and in the wrong clothes, and I couldn't help but worry that at any minute someone might try to come by and braid my hair or discuss the sexual symbolism of the pineapple bud.

What I'm trying to say is that I used to be a bit of a jerk about Santa Fe. On this trip, however, I found to my surprise that if you ignore the lackluster art and the overpriced jewelry and the ostentatious rich-lady self-actualization, Santa Fe is actually pretty nice. Take it from me: stick to the history and you'll be just fine.

The first official expedition into New Mexico was led by Juan de Oñate, the son of a silver baron who had received a contract from the Spanish crown to settle the area. Oñate left Zacatecas in 1598 with 600 to 700 settlers, 7,000 animals, 10 Franciscan missionaries, and 129 soldiers, and by April of that same year he had crossed the Rio Grande and claimed all land north of it for Spain. His first capital city was San Juan de los Caballeros, located at the junction of the Rio Grande and the Rio Chama, about halfway between Santa Fe and Taos. But by the mid-

seventeenth century the capital had been relocated to a city called La
Villa Real de la Santa Fe de San Francisco de Asís—The Royal City of
the Holy Faith of Saint Francis of Assisi. Now known simply as Santa Fe,
it has served as the administrative center of New Mexico ever since.

Though you can spend hours poking through the historical buildings
of Santa Fe or driving through the sparsely populated mountain towns to
the north, the best way to get a sense of what life was like in eighteenth-
century New Mexico is to head to a place called El Rancho de las Golon-
drinas, or "Ranch of the Swallows." Situated on 200 acres about fifteen
minutes south of Santa Fe, the ranch was originally built in the early
1700s as a stop along the Camino Real. Today it is more or less the Colonial Williamsburg of New Spain.

Though the ranch in many ways attempts to replicate as closely as possible conditions in historic New Mexico, it is so picturesque and well kept
that it can only be called a museum. Or, possibly, the setting for a photo
shoot. The adobe buildings are perfectly set off by the blue summer sky,
and everywhere you look you find artfully arranged period detail, from
religious artifacts to kitchen utensils to skeins of richly colored yarn. Two
of my favorite classmates from college had gotten married here at a time
when I couldn't afford the plane ticket to Santa Fe, and my first thought
when I walked in was how pissed I was I'd missed that party.

The ranch is a living history museum, which means that scattered
about the grounds are museum employees dressed in costume and ready
to explain the mechanics of the ovens or the water-powered mill. I spent
a happy few hours exploring the ranch, discovering how, among other
things, Hispanic mills "without exception" turn counterclockwise while
Anglo mills turn clockwise. (I am still unable to verify or explain this.)
In the kitchens I came across Annyssa, a fourteen-year-old museum
volunteer whose family had lived on the ranch for generations. Though
she was a little skeptical of my reasons for wanting to know about any
Spanish slang, she indulged me, teaching me a few phrases I later identified not as New Mexican Spanish but as Teenager Spanish.

At the schoolhouse, meanwhile, I met a woman named Judy Reed. She
had learned Castilian Spanish in school, and she spent some time telling
me about the difficulties she had understanding the local Spanish. She had
a friend who was born in Spain, she said, and even he had trouble

communicating. I was surprised. Although I had expected New Mexican Spanish to be different, I certainly hadn't expected it to be incomprehensible. I wondered if Ms. Reed wasn't telling me more about Castilian Spanish than about New Mexican Spanish.

As usual, I figured I'd better do some reading.

The first settlers to come to New Mexico, I found, spoke more than one kind of Spanish. There were Castilian-speakers, to be sure, but there were also Andalusians, Asturians, Galicians, and even a few Basques. And as soon as they settled in New Mexico, their language began to diverge from the forms spoken in Europe. Rubén Cobos, a native of Coahuila, Mexico, and a linguist who studied New Mexican and Colorado Spanish for more than seventy-five years, identified a few key grammatical differences between the new and old varieties. First of all, he writes, in New Mexico the second-person plural form fell out of use. But this is nothing new for anyone who has studied Latin American Spanish—usage of *vosotros* is these days limited to Spain.* The other morphological changes identified by Cobos are relatively minor, nothing that should confuse a native Spanish-speaker. There are, for instance, some slight changes in the formation of the preterit (i.e., the past perfective), a substitution in present-tense first-person-plural conjugations of -*emos* for -*imos*, and an occasional shift in accent and inflection that results in the change from *hablemos* to *háblenos*.

There are a number of phonetic divergences as well, but for non-linguists the most obvious differences between the dialects are lexical. Some New Mexican Spanish words are radically different from the Spanish words you'd find in Spain or even in Mexico.

New Mexican Spanish	English	Standard Spanish
ratón coludo	squirrel ("long-tailed rat")	*ardilla*
ratón volador	bat ("flying rat")	*murciélago*

---

* Most everyone else uses *ustedes*, the third-person plural. This is not to be confused with the use of *vos* as a second-person singular, which particularly common in Nicaragua, Argentina, Paraguay, and Uruguay.

ánsara	goose	*ganso*
chuparrosa	hummingbird	*colibrí*
jojolote	ear of corn; corn cob	*maȝorca de maíȝ*

These new words came from a variety of sources. Just as English adopted the names of local plants and animals from indigenous languages, so too did Spanish turn to the languages of the Americas when it needed to describe the novelties of the New World. The primary sources for these loanwords were the Nahuatl languages of Mexico and Central America. Though Mexican Spanish, too, has a large number of Nahuatl loans, the isolation of New Mexican Spanish resulted in some drastically different pronunciations. Cobos, in fact, suggests that these words are still pronounced as they would have been in the early seventeenth century. One of these words is *nesha*, which in New Mexican Spanish means "yellowish." It comes from the Nahuatl *nexectic*, a word used to describe corn tortillas that had turned grayish due to an excess of lime.

New Mexican Spanish was, of course, also subject to influence from English—more, certainly, than it would have been south of the border—and so a number of Americanizations have also crept into the lexicon. Some, such as *bequenpaura* ("baking powder"), were simple Hispanizations of English words. Others had more roundabout histories. From the word *honey* came the Spanish *jane*. This then became the verb *janear*, "to look for girls." Similarly, "how much" snuck into Spanish as *jamache*. This eventually evolved into the verb *jamachar*, "to talk business"—or, as Cobos puts it, "to talk turkey."

The existence of New Mexican Spanish owes much to the isolation of the area's first settlements. Although the Camino Real was used to supply the missions and scattered settlements, the supply trains were only scheduled to come through once every three years—six months out, six months there, six months back. But in practice they came through even less frequently. Moreover, ongoing hostilities between settlers and local Indian tribes discouraged new arrivals. Travel was also highly regulated by Spanish authorities, and until 1821 a law prohibited the Spanish from engaging in commerce with American or French traders.

In the early days of Spanish colonization, then, there was little traffic in or out of the area. Furthermore, as linguist John M. Lipski has pointed out, the area was underserviced by the institutions—schools, churches, government—that establish standard prestige dialects. It was, in other words, a linguistic power vacuum. There was no social or economic pressure on New Mexican settlers, then, to shift away from their regional dialect, either toward English or toward a more standard or elite form of Spanish. It's almost as if someone planned New Mexico as a way to establish and preserve a distinctive Spanish dialect.

In the years after the United States acquired the territory, this unusual linguistic environment was at first largely preserved. Because even though the territory came under U.S. control after the end of the Mexican-American War back in 1848, New Mexico was actually one of the last territories in the continental United States to be admitted to the Union. It wasn't granted statehood until 1912, nearly sixty-four years after the Treaty of Guadalupe Hidalgo. As such, the state was slow in acquiring an English-language bureaucracy. Spanish was, quite accidentally, protected so well in New Mexico that until the 1940s Spanish was still a viable school language.

All of these circumstances combined to make New Mexican Spanish something of an oddity. It is certainly highly unlikely that today a new dialect of Spanish could develop and survive in the United States for any period of time. For one thing, even existing dialects tend to lose their distinctiveness when they arrive in this country. Despite the tremendous diversity of Spanish dialects throughout the world, once they begin to interact with each other, something called dialect leveling occurs. When speakers of two (or more) dialects attempt to communicate, they typically do their best to stay away from any regionalisms that might not be understood. Over time, this process results in a version of a language that is mutually comprehensible but, all things considered, a bit bland. Like every other language to come to the United States, Spanish is not unaffected by the change of scene.

As it turns out, however, what is most unusual about New Mexican Spanish is not that it's different but that it even exists. The more I learned about Spanish in the United States, the more I began to understand that

despite its rapid growth and seeming omnipresence, Spanish is nevertheless being rapidly replaced by English.

There is in popular discourse a pervasive and powerful sense that the
population of Spanish-speakers is increasing not because of high Latino
birthrates or an uptick in immigration but because Spanish-speakers
have less and less incentive to learn English—and, in fact, because
many Spanish-speakers are no longer doing so. The consequences of
such a thing are, for some, far more alarming than the petty concerns of
people who hate having to press 1 for English. It suggests that the primacy of English in the United States is being threatened.

For this reason we have organizations such as U.S. English and English First.

This is far from the first time our nation's politicians have turned their
attention to language. Most early American language policy was largely
concerned with German. Although by 1790 Germans only made up 8.6
percent of the white American population, they were heavily concentrated in areas such as Pennsylvania, where they accounted for a full 33
percent of the state's population and maintained a vibrant language community and a robust German-language press. In fact, the first newspaper
to announce the adoption of the Declaration of Independence was a German paper called the *Pennsylvanischer Staatsbote*. The sheer size and visibility of the German population in Pennsylvania gave them a great deal of
clout when it came to political maneuvering. Accordingly, early U.S. language policy was actually pro-German. From 1774 to 1779, for instance,
the Continental Congress published its proclamations in English and German. Similarly, Pennsylvania printed all official announcements in English
and German. All in all, according to sociologist April Linton, of the fifty-
eight language policies adopted before 1880, thirty-three relate to German.

This early tolerance toward German has given rise to some misunderstandings about early American language policy, the most notable of
which is that German was very nearly the official language of the United
States. It wasn't. There was, it's true, some discussion of whether an official language other than English should be chosen. But this was mostly
the Americans' attempt to thumb their noses at the British, and apparently

it wasn't taken particularly seriously. Roger Sherman, a delegate to the Continental Congress from Connecticut, remarked, "It would be more convenient for us to keep the language as it was and make the English speak Greek." Though there was some deliberation on the matter, there was never a vote on making any language—be it English, German, or even Greek—the official language.

Not only was German never actually under consideration as the official language of the United States, it was even in the eighteenth century actually the target of some criticism by those who claimed that the language barrier between English- and German-speakers was a problem of national import. No less a personage than Benjamin Franklin held particularly strong views on the Germans. In a 1753 letter, Franklin, never one to mince his words, wrote the following:

> I am perfectly of your mind, that measures of great Temper are necessary with the Germans: and am not without Apprehensions, that thro' their indiscretion or Ours, or both, great disorders and inconveniences may one day arise among us; Those who come hither are generally of the most ignorant Stupid Sort of their own Nation, and as Ignorance is often attended with Credulity when Knavery would mislead it, and with Suspicion when Honesty would set it right; and as few of the English understand the German Language, and so cannot address them either from the Press or Pulpit, 'tis almost impossible to remove any prejudices they once entertain.

It is perhaps not irrelevant to note that Franklin attempted to start a German-language newspaper in 1732. It lasted only two issues.

The myth of this close brush with German as an official language dates to 1795, when Congress considered a proposal based on a petition from a group of Virginian Germans. They were asking, simply, for federal laws to be published in both English and German. The proposal was voted down, but somewhere in the debate there was a motion to adjourn in order to consider an alternative recommendation involving the distribution of German translations of laws and statutes to each state. This motion failed by one vote. It was this motion that somehow gave rise to the idea that German was one vote short of becoming the official language of the United States. To this day the United States has refrained from naming any language "official."

This is not the case at the state level, however.

Though the nineteenth century was hardly free of nativist legislation and anti-immigrant sentiment, tensions rarely affected language policy on the federal or state level, with the notable exception of assimilationist policies toward American Indian languages. In fact, early language policy generally encouraged language diversity. In California, the public "cosmopolitan schools" of the 1860s taught French and German alongside English. In Iowa, Kansas, and Nebraska, schools were required to teach German if parents requested it. In 1889 New Mexico passed a law requiring that lower-level government employees be bilingual in English and Spanish.

When the political tide turned toward restrictive language policy, the language at the center of the debate was, again, German. The nativist stirrings of the late nineteenth century set the stage, ushering in legislation such as the 1906 requirement that naturalized citizens speak English and, subsequently, the Immigration Act of 1924. This generalized nativism intensified during World War I, when anti-German sentiment swept through the country.

In 1919, Nebraska passed a law that declared, "No person, individually or as a teacher, shall, in any private, denominational, parochial or public school, teach any subject to any person in any language than the English language." It further ordered that instruction of foreign languages was illegal unless students had finished eighth grade. Then, on May 25, 1920, a teacher in a one-room parochial school named Robert T. Meyer was caught reading German Bible stories to a fourth-grade pupil. He was tried, convicted, and fined $25. He appealed, and in the case that would forever after be known as *Meyer v. Nebraska*, the U.S. Supreme Court overturned the verdict on the grounds that the Nebraska law violated due process. Speaking for the majority, Justice James Clark McReynolds remarked somewhat famously, "Mere knowledge of the German language cannot reasonably be considered as harmful."

This wasn't Nebraska's only stab at restrictive language legislation. In 1920 Nebraska also became the first state to declare English its official language, which it did by constitutional amendment. This would be the only real official-English legislation in the United States for decades.*

The most recent wave of official-English legislation kicked off in 1981, when Senator S. I. Hayakawa (R-Calif.) introduced a constitutional amendment declaring, "Neither the United States nor any State shall make or enforce any law which requires the use of any language other than English. This article shall apply to laws, ordinances, regulations, orders, programs, and policies." When this amendment failed to progress to a vote, he tried another tack, introducing an amendment to immigration bill S. 2222: "It is the sense of the Congress that (1) the English language is the official language of the United States, and (2) no language other than the English language is recognized as the official language of the United States." The Senate passed the amendment 78–21, but the bill it was attached to never passed the House.

Senator Hayakawa didn't run for reelection that year, but he was far from finished in politics. In 1983 he founded the group U.S. English, which bills itself as the "nation's oldest, largest citizens' action group dedicated to preserving the unifying role of the English language in the United States." Though U.S. English and similar groups such as English First, the American Ethnic Coalition, and ProEnglish have yet to effect passage of any legislation on the federal level, since 1981 twenty-six states have passed official-English laws.[†]

What is the impetus for this type of legislation? Lucy Tse, an expert in second-language acquisition, looked at congressional speeches made regarding English-language-related amendments between 1981 and 1998 and found that of fifteen speeches, thirteen referred to English as a "uni-

---

* With one quasi-exception: in 1923 Illinois declared "American" its official language. The measure was brought to the floor by Frank Ryan, an Irish-born legislator from Cook County who may have been taking his cue from a similar bill that had been introduced that year in Congress. According to language policy expert James Crawford, the measure was not taken seriously at the federal level. But the state bill passed by large margins in both the Illinois House and Senate, and it remained on the books until 1969 when the General Assembly approved an amendment replacing "American" with "English."

† Only twenty-five of these laws are still in effect: Alaska's official-English initiative, passed in 1998, was overturned in state superior court in 2002.

fying and stabilizing force" in American society. Another ten suggested that such legislation would help new arrivals. The 1995 testimony of Senator Richard Shelby (R-Ala.) is representative of this stance: "By encouraging people to communicate in a common language, we actually help them progress in society. A common language allows individuals to take advantage of the social and economic opportunities America has to offer."

Politically, then, the issue is framed in terms of national unity and economic growth, a savvy choice given the near-universal appeal of such concepts. You might as well argue that official English saves puppies and cares for babies. (What? You don't support official English? Well, you might as well just go kick a puppy and bomb the Capitol. See how that works?) The English-only and official-English movements are, as a result of this rhetorical success, able to point to public polling that repeatedly shows substantial support for the general idea of official English.

The problem is that when you actually bother to study the issue, you discover fairly quickly that these types of arguments simply don't hold water.

Standard reasoning holds that making English an official language will result in economic benefits for struggling immigrants. Now, in the United States, all other things being equal, fluency in English is unquestionably economically preferable to limited English proficiency. Official-English legislation isn't going to make it significantly more advantageous. Nor, to be fair, do supporters of such legislation frequently argue that it will. They do, however, imply that the provision of government services in multiple languages makes it easier to put off learning English. An official-language policy would remove that disincentive, thereby making the economic incentive that much more powerful.

This, of course, is foolish on a number of levels, the most obvious of which is that if the potential economic gains are great enough, it won't matter a bit what language you can or can't vote in. The economic realities at present are far more persuasive than anything that can or can't be found at the DMV. And the fact of the matter is that non-English-language communities are already perfectly well aware of the benefits of learning English. In fact, they might even be more sensitive to the issue than English-speakers themselves. According to a 2003 Pew Hispanic Center survey, 92 percent of Latinos believe it is "very important" for immigrant children to be taught English. Only 87 percent of non-Hispanic whites said the same.

The proposition that a single official language would promote national unity is no more defensible. The implication, of course, is that bilingualism somehow erodes unity, something politicians like to suggest with sly allusions to Quebec, Belgium, and India. But the evidence simply doesn't support this. Nevertheless, politicians continue to reference it in their speeches, alluding to modern-day Towers of Babel as if bilingualism were the evening entertainment in Sodom and Gomorrah.

The more I read about the official-English debate, the more confused I got. I had to be missing something. How could something be so popular and yet so seemingly indefensible? These were the questions flitting about my head as I headed out of Santa Fe and made my way to Laredo, Texas, the closest thing I could find to a bilingual town.

OK, so it wasn't exactly the *closest* thing I could find. But I'm not going to lie: I didn't want to go to El Paso. Like Laredo, El Paso is a bustling border town with a majority Spanish-speaking population. Unlike Laredo, however, El Paso is just across from Ciudad Juárez, the epicenter of the violence that is currently plaguing Mexico. The last time I had driven through El Paso I had been shocked by the crackle of energy and anxiety along the border, an impression that was only reinforced when I drove past a large-scale police operation involving a lot of cars and a lot of flashing lights. It seemed like it would be only a matter of time before there were also a lot of guns. There are few things in life I'm less keen on than a twitchy cop with an expansive mandate, so I decided to skip El Paso and head farther west.

As I made my way through Texas, visiting museums and monuments and out-of-the-way little towns recommended for their chiles rellenos, it became almost commonplace for me to happen upon Homeland Security border checkpoints. In one sense they were trifling things; the livestock and agriculture inspection stations on your way into California are more substantial. And though I probably drove through a dozen of these things—maybe as many as twenty—I was always waved through.

Even so, I felt an anxious twist to my stomach every time I approached one. The weapons on display at each checkpoint let me know they meant business. And every time I saw them stop a pickup truck driven by someone who appeared to be Latino—as they did every time—I couldn't help but wonder about the calculations made by each checkpoint guard when deciding whether or not to wave a vehicle through. I suspected I would rather not know. Part of me began to wish I'd gone to El Paso instead.

But once I got to Laredo I was glad to be there. It was hotter than Satan's sweaty ball sack, and I had to find a bottle of water and a spot of air-conditioning every twenty minutes or so or risk serious dehydration, but I was delighted by the downtown area. It felt very much like the liminal space I had been hoping it would be. I realized that if I took off my glasses, leaving me able to see but unable to read any signs or license plates, the streets of Laredo looked just like Mexico. It felt very much like a Mexican city with American laws.

Established in 1755, Laredo is famously the only part of Texas to have flown seven different flags. Six are well known to Texans: the Spanish flag, the French flag, the Mexican flag, the Texas Republic flag, the Texas Confederate flag, and the U.S. flag. The seventh is the flag of the Republic of the Rio Grande, a short-lived nation established in 1840 by Mexican insurgents, and the second-best example of the town's independent streak. The best example occurred when the city was given to the United States after the Mexican-American War. Laredo voted to petition the government to allow them to continue to be part of Mexico, but the petition was denied, and many of the town's residents moved across the river to found Nuevo Laredo.

Today Laredo is the largest inland port in the country, and along with Nuevo Laredo it handles a huge percentage of the trade between the United States and Mexico. Trade, then, is Laredo's main business—and also its main tourist attraction. As far as I could tell, most people come here to shop. The city, particularly near the border, is chock-full of presumably Western/vaguely Mexican/ambiguously tribal handicrafts at stores with names like El Alamo Pottery and Los Chiles Imports. Farther north is an even more popular shopping district of utterly generic big-box American retailers. Admittedly, I found it hard to get excited about shopping in Laredo. But then, I wasn't there to find a Mexican floor candelabra. I was there to experience *la vida bilingüe*.

I was expecting Laredo to be something like Montreal. About half of Montreal's population is fully bilingual in French and English, a wonderful thing if you don't speak French but incredibly exasperating if you're trying to speak French. The moment you slip up or stumble, Montrealers switch fluidly and almost apologetically into English, like they're a little sad you don't have the benefit of their language skills. Every time I've been there I've played a game I call How Long Will It Take Them to Figure Out I'm a Native English-Speaker. My record so far is five French words.

Percentage-wise, the makeup of Laredo's language community isn't that different from Montreal's. As of the 2000 Census, almost 92 percent of Laredo's population reported speaking Spanish, with just over 88 percent of this group reporting speaking English "well" or "very well." These high levels of bilingualism led me to assume that my experience in Laredo would be similar to my experience in Montreal—that is to say, I thought they'd all make fun of my Spanish.

What I found was very different.

Almost everyone I encountered in Laredo spoke Spanish and English. This was true whether I was talking to a guide at the visitor center, the curator of a museum, or the cashier at Walgreens. I was frequently greeted in Spanish despite the fact that I don't look at all Latina. Wherever I went, Spanish words were used as a matter of course, almost as if no one stopped to consider I might not know them. It was the first time in my life outside of language class I'd ever been assumed to speak any language besides English. And I was, I have to admit, totally flattered.

But it's important to note that although Laredoans used *some* Spanish with me, they didn't use *only* Spanish. I was surprised to find that many Laredoans used Spanish and English, sometimes in the same conversation. I had thought that the everyday language here might be like the souvenirs, stereotypically Mexican products marketed to American tourists, a melding of the most well-known qualities of each into some third thing that is entirely different. I expected to find a creole, in other words—or at least a pidgin.

Navigating the languages of Laredo made me think back to a book I had read recently, Bill Santiago's *Pardon My Spanglish*, which I purchased under the impression that it might help me make my way through old Laredo. Here's a paragraph I think is particularly relevant to the point at hand:

> As a descriptive term, code-switching, *como se dice* . . . sucks. *No se trata de* codes, *sino de idiomas* and everything they embody: culture, heritage, emotional frequencies, ways of thinking and feeling. *El switcheo* is actually between co-dependent realities. *Así que* code-switching is obviously code for: *Estos chingados académicos* have no idea *de lo que están* talking about.

This paragraph is a great example of the type of language I frequently heard in Laredo, a way of speaking known—however inadequately, prosaically, or in this case ironically—as code-switching. Code-switching occurs when multilingual speakers elect to draw from different languages within a single conversation. Sometimes the language shift will occur because the speaker is searching for a word. But just as frequently the language they choose is a reflection of the subject, the situation, and the interlocutors. It is like the way you might elect to use jargon with a work colleague or an SAT word in an interview—or, for that matter, like the way you might elect *not* to use slang with your grandmother or profanity in front of your little sibling. Code-switching is a similar phenomenon. Multilinguals just have more registers to draw from.

A distinctive feature of code-switching is that speakers don't just switch to the vocabulary of another language; they also switch to its grammatical and phonological rules. You can see, for instance, that though Santiago switches between Spanish and English, the grammar of each language is preserved—in Spanish, for instance, *estos* and *chingados* agree with *académicos*. When English is used, *is* agrees with *code-switching* and *embody* agrees with *they*. You don't see grammatical rules bleeding from one language into the other; neither do you see rules independent of either language.

Even so, I agree that *code-switching* isn't the most descriptive or transparent term. It certainly has no poetry to it. But then, I often suspect that there is a secret cabal of linguists who meet each year to make sure linguistic terminology remains as impenetrable and unpleasant as possible. This way they can make sure that anyone with an interest in language feels compelled to pursue graduate studies, thus preserving their supply of low-cost teaching assistants. And I can certainly understand not wanting to reduce a way of talking and interacting to something as sterile-sounding as *code-switching*. It sounds more like the province of machine than man, like something the IBM programmers taught Watson.

But code-switching is so much more interesting than that. Like creoles, pidgins, and jargons, it's a creature of language contact. But unlike creoles, pidgins, and jargons, code-switching occurs in—and is therefore evidence of—environments more conducive to bilingualism than, for instance, the slave-based societies of the colonial Americas. Though code-switching is not a phenomenon that connotes anything close to perfect social equality, at the very least it must be a sign of relative social mobility.

When I went to Laredo, I expected to find one of three things, in descending order of probability: (1) a community that had developed an English-Spanish creole, (2) a community that was assimilating to Spanish, or (3) a community that was assimilating to English. I thought I would be able to deduce from this what we might be able to expect from American cities with growing Spanish-speaking populations. As it turned out, I wasn't quite sure how to interpret my actual observations, though I was certainly aware that they represented only one small part of the city's complex linguistic reality.

I knew one thing for sure, though. If English was still somehow managing to hold its own in a city where 92 percent of the population spoke Spanish, then groups such as U.S. English were tilting at windmills even more than I had thought.

Admittedly, even my own travels may seem to perpetuate the idea that English is spoken less and less in the United States. In Miami, for instance, I felt like I was living in three different languages, none of them English, and in Laredo it was frequently assumed that I understood Spanish. But my experience was anything but random. I chose to visit these cities because I knew that their language communities were supported by their particular immigration patterns and policies. And even in these cities—cities I had selected specifically for their vigorous Spanish-language communities—I was never without linguistic recourse. With very few exceptions, everyone I met spoke at least some English. With *no* exceptions, everyone I encountered in any sort of official capacity spoke excellent English.

My experience may be anecdotal, but it is supported by hard data. Although not everyone who comes to the United States manages to learn fluent English, it is exceedingly rare for the second generation to avoid doing it. According to Calvin Veltman, an expert on language demographics, there are a few determinants of the rapidity with which English is acquired. Economic motivators are, of course, hugely important. But Veltman has found that the younger a person is at the time of immigration, the more extensive the language shift. Furthermore, the longer a person has been in the United States, the more extensive the shift. He ultimately concludes that "the language shift process of immigrants begins *immediately upon arrival* in the United States, progresses rapidly and ends within approximately fifteen years" (italics mine).

Empirical evidence demonstrates not only that immigrants are still learning English—and learning it well—but also that they are learning it quickly. A 1998 survey of eighth- and ninth-grade students in San Diego and Miami, two cities with extremely large immigrant communities, found that an overwhelming majority of students were extremely proficient in English. Of more than 5,000 students surveyed, 93.6 percent spoke English "very well" or "well." Haitian and Latin American students logged slightly higher numbers—95.4 percent and 94.7 percent, respectively. Meanwhile, in an analysis of data from the Immigration and Intergenerational Mobility in Metropolitan Los Angeles survey and the third wave of the Children of Immigrants Longitudinal Study, Rubén G. Rumbaut, Douglas S. Massey, and Frank D. Bean found that 96 percent of third-generation Mexican Americans prefer to speak English at home—which is to say that only 4 percent were still speaking Spanish.

If Spanish-speakers are assimilating to English so completely, why, then, is there such a strong sense in the United States that the opposite is true? Well, it's not entirely imagined. Though retention of Spanish in the second and third generations is certainly not high by any standards, it is nevertheless slightly higher than language retention rates seen in other groups today and historically. In *Legacies: The Story of the Immigrant Second Generation*, sociologists Alejandro Portes and Rubén Rumbaut conclude, "Children whose cultural background includes Spanish are more likely than other second-generation youths to preserve that language, regardless of what school they attend or what type of family they come from."

But perhaps most important, the Latino population in the United States has been rapidly increasing. Though rates of Spanish retention are low and the speed of English acquisition is high, the massive influx of foreign-born Spanish-speakers is naturally going to affect the immediate language environment. As a result of immigration, there has, very broadly, been a slight increase in limited English proficiency in the United States over the past thirty years. The proportion of the population ages five and over who spoke English less than "very well" grew from 4.8 percent in 1980 to 6.1 percent in 1990 to 8.1 percent in 2000. According to the most recent available estimates, this number has now crept up to 8.6 percent.

These numbers probably underestimate the perceived language shift. As ethnic communities welcome steady inflows of immigrants, the usual process of language shift—limited English in the first generation, bilingual in the second generation, monolingual English in the third—is obscured, at least on the surface. When families acquire English proficiency, their economic circumstances typically improve, allowing them to move out of the gateway neighborhoods favored by new arrivals. If you walk into a border town or ethnic enclave and look around, it's not hard to come to the conclusion that these communities "just aren't learning English."

I would suggest, however, that the rise in alarmism about the English language is also driven by factors beyond an exaggerated perception of demographic trends. As it turns out, most of the states that have passed official-English legislation are not what I would call our more multicultural regions. Despite this—or, indeed, perhaps because of this—official-English proposals in these states have garnered overwhelming support. In Alabama, 89 percent of voters supported an official-English measure at a time when less than 3 percent of the state's population spoke a language other than English at home. Of the ten states with the highest percentages of English-speakers, eight have passed legislation declaring English the official language.

Official-English Legislation in States with High Numbers of Native English-Speakers

State	Year	Type of legislation, if any	State population estimates	
			Native English-speakers	% native English-speakers
WV	n/a	None	1,648,821	97.69%
MS	1987	Statute	2,533,909	96.75%
KY	1984	Statute	3,643,719	96.06%
AL	1990	Amendment by initiative	3,990,180	95.92%
MT	1995	Statute	805,964	95.71%
VT	n/a	None	549,245	95.28%
TN	1984	Statute	5,130,671	94.55%
MO	1998	Statute	4,954,916	94.52%
SC	1987	Statute	3,612,219	94.03%
WY	1996	Statute	435,660	93.94%

Sources: Crawford, "Language Legislation in the U.S.A."; U.S. Census Bureau, "S0501 Selected Characteristics of the Native and Foreign-Born Populations," generated by American FactFinder.

What official-English legislation has going for it is political opportunity. This is particularly true in states with mostly English-speaking populations, where a legislator can, with very little risk of censure, rally support and goodwill based on the measures' superficial appearance of universal appeal and inarguable benefit. Indeed, in his study of American language legislation, political scientist Raymond Tatalovich concluded that "the movement for an official English language—in most states—was elite driven, not a result of grass-roots agitation." This is not a trend driven by the people of the United States; it is driven by opportunistic legislators. Official English is, politically, a cheap but effective shot. And while it has a great deal of upside and very little downside for legislators, the opposite might be true for the country's speakers of languages other than English.

Though the costs of bilingualism are apparently debatable, its cognitive benefits are far from controversial—at least they are today. Very early research on bilingualism suggested that cognitive abilities were diminished by the attempt to speak more than one language. However, as Alejandro Portes and Lingxin Hao (and numerous others) have pointed out, these early analyses failed to account for socioeconomic differences or to distinguish fluency levels among their subjects. Researchers looked at the poor children of immigrants and the middle-class children of natives and concluded that discrepancies in educational achievement had nothing to do with economic privilege and were solely determined by linguistic confusion. Then came a 1962 study—properly designed—on bilingualism in French Canadian students. It found that bilingual students routinely outperformed monolingual students. Since then, dozens of studies have confirmed that bilingualism ultimately improves academic performance.

This does not mean, however, that bilingual communities such as Laredo are somehow exempt from the educational challenges faced by the country's immigrant population. Although the vast majority of Laredo's population speaks at least some English, the English literacy rate is shockingly low—only 47 percent in 2000, the lowest of any city surveyed. This is in no small part a function of socioeconomic disadvantage. Median household income in the Laredo metropolitan area is $36,784 (in 2009 dollars), $14,641 less than the national average, and a full quarter of the city's families live below the poverty level. As of the 2000 Census 45 percent of Laredoans lack a high school diploma; 28 percent have no education beyond eighth grade.

I don't believe English needs institutional support to maintain its place as the nation's primary prestige language, and I don't believe that immigrants are in any way reluctant to learn English. We don't have to do anything special in the long term to make sure that English remains the de facto national language of the United States. All those who are wary of waking up one day and not being able to order their Egg McMuffin in English can rest easy. Even so, we can't afford to ignore the issue of language instruction in public schools. Language shift may begin upon arrival in the United States, but it is not complete for generations. Third-generation immigrants typically become fluent English-speakers quite naturally. The first and second generations, however, are vulnerable, and without support they face all the challenges of a minority-language-speaker in an English-driven world.

The statistics may imply that Laredoan children are learning to speak English with ease, but speaking a language is a very different thing from reading and writing one. Academic achievement does not come so easily. Moreover, first- and second-generation immigrants are more likely to come from economically disadvantaged households, which means that their parents are less likely to be able to provide academic resources, to be involved with their school, or to help with homework. Furthermore, their parents are more likely to have limited English proficiency themselves, which makes getting help with schoolwork even more challenging.

The problem of illiteracy in Laredo serves as an important reminder that the first generations to arrive in the United States are in many ways facing an uphill battle, particularly with regard to academic achievement. Unfortunately, some policy makers would like to make things even more difficult.

So far, official-English legislation has had few pronounced effects on the country's immigrant population. There are protections already in place to ensure that those with limited English proficiency are not excluded from the workings of government. For instance Title VI of the Civil Rights Act of 1964 allows the government to withdraw federal funding from any agency that shows evidence of discriminatory practices, and Executive Order 13166 requires that federal agencies comply with certain Department of Justice guidelines and make "reasonable steps to ensure meaningful access" for those with limited English proficiency. The Voting Rights Act of 1965, meanwhile, has a provision for multilingual ballots, and the Supreme Court decision in *Lau v. Nichols* requires public schools to provide support to ensure equal educational opportunity for students with limited English skills. As a result, even states with official-English laws provide services in other languages.

Nevertheless, it would be pure folly to ignore the very real downsides to official-English legislation. First and foremost, it risks alienating the immigrant community. There is, after all, a crucial difference between integration and assimilation, and America's comparatively low level of naturalization may be a sign that American language policy is negatively impacting immigrants' attitudes toward the government. Furthermore, I don't see how depriving limited-English-proficient residents of government services and assistance could possibly help them learn English.

It is for this reason that I am particularly troubled by the official-English movement's recent strategic shift away from official-English legislation and toward restrictions on bilingual education.

When the Elementary and Secondary Education Act was passed in 1968, bilingual education was thought by many to be an important tool in the effort to promote equality across cultural and ethnic lines. By 1994, however, attitudes toward bilingual schooling had changed, and Congress reduced funding for the Bilingual Education Act by 38 percent. Then, in 1998, California became the first state to ban bilingual education programs when Proposition 227, a measure backed by Ron Unz, the successful founder of a financial services company and a failed gubernatorial candidate, was supported by 61 percent of voters. After his victory in California, Unz spearheaded initiatives in Colorado, Arizona, and Massachusetts. The latter two states passed similar measures in 2000 and 2002, respectively. In these states, bilingual education—where students with limited English proficiency are taught at least partially in their native language before eventually being transitioned into the general population—was replaced with something called structured English immersion, which generally allows students one year of rigorous English study.

Many of the arguments in favor of immersion programs use language that is markedly similar to that used to support official English, suggesting that bilingual education slows or prevents integration or, more damningly, that it fosters disunity. But the most difficult argument to counter is the most seemingly well-intentioned one: that we're doing it for their own good. However, just as research provides little support for the contention that modern-day immigrants are not learning English, so too is it difficult to find empirical evidence that favors structured immersion over bilingual education. In what they call a "meta-meta-analysis" of existing bilingual education studies, Stephen Krashen and Grace McField conclude that "the strikingly similar results from different meta-analyses provide clear support for bilingual education as a means of helping succeed academically in English. They also cast strong doubt on claims that all-English approaches are superior and should be mandated by law."

Despite this, many believe the evidence is inconclusive or even that it supports English-only education. This belief is not limited to fringe groups or vaguely risible organizations such as U.S. English or English First. It is shared—or at least espoused—by prominent politicians who are in a place to affect not only educational policy but also popular discourse and the public perception of multiculturalism.

Newt Gingrich, ever a presumptive presidential hopeful, caught flak in 2007 for declaring, "We should replace bilingual education with immersion in English so people learn the common language of the country and they learn the language of prosperity, not the language of living in a ghetto." What people objected to, however, was not his support for English-only education but his use of the word *ghetto*. Hispanic groups were particularly outraged.

In a post on *Language Log*, lexicographer Ben Zimmer came, somewhat reluctantly, to Gingrich's defense. He pointed out that in this case Gingrich was not using *ghetto* in a pejorative sense; rather, he was clearly referring to the idea of a "linguistic ghetto," a phrase commonly used by English-only advocates. Nevertheless, Zimmer noted, "I still feel that the use of the term '(linguistic) ghetto' by English-only advocates is intended to evoke the 'urban slum' sense, at least implicitly. . . . It's part of an arsenal of scare tactics with little or no empirical basis in the social realities of bilingualism."

He makes an important point. Language legislation in the United States might not be explicitly driven by racism or xenophobia, but the arguments used in favor of official-English and English-only policies reinforce derogatory stereotypes that absolutely encourage prejudice and discrimination. Politicians present as incontrovertible truth the fiction that language is necessarily divisive and that, more and more, immigrants are not learning English. The most positive possible interpretation of this is that immigrants are loyal to their home country and mother tongue.

But let's be honest about the real implication here, which is that immigrants are choosing not to learn English because they are lazy, stu-pid, unpatriotic, or some combination of the three. Scoff all you want at the pearl-clutching that characterizes political correctness, but words matter. Public discourse is like a giant game of telephone, and a few seemingly harmless words on one end can become malignant supposi-tion on the other. No one today—particularly in public office—can in good conscience pretend to be ignorant of this.

The supporters of official-English and English-only legislation claim they are fighting for national unity. And perhaps they truly believe that's what they're doing. But everything I've seen and heard over the course of my travels suggests to me that they are doing precisely the op-posite. Losing a language is, I think, not unlike losing a limb, and the phantom pain is passed down from generation to generation. It can be as mild as nostalgia or as excruciating as shame. None of us have truly cho-sen this of our own accord, but deliberate and targeted cultural coercion of any form is nevertheless a most vile betrayal of what we were led to believe by those we chose to lead us. And whatever English First may say, I find it impossible to imagine that any true and lasting unity could ever spring from such legislation.

Los Angeles: English

THIS IS NOT THE BOOK I thought I was going to write. When I first decided to hop in my car and set out across the country in search of the languages of the United States, I'd expected it would be a bit of a romp, an opportunity to combine two of my favorite activities, road-tripping and language-learning. I'd anticipated putting together something of a field guide, a bit of whimsical reference for my fellow travelers and linguaphiles. I thought, in short, that it would be fun.

It wasn't.

Oh, sure, it had its moments. I mean, I spent two years periodically driving about the country, fishing through its libraries and engaging its residents in shy, awkward conversation. I discovered a passion for Athabaskan languages and a renewed interest in French. I discovered something about the first African American linguist, and I learned my first words in Norwegian. I picked up some Haitian Creole; I practiced my Spanish. I still entertain vague notions of moving to New Orleans, I send everyone I can to Hobuck Beach Resort in Neah Bay, and I fully intend to get myself back to those two-dollar blackjack tables in Elko one day. Unless you are a genuine curmudgeon or totally lacking in self-awareness, it's impossible to be miserable while being paid to flit about the country doing what you love. Road weariness and homesickness are trivial things in the grand scheme of reckless ambition.

But as much as this has been an exploration of the history of language in the United States, it has also turned out to be an examination of prejudice and privilege. I was not the most attentive of high school history students, and so when I set out I had what I now recognize as a shamefully juvenile sense of American history. I think I half expected to bounce from one grand patriotic story to the next. But history is, to quote the great Alan Bennett, just one fucking thing after another, and American history is certainly no different. It is genocide and slavery and discrimination. And in attempting to make sense of the hugely complex set of interactions that create and perpetuate these inequalities, I couldn't help but begin to acknowledge the ways in which I myself am complicit.

Privilege is such a sly creature, so often hiding in plain sight. I know I personally am typically hugely successful at convincing myself I don't have it. Going to private schools and Ivy League universities will give you an incredibly acute awareness of social and economic inequalities, but unless you are one of the extremely rich (as opposed to just regular old rich), it is easy to graduate from these institutions with a sense that you are actually part of the hardscrabble proletariat. It is a seductive notion, particularly appealing to those of us who would like to believe that our achievements are wholly the result of hard work and talent. If you ask someone where he or she went to college and that person is oddly reluctant to answer any more specifically than "in Boston," chances are you have met one of these people. They are not necessarily being coy about their achievements; they are often attempting, however futilely, to downplay their privilege.

Over the years—and this may or may not be related to significant amounts of psychotherapy—I've tried to become more aware of the ways in which my own assumptions and opinions cloud my ability to interpret the world around me. And I've found that, for me, the most reliable way to shake loose the shackles of narrow, complacent thinking is to travel. Until I began to venture outside the United States, I don't think I ever really thought about what it means to be different. I don't mean *quirky* or *outlandish* or *idiosyncratic* or any of those other words used to describe questionable fashion choices or secondary characters in independent films. I mean different as in "not one of us." As in the high school clique taken to its sociological extreme. As in different bathrooms and different fountains and different rules.

I first got an inkling of the true scope of cultural difference when I was working in China. With my Nordic height and Celtic pallor, I was the very definition of conspicuous. On occasion, local response to my presence was favorable. Countless older Chinese ladies approached me and asked if they could introduce me to their sons or grandsons. Then they would gesture at my hips, which until then I had only really taken notice of when shopping for jeans. "Wide hips," they would say. "Very fertile. Good for breeding."

Other times the reactions were less complimentary. Whispers and murmurs would follow me as I moved through cities and villages. More than once I overheard sibilant speculation that a foreign woman traveling alone had to be a prostitute.

Many languages have two forms of the first-person plural pronoun: one for "we-including-you" and one for "we-and-not-you." It seemed strange to me that Mandarin wasn't one of these languages, because it was clear that the non-inclusive "we" was in full and incessant effect. Each and every interaction emphasized the fact that I was, in their eyes, very, very different. It didn't matter if we had interests, opinions, or experiences in common. I was always "them." I was never "us."

Even my most gracious and patient hosts—a group of Buddhist monks living on the slopes of Jiuhuashan, a sacred mountain in Anhui province—couldn't contain their curiosity for long. When I arrived, they offered me a snack of fruit and tea, which we consumed as we chatted about the brutal humidity of the Chinese summer and the cheeky manners of the local monkey population. As soon as I finished, a novice spoke up: "Just how tall *are* you?"

At this point I was forced to reveal my total ignorance with regard to the metric system. So the monks formed a line and had me stand at the front of it. The novice went from monk to monk to me, murmuring as he measured with his hands. After a moment he announced I was 1.8 meters tall. The assembled group gasped, and not precisely in appreciation. Once again I was reminded that while I was there, I was first and foremost a bit of a freak.

I withstood the pointing, the staring, and even the occasional request to pose for photographs with exceptional goodwill. I was, after all, a guest in their country. But after two months, my patience had worn thin. I had originally planned to tour the western half of the country when I finished my work. Instead, as soon as I filed my last batch of copy, I hightailed it back to the States. When I arrived in Chicago, my sigh of relief was so ostentatious the customs agent couldn't help but laugh, and said, "Glad to be home, are you?"

A few years later I moved to Italy, certain that my time in China had prepared me for the difficulties of cultural integration. In one respect my time there was much easier—which is to say that it wasn't immediately visually apparent that I wasn't Italian. But when I first arrived, I didn't speak a word of Italian that didn't involve pasta, wine, or profanity. And, tragically, there's more to daily life than those three things. Each time I went to the grocery store, the post office, the bus station, or a café, I faced the struggle of figuring out how to express myself with my limited vocabulary. Even something as simple as ordering a slab of cheese became a monumental struggle.

And so I applied myself to my language study, attacking dictionaries and grammars with a vigor that alarmed my Italian roommate. "You speak very well for a beginner," she told me one day. "Why must you go so fast?"

I needed to "go fast," as she put it, because I needed to fit in. Or, more precisely, I needed not to stick out.

Even these efforts were for naught, however. By the time I left I was nearly fluent, but my American accent was a dead giveaway. No matter how perfect my grammar, no matter how advanced my vocabulary, I would still see a look in the faces of those I spoke with—a look I was becoming accustomed to, a look that meant I was still on the outside.

The only time I've ever truly blended in while abroad was in Hungary, where my eastern European bone structure and full-coverage winter coat finally accorded me the anonymity to which I'd always aspired. I think I might have actually preened when a friend of my father-in-law's looked me in the eye and said, "With that face, you could be Hungarian." I'd never been mistaken for a native on sight. To Italians, I was blatantly American; the Chinese usually assumed I was Australian. To be told by a Hungarian that I *looked* Hungarian—I couldn't have been more flattered had he informed me I was the most beautiful woman alive.

Of course, this turned out to be a mixed blessing. While walking the streets of Budapest I was stopped at regular intervals by the city's residents. Except this time it wasn't to comment on my stature or unfortunate footwear. No, this time they wanted obscure, neighborhood-specific directions. Apparently, I looked so Hungarian I even confused the locals.

I knew enough of the language to understand what they were asking, but I could no more give directions in Hungarian than I can land a triple axel. I had the looks, but I didn't have the language. So I would simply say, in my most penitent tone, *nem beszélek Magyarul*—"I don't speak Hungarian." And invariably the man or woman in question would then switch effortlessly into English and apologize, wishing me the best during my stay in Budapest. No one was ever anything less than impeccably friendly and polite, but I could always sense that delicate but unmistakable retreat: *not one of us.*

Again, here I am exaggerating my disadvantages to distract you from my advantages. The trials, tears, and tribulations I endured in China, Italy, and Hungary were just a drop in the cross-cultural bucket. I knew I was going to go home eventually. I didn't have roots to plant; I didn't have a family to provide for. From time to time my language skills would fail me, but I was almost always able to find an English-speaker nearby. And if I wasn't, I just pulled out my phrasebook—not, to be honest, that anyone really expects you to know the language anyway. I was exhausted day in and day out. I complained a lot. I drank more. But at no point was my ability to fit in ever anything that might have had an impact on my long-term future. I can only imagine the frustration of having to surmount linguistic and cultural difficulties indefinitely.

Traveling outside the United States made me think about the ways that we are divided by language. It was the trip I took for this book, however—a trip entirely within the United States—that made me think about the ways we are divided by the *perceptions* of language. Throughout my travels I found myself thinking back to my very first class in Ancient Greek. That day I learned that the English word *barbarian* ultimately owes its existence to the Greek βάρβαρος (*barbaros*), "uncouth foreigner." The origin of the Greek word itself is particularly revealing:

it's onomatopoetic. To the Greeks, foreign languages sounded like a succession of nonsense syllables: *barbarbarbarbarbarbar*. Our concept of "barbarian"—a term that has an unabashedly negative connotation and is almost always used to refer to those other than ourselves—evolved from a word that basically meant "people who talk funny." Language, I was reminded, is as powerful a means of discrimination as any.

The United States has, from the very beginning, been a country of extraordinary linguistic diversity. Its economy and resources drew millions of immigrants from all over the world, and over the years it has been home to speakers of more immigrant languages than any other developed nation. These languages intermingled not just with each other but also with the wide variety of indigenous languages that were already here, and the vast territory of the United States allowed for the development of unique language communities—and, sometimes, for their preservation.

Far more remarkable than the historical diversity of language in the United States, however, is the fact that English has always maintained its position as the nation's dominant language. It hasn't managed to do so in a suspenseful, edge-of-your-seat kind of way; there were never years where things were looking kind of dicey. When I say English is dominant, I mean it has dominated. In fact, a 1975 paper by Stanley Lieberson, Guy Dalton, and Mary Ellen Johnston looked at longitudinal data from thirty-five countries and found that in no other country did language assimilation happen so quickly.

There are exceptions. There are pockets of New Mexican Spanish and Louisiana French. Gullah still survives, as do Navajo and Crow. But even these languages have experienced significant declines and are at constant risk of extinction. Sometimes assimilation has been precipitated by policy; sometimes it has been precipitated by opportunity. Sometimes simple prejudice is to blame. Sometimes it takes decades; sometimes it happens right away. Whatever the reason and whatever the process, the history of language in America is—in North Dakota, in South Carolina, and even in Queens—ultimately a history of language loss.

This is, I believe, a testament not only to the power of linguistic discrimination but also to the extent of social, economic, and political inequality in the minds and institutions of America.

It took two years of travel for me to begin to understand this on an intellectual level. But there was one more trip I had to take before I could understand it on an emotional one.

In 2010, my husband and I did the unthinkable: we moved to Los Angeles.

Los Angeles and New York are the Beatrice and Benedick of American cities. They need the tension between them to conjure charm out of what would otherwise be a smug sort of bitchiness. Each claims to want to have nothing to do with the other, but secretly that's not true. They give each other their best material, after all. But woe betide the New Yorker who defects to L.A. or the Angeleno who leaves for New York. According to our friends in New York, we were abandoning all that is good for all that is bad, leaving culture for commerce, substance for superficiality, the vagaries of the MTA for the frustrations of the 405. We might as well have been moving to Mars.

Here's the thing, though. L.A. is not so different from Queens. It's wildly multicultural. It has great food. It's not what I would call pretty. The subway lines are few and far between, and although there are parking lots, the spaces are always smaller than you'd like. L.A. is not particularly skilled at snow removal or professional baseball.

And, much to my delight, the languages of Los Angeles, like the languages of Queens, are incredibly compelling. A majority of Angelenos speak languages other than English, and even though L.A. doesn't have anything like the pedestrian culture of New York, you can never go long here without seeing evidence of another language. I'm getting used to seeing Korean signage wherever I go. I'm learning to distinguish between sounds I never heard in New York, languages such as Armenian and Persian and Amharic. I'm picking up Spanish translations of English marketing copy.

I am also, for the first time, watching someone else learn English. Because just three months before I moved across the country, I gave birth to a baby boy.

Part of me always assumed that if I ever had children I would raise them bilingually. This assumption was not based on any ideas about academic achievement or how a second language would look on a college application. It was much more selfish than that. Part of the great promise of being a parent is the prospect of introducing your children to all the things in the world you love and having the chance, through them, to fall in love all over again. So, yes, I hope that my son finds joy in the things I do. I hope that he likes books and baseball and Mel Brooks. It's OK if he doesn't, but I won't pretend I'm not trying to nudge him along. And this is why, during my pregnancy, I began to plan out a Spanish-language curriculum. My Spanish is good enough for the basics, and I was happy to have a reason to study up and get my *patos* in a *fila*.

But then the strangest thing happened. When my son was born, I discovered I didn't want to speak to him in Spanish. I didn't want to speak to him in Chinese, French, Italian, or any language I'd ever studied. I just wanted to speak to him in my language.

I'd never thought of English as mine before. The fact that I spoke English was just a quirk of genetics and geography, no more or less interesting to me than the fact that I have brown hair. Like I've said, for most of my life I thought English was total dullsville. It's one of the reasons I was so drawn to every language but English. But, as with all new parents, those first few weeks were a blur not just of diapers and blankets and impossibly tiny nail trimmers but also of profound reappraisal.

I had underestimated the fierce intimacy of the murmurings between a mother and her child. I'm giving him my language, a language that isn't just Standard English or even Midland American English. Every word I use is a by-product of the sum total of my experience. It's St. Louis and Boston and New York and a little bit of Canada. It's the weird way I say *Tuesday* and the trouble I have pronouncing *bagel*. It's the words I learned from reading cold war suspense novels and watching *Young Frankenstein*. The idea of not being able to share these words with him absolutely breaks my heart.

I now understand in a visceral way what it means to have a family— and the incalculable, helpless fear that comes with it. I want nothing more than to make sure my son has as many opportunities as possible, and as a result, I'm achingly, incessantly aware that there are things about the world that I cannot fix or control. I know, too, that I would sacrifice anything for him. If I needed to make sure he grew up with a language other than my own, I would do it in a second, no matter how painful a personal loss that might be.

Fortunately—oh so fortunately, I know now—I don't have to. I may have spent most of my life trying to deny the realities of my own privilege, linguistic and otherwise. My son makes me realize how incredibly lucky I am to have it.

So, I have a new plan now.

Instead of teaching my son another language, I will teach him about language. I will tell him about evidentials and ergatives, code-switching and switch-reference; I will discuss the difference between creoles and pidgins, between prestige and value. I will be honest and upfront about all the ways that I have misjudged the languages of others. I will see if I can't convince someone to mock up an illustrated board-book version of *Language Log*.

And I hope that someday in the future we will take a drive together, traveling once more through the sounds and stories of American language.

ACKNOWLEDGMENTS

It is a great privilege simply to be given the chance to publish a book, but I have been particularly blessed with the opportunity to work with an incredible group of editors at Bloomsbury all the way from acquisition to production. Colin Dickerman saw in a far-reaching and mildly hyperactive proposal the potential for something special. Benjamin Adams, my long-suffering and infinitely patient editor, kept me going through dozens of drafts and twice as many nervous breakdowns. Without the benefit of his editorial acumen, this would be less a book than a chaotic jumble of meaningless paper. Thank you, Ben, for sticking with me.

I am also indebted to my copy editor, the talented and meticulous Sue Warga, and my managing editor, the magnificently helpful Mike O'Connor.

Any mistakes in the text are, of course, entirely my own.

Many thanks as well to everyone who took the time to talk to me during my travels, particularly Tim McCleary at Little Bighorn College; Crystal Thompson at the Makah Language Center; Alphonso Brown, Al Miller, and Seretha Tuttle in South Carolina; and David Brown, David Barry Daniels, Barbara Eisenhower, and Jan Mapou in Miami.

My apologies, however, to Robyn Hughes of the Jewish Museum of Baltimore. She was the best docent I've ever had the pleasure of meeting. And I'm sorry I didn't end up including Baltimore in the text. This is no reflection on my time there, merely on my ability to do the city justice. (Not that it needs me so long as David Simon is around.)

I could not have survived my travels without Vania and Nate Kent Harber, Damian Wisniewski, and Jon Beckman and Naomi Straus. After spending six consecutive weeks schlepping from hotel room to hotel room, there is no greater comfort than the company and hospitality of friends. All that wine didn't hurt, either.

I also had considerable support networks in New York, Los Angeles, and everywhere in between. My parents continue to encourage and inspire me in every way they can. Ellen Amato, Scott Korb, Annie Ronan, David Lapidus, George Hamilton, Lewis McVey, Deborah Shapiro, John Herndon, and many others listened patiently to my prattling and more often than not asked insightful questions that helped lead me to new and unexpected conclusions. And I cannot imagine the past three years without the sound advice, wicked humor, and very dear friendship of Sara Burningham.

Kate Garrick, meanwhile, is necessarily underrepresented in these pages, as it's impossible to account for all the ways in which my life and work are richer for having met her.

But it's Dylan Kidd—my partner, my conspirator—who makes this whole thing worth doing. In case it isn't clear by now, I'm sorry I made fun of you for living in Queens.

Introduction: New York City

2   At the time of the 2000 Census: U.S. Census Bureau, "QT-P16 Language Spoken at Home," generated by American FactFinder for ZIP code 11104.

3   a population of almost 2.3 million: U.S. Census Bureau, "DP-1 Profile of General Population and Housing Characteristics: 2010," generated by American FactFinder for Queens County.

3   In 1927: *Queens Immigrant Guide: Common Threads*, "Through Their Eyes: Greeks."

3   by the mid-1990s: Jackson, *Encyclopedia of New York City*, s.v. "Astoria."

3   at least ten mosques: Bilefsky, "Converging on Little Egypt."

3   several thousand Arabic-speakers: U.S. Census Bureau, "QT-P16 Language Spoken at Home," generated by American FactFinder for ZIP codes 11102, 11103, 11105, and 11106.

3   The Bohemian Citizens' Benevolent Society: Bohemian Beer Garden, "History."

4   more Argentineans than anywhere else in the city: Jackson, *The Encyclopedia of New York City*, s.v. "Jackson Heights."

4   Queensboro Realty: Ibid.

4   50 percent of the borough's Chinese population: *Queens Immigrant Guide: Common Threads*, "Through Their Eyes: Chinese."

4   The Flushing community library: Queens Library, "Community and Library History."

4   According to library statistics: Ibid.

6   This treatment was soon the therapy of choice: Munger, "Guaiacum," 209.

6   a word borrowed from the Taíno language: Bailey, "American English," 4.

7   the widely accepted translation is "hilly island": See, for instance, Shorto, *The Island at the Center of the World*, 42, or Burrows and Wallace, *Gotham*, 15.

8   "The Lenape gave a Pennsylvania missionary": Burrows and Wallace, *Gotham*, 15.

8   "Facts are all I aim at": Review of *Collections of the New York Historical Society*, 311.

8   In 1886 a coffee broker named James Potter: Flusser, *Dressing the Man*, 92.

8   The word *tuxedo* itself, meanwhile: Bright, *Native American Placenames*, s.v. "Tuxedo."

9   It wasn't until Henry Hudson: Burrows and Wallace, *Gotham*, 14.

9   Dutch remained the official school language: Dillard, *A History of American English*, 29.

9   "English is the most prevailing Language": Smith, *History of New-York*, 323.

9   *Stoop*, for instance: Dillard, *A History of American English*, 26.

9   Dutch words used outside the five boroughs: Marckwardt, *American English*, 48.

10   "The most credible [etymology]": Ibid., 49.

10   New Netherland was home to: Dillard, *A History of American English*, 22.

10   In 1748, Manhattan boasted: Kalm, *Travels in North America*, 1:132–33.

10   Between 1815 and 1915: Jackson, *The Encyclopedia of New York*, s.v. "Immigration."

10   Today the city is home: New York Community Media Alliance, "Members."

10   More than 150 languages: Roberts, "Listening to (and Saving) the World's Languages."

Chapter One: Montana

21   The first treaty the Crow signed: This and general details about diplomatic relations between the Crow and the U.S. government from Medicine Crow, *From the Heart of the Crow Country*, 3–4.

22   there still exists some discord between the groups: Perrottet, "Little Bighorn Reborn."

22n Fewer than 4 percent: Rhodes and Pufahl, *Foreign Language Teaching in U.S. Schools*, 3.

22   Interestingly, Harvard might not still exist: Peabody Museum of Archaeology and Ethnology, "The Harvard Indian College."

23   reputable sources have suggested: For a general overview of estimates on the numbers of pre-contact languages in North America, see Yamamoto and Zepeda, "Native American Languages," 174. Estimates on the low end of the spectrum hover around 300–400 (see Mithun, *The Languages of Native North America*, 1, and Krauss, "The Condition of Native North American Languages," 9). On the other end is Silver and Miller's estimate. They list more than 550 Native languages, about 250 of which are or were spoken in what is now Canada and the United States. They warn, however, that because of language extinction and dialect confusion even this relatively generous estimate probably falls short: "The number of distinct languages at the time of European contact clearly must have been much greater, with the total for North America probably closer to 750." Silver and Miller, *American Indian Languages*, 7:359–65.

23   Michael Krauss of the Linguistic Society of America: Krauss, "The Condition of Native North American Languages," 12.

24   "covers the widest territory": Mithun, *The Languages of Native North America*, 328.

24   which encompasses more languages and more modern-day speakers: Ibid., 347.

25   while SIL International's Ethnologue: Lewis, ed., *Ethnologue*, 16th ed., "Languages of Papua New Guinea."

25   In a 1946 article: Sapir and Swadesh, "American Indian Grammatical Categories," 136.

26   a "beast in bignes[s] of a pig": Harrington, "The Original Strachey Vocabulary," sheet 2.

26   "An Opassom hath a head": Smith, *The Generall Historie of Virginia*, 2:27.

26   *Squaw, papoose*, and *wigwam*: Oxford English Dictionary, 2nd ed., s.v.v. "squaw," "wigwam," and "tipi"; 3rd ed., s.v. "papoose."

27   an Algonquin word meaning "marshy meadow": Tooker, *The Indian Place-names*, 196–97, quoted in Read, "The Rationale of 'Podunk,'" 103. Tooker notes that *podunk* is likely derived from *pot-*, "to sink," and the locative *-unk*—i.e., "sinking place" or "marsh."

27   Maine place names such as *Ogunquit*: Bond, *Native Names of New England Towns and Villages*, 8.

27   *Swampscott*: Ibid., 54.

27   *Cohasset*: Ibid., 41.

27   The notorious *Chappaquiddick*: Ibid., 39.

27   *Alaska*, for instance: Bright, *Native American Placenames*, s.v. "Alaska."

27   *Texas*: Ibid., s.v. "Texas."

27   The name *Oklahoma*: Oxford English Dictionary, 3rd ed., s.v. "Oklahoma."

28   In the Munsee language: Bright, *Native American Placenames*, s.v. "Wyoming."

28   There is some debate: Metcalf, "How 'OK' Took Over the World."

28   In *Made in America*: Bryson, *Made in America*, 24.

29   Their ancestors migrated to the plains: This and other basic details of Crow history from Medicine Crow, *From the Heart of the Crow Country*, and Frey, *The World of the Crow Indians*.

29   scholars such as the linguist G. Hubert Matthews: Matthews, "Glottochronology and the Separation of the Crow and Hidatsa," 113–25. Quoted in Frey, *The World of the Crow Indians*, 11.

30   Consider *baawaashbaaléewiawaassaak*: Graczyk, "Crow," 269.

30   Switch reference was first observed: Mithun, *The Languages of Native North America*, 269.

31   In Crow, however: Graczyk, *A Grammar of Crow*, 404.

31   In Crow this is accomplished: Ibid., 328.

31   a survey showed: Dracon, *The Extent of Spoken Crow and Cheyenne*, referenced in Watts, "Crow Language Teachers' Views," 3–4.

31   Only 25 percent of children ages three to nineteen: Watts, "Crow Language Teachers' Views," 3. These survey results are from Watts's personal communication with Sharon Stewart-Peregoy, November 21, 1997.

33   The exit off I-90 for Crow Agency: Bohrer, "Tribal Words Highlight Exit Signs."

34   Most of the bodies: This and other details about the administration of the battlefield and its monuments are from Perrottet, "Little Bighorn Reborn."

Chapter Two: *Arizona*

36   more than 150,000 speakers: U.S. Census Bureau, 2005 American Community Survey, generated by the MLA Language Map Data Center, www.mla.org/map_data.

38   To give you a better idea: My own understanding of Young and Morgan's system was largely facilitated by Joyce Mary McDonough's indispensable paper, "How to Use Young and Morgan's *The Navajo Language*."

38   here's a standard Navajo verb template: Young and Morgan, *The Navajo Language*, 37–38. Note that this verb template varies slightly from the one outlined by Young in *The Navajo Verb System*. In this template Young also includes the disjunct prefix Ie for the semeliterative.

38   the stem for "cry": Faltz, *The Navajo Verb*, 440.

38   Some verbs require not just the stem: Faltz, *The Navajo Verb*, 22.

39   There are groups of "solid roundish objects": Young, *The Navajo Verb System*, 3–17.

40   Danny Hieber, a content editor: Hieber, "Rising to the Challenge."

40   home to nearly 170,000: U.S. Census Bureau, "DP-1 Profile of General Population and Housing Characteristics: 2010," generated by American FactFinder for Navajo Nation Reservation and Off-Reservation Trust Land.

40   the tribe's 300,000-plus members: Donovan, "Census: Navajo Enrollment Tops 300,000."

41   Inhabited for nearly 5,000 years: National Park Service, "Canyon de Chelly National Monument: History and Culture."

42   It was named in 1882: National Park Service, "Canyon de Chelly National Monument."

42   By the eighteenth century: Iverson, *Diné*, 22.

42   The first Spanish references: Ibid., 26.

42   The word *Navajo* itself: Ibid., 26; see also Franciscan Fathers, *An Ethnologic Dictionary of the Navajo Language*, 23–25.

43   According to Navajo oral tradition: Iverson, *Diné*, 29.

43   General Edward Canby: Ibid., 47.

43   "The old Indians will die off": Thompson, *The Army and the Navajo*, 28.

43   Despite being advised: Iverson, *Diné*, 50.

44   "The Navajo Indians have got to be whipped": James Carleton to J. Francisco Chavez, August 7, 1868, in *Reports of the Committees of the Senate of the United States for the Second Session Thirty-Ninth Congress, 1866–67*, 126.

44   Carson ordered the complete destruction: Brown, *Bury My Heart at Wounded Knee*, 27.

44   It was this attack: Houk and Andrews, *Navajo of Canyon de Chelly*, 15.

45   "Naturally the Indian has many noble qualities": Taylor et al., "Report to the President," 43.

46   "A great general has said": Pratt, "The Advantages of Mingling Indians with Whites," 260–71.

46   In 1883, for instance: Montana Office of Public Instruction, "Crow Reservation Timeline."

46 nineteen Hopi men: Reyhner, "Cultural Survival vs. Forced Assimilation."

47 Some students suffered more severe punishments: House, *Language Shift Among the Navajos*, 18.

47 "Children were taught": Kneale, *Indian Agent*, 169.

47 "My grandchild": It is widely accepted that Manuelito said this to Henry Chee Dodge in the early 1880s. The English translation used here can be found throughout the literature—not to mention throughout Navajo Nation. See, for instance, Moore, *Chiefs, Agents, and Soldiers*, 258–59.

47 Native-language instruction was banned: Lockard, "New Paper Words," 25.

47 In 1882 Manuelito sent his two sons: Moore, *Chiefs, Agents, and Soldiers*, 259.

48 Although the land for St. Michael's: This and other details about the early days of St. Michael's and its early English-Navajo dictionary are from Lockard, "New Paper Words," 21.

48 "he might have been more Navajo than Anglo": Austin-Garrison et al., *Diné Bizaad Yissohígíí*, 356, quoted in Spolsky, "Prospects for the Survival of the Navajo Language," 148.

49 At this point there were three kinds of schools: Mizuno, "*Diné bi Olta*," 143.

49 Rough Rock Demonstration School was the first BIA school: U.S. Department of the Interior, "$52.5 Million Recovery Project Gets Underway"; Mizuno, "*Diné bi Olta*," 155.

49 where students in grades K–8: Window Rock Unified School District, "About Us."

52 A 1990 study: Platero, "Navajo Head Start Language Study," quoted in Spolsky, "Prospects for the Survival of the Navajo Language," 141.

53 A survey by the Window Rock school district: Zehr, "A Culture Put to the Test."

53 "the use of the Navajo language": House, *Language Shift Among the Navajos*, 79.

53 they were anything but immediately effective: Spolsky, "Prospects for the Survival of the Navajo Language," 143.

53 "Interestingly, absent from the students' counter-narratives": Lee, "Language, Identity, and Power," 313.

53 Meanwhile, the high visibility of Navajo-language instruction: This insight—that effective top-down PR can undermine bottom-up proactivity—comes from House, *Language Shift Among the Navajos*, 48. She notes pointedly that "well-crafted, effective discourse can cause us to deny the meaning of what we see or hear."

54 only 10 percent of Navajo pupils: Lee and McLaughlin, "Reversing Navajo Language Shift, Revisited," 34–35.

54 "the language associated with access": House, *Language Shift Among the Navajos*, 28.

Chapter Three: Washington

55 with twenty-nine federally recognized: "Indian Entities Recognized," 60810–4.

59 In a 1921 issue: Meany, "Origin of Washington Geographic Names," 217–18.

59 On December 18, 1955: "Indians Named Puyallup."

61 decidedly mundane translation of *Puyallup*: Puyallup Tribal News Language Page, January 2008, www.puyallup-tribe.com/assets/puyallup-tribe/learning/langpg/january.2008.pdf.

62   their language program suggests otherwise: Puyallup Tribal News Language
     Page, February 2008, www.puyallup-tribe.com/assets/puyallup-tribe/learning/
     langpg/january.2008.pdf.

62   I looked up *Puyallup*: Hess and Hilbert, *Lushootseed Dictionary*, s.v. "puy."

62   *alap*, which has the rough meaning: Ibid., s.v. "alap."

63   In a 1990 letter: Goddard, "Time to Retire an Indian Place-Name Hoax."

64   There is not, by the way, a single language: Holton, "Inuit or Eskimo"; Qitsualik,
     "Are Eskimo and Inuit the Same People?"

64   "supposed literal translations": Goddard, "Time to Retire an Indian Place-Name
     Hoax."

64   "English knifemen and Nipmuck Indians": Belluck, "What's the Name of That
     Lake?"

65   But then, in 2003: Meyer, "The Story Behind Twilight."

67   *la bouche* became *la push*: Powell and Jensen, *Quileute*, 15.

67   Quileute is one of only two Chimakuan languages: Mithun, *The Languages of Na-
     tive North America*, 377.

67   Edward Sapir first observed this phenomenon: Ibid., 273–74. The article she is re-
     ferring to is Edward Sapir's "Abnormal Types of Speech in Nootka," which can be
     found in Sapir, *Selected Writings of Edward Sapir in Language, Culture, and Personal-
     ity*, ed. David G. Mandelbaum (Berkeley: University of California Press, 1949).

67   For instance, if you were talking to someone: Frachtenberg, "Abnormal Types of
     Speech in Quileute," 298.

67   By the mid-1970s, the population of native Quileute-speakers: This and the 1977
     and 1900 population estimates are from Powell and Jensen, *Quileute*, 58.

70   "For this reason you Quileute": Andrade and Frachtenberg, *Quileute Texts*, 85,
     quoted in Powell and Jensen, *Quileute*, 17.

71   "Dear Fans": Facebook page of the Quileute Nation of La Push, Washington,
     www.facebook.com/permalink.php?story_fbid=187322547390&id=197450
     675626.

74   Ruth E. Claplanhoo: Barber, "Basket Weaver's Legacy Is Woven into Fabric of the
     Makah."

74   "A glottal stop is produced simultaneously": Jacobsen, *First Lessons in Makah*, 2.

75   in Makah there exists a series of suffixes: This and additional details and examples
     of Makah evidentials from Jacobsen, "The Heterogeneity of Evidentials in
     Makah," quoted in Mithun, *The Languages of Native North America*, 185–86.

76   When parsed out, it becomes: From the exhibit notes at the Makah Cultural and
     Research Center in Neah Bay (visited July 2008).

77   The Makah called the outsiders: Erikson, *Voices of a Thousand People*, 24.

77   "They were asked": Ibid., 9–10.

78   he wrote, for instance: Swan, *The Indians of Cape Flattery*, 1.

79   "We had to go through": Erikson, *Voices of a Thousand People*, 52, from a 1995 in-
     terview with Helma Ward.

79   "I have taken the buildings at Bahada Point": C. A. Huntington to Commissioner
      of Indian Affairs, September 5, 1874, in *Annual Report of the Commissioner of Indian
      Affairs to the Secretary of the Interior for the Year* 1874, 333.

79   "When he was caught [speaking Makah]": Erikson, *Voices of a Thousand People*, 78.

80   archaeologists uncovered more than 55,000 artifacts: Renker, "The Makah Tribe."

80   The Makah employed an exhibit designer: Erikson, *Voices of a Thousand People*, 173.

81   In 1978, the tribe received a grant: "U.S. Helps Small Tribe to Save Its Language."

82   Between 2000 and 2007: U.S. Department of Health and Human Servies, "ANA
      Grant Awards."

82   Jessie Little Doe Baird: MacArthur Foundation, "Jessie Little Doe Baird."

83   Michael Krauss estimated: Krauss, "The Condition of Native North American
      Languages," 10.

84   the life expectancy for men on the Crow reservation: From interview with Profes-
      sor Tim McCleary, July 2008.

84   on par with countries such as: World Bank, *World Development Indicators*, 119–20.

84n   teenage Navajo girls are significantly more likely: Russell, "Environmental Rac-
      ism," quoted in Wenz, "Just Garbage," 66.

84   The suicide rate: U.S. Department of Health and Human Services, *Trends in Indian
      Health*, Table 4.22, 77.

85   "*Not* learning a language": This quotation was taken from an exhibit at the Makah
      Cultural and Research Center (visited July 2008).

85   "which flattered us": Cook, *The Voyages of Captain Cook*, 2:260.

Chapter Four: Louisiana

87   at the time of the American Revolution: Bailey, "American English: Its Origins
      and History," 11.

88   "a considerable oversimplification": Crystal, *The Stories of English*, 425.

88   an estimated 100,000 speakers: Mithun, *The Languages of Native North America*,
      587–88.

90   In 1718, Jean-Baptiste Le Moyne de Bienville: Stewart, *Names on the Land*, 135.

91   The Good Friday fire of 1788: Reeves, "French Quarter Fire and Flood."

91   "By the end of Reconstruction": Brasseaux, *French, Creole, Cajun, Houma*, 100.

91   Because residents of the area couldn't afford : Hirsch and Logsdon, *Creole New Or-
      leans*, 119.

92   At Galatoire's: Claverie, "Trout Meuniere Amandine."

92   *beignet* can be traced back: *New Oxford American Dictionary*, 2nd ed., s.v. "beignet."

94   *Lagniappe* derives from the Spanish *la ñapa*: *Oxford English Dictionary*, 2nd ed., s.v.
      "lagniappe."

94   "We picked up one excellent word": Twain, *Life on the Mississippi*, 316.

94n   The Spanish, in turn, comes from the Quechua: This is a widely accepted etymology.
      See, for instance, *Collins English Dictionary*, 10th ed., or *Random House Dictionary*,
      2011.

95   Its etymology is fairly straightforward: *Oxford English Dictionary*, 2nd ed., s.v. "Creole."

96   The SIL Ethnologue currently lists eighty-two creoles: Lewis, ed., *Ethnologue*.

96   With nearly 8 million speakers: Ibid., s.v. "Haitian."

97   The words and structure of the language: Holm, *An Introduction to Pidgins and Creoles*, 5–6.

97   According to the most recent scholarship: This and other details and quotations in this paragraph from Brasseaux, *French, Cajun, Creole, Houma*, 89.

97   "the earliest published reference": Domínguez, "Social Classification in Creole Louisiana," 591.

97   "There are four types of inhabitants": Bossu, *Travels in the Interior of North America*, 22.

98   according to Domínguez: Domínguez, "Social Classification in Creole Louisiana," 593.

99   Historian Gary Mills: Mills, *The Forgotten People*, xii–xiv.

99   "paper bag test": Brasseaux, *French, Cajun, Creole, Houma*, 111.

100   in Louisiana the term *Creole* is used most commonly: Dubois and Melançon, "Creole Is, Creole Ain't."

100   This definition persisted: Domínguez, *White by Definition*, 45–46.

106   Laura met a man from St. Louis: Gore, *Memories of the Old Plantation Home*, 152.

106   moved with Gore to what is now St. Louis's Central West End: Ibid., 156.

106   Her memoir, published as *Memories of the Old Plantation*: Ibid., 1.

106   Of Laura's three first cousins: Ibid., 152.

107   a "perfect command": Ibid., 24.

107   Nicolas de la Salle: Hall, *Africans in Colonial Louisiana*, 57.

107   by 1800: Ibid., 279.

108   When the plantation commenced production: Laura Plantation, "5 Centuries of Habitation."

108   Elisabeth came up with a cheaper solution: Gore, *Memories of the Old Plantation Home*, 137.

108   by the time of the Civil War: Laura Plantation, "5 Centuries of Habitation."

109n   In her memoir Laura recounts: Gore, *Memories of the Old Plantation Home*, 78.

110   "In jou in chien acheté": Fortier, *Louisiana Folk-tales*, 32.

110   *One day a dog*: This translation is my own, but it differs only minimally from Fortier's, found on page 33 of *Louisiana Folk-tales*.

110n   A literal modern Standard French translation: This translation is also my own, with assistance from Nadia Garrick.

111   Fortier himself acknowledges this tendency: Fortier, *Louisiana Folk-tales*, x.

112   "It is curious to see": Ibid.

113   Indeed, after a little digging: Hall, *Africans in Colonial Louisiana*, 188.

113   As colonial records show: Brasseaux, *French, Cajun, Creole, Houma*, 12.

113   Afterward, economic and political realities: Ingersoll, "The Slave Trade and the Ethnic Diversity of Louisiana's Slave Community," 141.

113   As documented: Hall, *Africans in Colonial Louisiana*, particularly Table 2, 60.

115   During the years of Spanish rule: Brasseaux, Fontenot, and Oubre, *Creoles of Color in the Bayou Country*, 4.

115   It was this latter route in particular: Ibid., 4.

115   Born in 1742 to the household of Louis Jucherau de St. Denis: This and other basic details of Coincoin's life are from Mills, *The Forgotten People*, 23–49.

116   Eventually she and her children: Mills, "Forgotten People of America."

117   When I read that the name *Coincoin*: Mills, *The Forgotten People*, 3, from Mills's May 12, 1973, correspondence with Dr. Jan Vansina.

117   "The vocabulary of Louisiana Creole": Hall, *Africans in Colonial Louisiana*, 188.

117   "so far no scholar has demonstrated": Valdman and Klingler, "The Structure of Louisiana Creole," 140.

119   There are legions of petty differences: Grammatical differences from Lane, "Notes on Louisiana-French," 323–33; lexical differences from LaFleur, "Faux Amis Cadiens."

119   The origin of the word *Acadia*: Griffiths, *From Migrant to Acadian*, 467.

119   The linguist Ingrid Neumann-Holzschuh has described this: Neumann, *Le créole de Breaux Bridge*, as summarized in Valdman and Klingler, "The Structure of Louisiana Creole," 123.

120   By the 1840s: Estaville, "The Louisiana French Language," 109–10.

121   A notice published in *L'Abeille*: Laura Plantation, "Slave Registry."

121   She writes in her memoir: Gore, *Memories of the Old Plantation Home*, 33.

121   Though Louisiana had been forced: Linton, "Language Politics and Policy in the United States," 12–13.

121   the language of "general exercises": Louisiana Constitution of 1868, article 109.

121   illegal to pass legislation requiring the publication: Ibid., article 138.

121   the 1901 discovery of oil: Brasseaux, *French, Cajun, Creole, Houma*, 76.

122   In a 1999 article: Natsis, "Legislation and Language," 326.

122   a student was forced to kneel on grains of corn: Yardley, "Minding Our Tongues," from Yardley's interview with Elmo Authement.

122   This latter student: Andersson and Boyer, *Bilingual Schooling in the United States*, 2:173–74.

122   often referred to derisively: Valdman and Klingler, "The Structure of Louisiana Creole," 110–11.

123   According to the American Community Survey: U.S. Census Bureau, 2005 American Community Survey, generated by the MLA Language Map Data Center, www.mla.org/map_data.

123   The best and most recent guess: Neumann, *Le créole de Breaux Bridge*, 20.

123   In 1969, for instance: Council for the Development of French in Louisiana, "Louisiana's French History."

123   And in 1984: Lafayette, "États-Unis," 41. This measure applied, specifically, to grades 4–8.

123   Leblanc's grand plan: Nadeau and Barlow, *The Story of French*, 226.

Chapter Five: South Carolina

126 "Buh Wolf and Buh Rabbit": Jones, *Gullah Folktales*, 29.

127 "Michael Row the Boat Ashore": Allen, Ware, and Garrison, *Slave Songs of the United States*, 23–24.

128 The *Charleston News and Courier* noted: Fordham, *True Stories of Black South Carolina*, 102.

128 The production also ran into difficulties: Standifer, "The Complicated Life of Porgy and Bess."

129 "Folklore subjects": Thomson, "George Gershwin," 151.

129 In the 1930s, for instance: Fraden, *Blueprints for a Black Federal Theatre*, 177–78.

129 "I saw the primitive Negro": Standifer, "The Complicated Life of Porgy and Bess."

135 Sometimes they were merely forced: Brown, *A Gullah Guide to Charleston*, 91.

135 if their owners were willing: Egerton, "The Material Culture of Slave Resistance."

136 William Aiken Jr. owned more than 700 slaves: Aiken-Rhett House, "African Americans."

139 The current statue is the second: Fields, "What One Cannot Remember Mistakenly," 157.

140 "But let me not be understood": Calhoun, "Speech on Slavery," 159.

140 In his book, Alphonso Brown relates: Brown, *A Gullah Guide to Charleston*, 46.

141 The conditions were so difficult: Turner, *Africanisms in the Gullah Dialect*, 5.

142 It was here that King planned: McMillan, "An Island of Gullah Culture."

143 The linguist George Philip Krapp: Krapp, "The English of the Negro," 191.

143 When it was initially founded: Nichols, *Voices of Our Ancestors*, 52.

143 as linguist Patricia Causey Nichols points out: Nichols, *Voices of Our Ancestors*, 91.

143 Many of these names do have English roots: These and other names found in Baird and Twining, "Names and Naming in the Sea Islands," 28–36.

144 Similar names found in Gullah include: Turner, *Africanisms in the Gullah Dialect*, 43.

144 the lack of passive voice in Gullah: Ibid., 209.

145 "As regards numerals": Ibid., 254.

145 Then the historian P. E. H. Hair: Opala, "The Gullah: Rice, Slavery, and the Sierra Leone–American Connection."

146 And more recently a linguist at the University of Texas: Ibid. For more information, see Hancock, "A Provisional Comparison of the English-Based Atlantic Creoles."

149 "In fact, during my first few years": Jones-Jackson, *When Roots Die*, 136.

149 In an interview with National Public Radio: National Public Radio, "'New Testament' Translated Into Gullah."

150 there had been little to no reputable research: Mille and Montgomery, "Introduction," xix–xxii.

150 "is the worst English in the world": Smith, *Gullah*, 18, quoted in Mille and Montgomery, "Introduction," xiii. Mille and Montgomery note that Smith attributed this opinion to an unidentified source.

150 "Slovenly and careless of speech": Gonzales, *The Black Border*, 10.

150 "When I was 16": "The 43rd President: In His Own Words."

152 Even though it has fewer than 10,000 monolingual speakers: Lewis, ed., *Ethnologue*, s.v. "Gullah."

153 there are reports from as late as 1949: Jones-Jackson, *When Roots Die*, 133.

153 As Patricia Jones-Jackson writes: Ibid., 133.

153 "Many speakers learn and use [Gullah]": Nichols, "Creole Languages," 139.

Chapter Six: Nevada

160 according to *A Basque History of the World*: Kurlansky, *The Basque History of the World*, 22.

162 Archi, a Caucasian language: Kibrirk, "Archi," 467.

162 ἀφύη, a generic term for a small fish: Liddell, Scott, Jones, *Greek-English Lexicon*, 9th ed., s.v. "ἀφύη."

162 one etymology cited if not endorsed by the *Oxford English Dictionary*: *Oxford English Dictionary*, 2nd ed., s.v. "bizarre."

163 And although the word *honcho*: Ibid., s.v. "honcho."

163 There are several plausible explanations: Ibid., s.v. "silhouette."

163 "[Silhouette] is a French spelling": Trask, "FAQs About Basque and the Basques."

164 at least two words in the Mi'kmaq language: Bakker, "Two Basque Loanwords in Micmac," 260.

164 In 1911 the *New York Times* reported: "Basque Language Balks Inspectors."

172 the Basques first learned to herd: Douglass, *Amerikanuak*, 223–24.

172 and by 1901: Lane, "The Cultural Ecology of Sheep Nomadism," 52–61, quoted in Lane, "Trouble in the Sweet Promised Land," 35.

173 William A. Douglass cites a number of examples: Douglass, *Amerikanuak*, 265–70.

173 Testifying in Congress in 1913: Ibid., 268.

173 When Nevada's many Basque supporters: Ibid., 269. See also Lane, "Trouble in the Sweet Promised Land," 38.

174 The latter act: U.S. Department of Labor, *Annual Report of the Commissioner General of Immigration to the Secretary of Labor*, 26.

175 The Basques were the first: Kurlansky, *The Basque History of the World*, 14.

178 Over the past three decades: Eustat, "Evolution of the Distribution of the Population."

178 In Gipuzkoa, meanwhile: Eustat, "More than Half the Population Claimed to Have Some Knowledge of the Basque Language in 2001."

179 UNESCO's most recent *Atlas of the World's Languages in Danger*: Moseley, ed., *Atlas of the World's Languages in Danger*, 3rd ed., s.v. "Basque."

179 57,793 people identified themselves as "Basque": U.S. Census Bureau, "PCT018 Ancestry," generated by American FactFinder for the United States.

179 Only 2,513, however: This and the following two data points from U.S. Census Bureau, 2000 Census Summary File 3, generated by the MLA Language Map Data Center, www.mla.org/map_data.

180 Idaho was the only state in 2000: Ibid.

Chapter Seven: North Dakota

184 Minot . . . was founded in 1886: This and other details of Minot's early history from *The WPA Guide to 1930s North Dakota*, 160–61.

187 The first Høstfest: This and other details about the history of Høstfest from Fiske, *The Best of the Norwegian Heritage*, 230.

192 in which he discusses the idea of "chamber of commerce ethnicity": Lovoll, *Norwegians on the Prairie*, 262–69.

194 Some years would see: Semmingsen, *Norway to America*, 32–33.

194 By the end of the 1860s: Zempel, *In Their Own Words*, ix.

194 Between the 1860s and the 1920s: Ibid., ix.

194 by 1920, the Norwegian population: Semmingsen, *Norway to America*, 132.

196 In 1869, a Norwegian journalist: Lovoll, "The Norwegian Press in North Dakota."

196 Between 1878 and 1890: Robinson, *History of North Dakota*, 146.

196 According to Ingrid Semmingsen: Semmingsen, *From Norway to America*, 138–39.

196 *Normanden* (The Norsemen): Details about *Normanden* and *Fram* from Lovoll, "The Norwegian Press in North Dakota."

197 Some papers, of course, served more practical purposes: Semmingsen, *From Norway to America*, 84.

197 As Haugen writes: Haugen, *The Norwegian Language in America*, 1:76.

197 H. L. Mencken lists a number of these words: Mencken, *The American Language*, 411–14.

197 "mutilated beyond recognition": Ibid., 412.

198 Ingrid Semmingsen relates the frustration: Semmingsen, *Norway to America*, 88.

199 "In early years the cows had their proper names": Haugen, "Language and Immigration."

199 "His name was Gunder": Zempel, *In Their Own Words*, 52.

199 "Pastor H. thinks": Ibid., 77.

199 among those arrested under the proclamation: Sage, *A History of Iowa*, 252.

200 Linguist Joshua Fishman estimates: Lovoll, *The Promise Fulfilled*, 335.

200 in the 1910 U.S. Census: U.S. Census Bureau, "Table 6. Mother Tongue of the Foreign-Born Population."

200 The latest estimates, from 2000: U.S. Census Bureau, 2000 Census Summary File 3, generated by the MLA Language Map Data Center, www.mla.org/map_data.

202 "The Synod spent considerable time": This quotation and other details about the Norwegian Church's educational efforts in the United States from Nelsen, "The School Controversy Among Norwegian Immigrants."

202 As late as 1925 the Norwegian Lutheran Church of America: This and further details about the decline of the Norwegian language in the Norwegian-American church from Lovoll, *Norwegians on the Prairie*, 245–46.

203 There are today in the United States only two churches: Lovoll, *The Promise Fulfilled*, 96.

Chapter Eight: Florida

207 Current population estimates suggest: U.S. Census Bureau, "QT-P16 Language Spoken at Home," generated by American FactFinder.

207 By 2050 it could be the largest: Mantilla, "Más 'speak spanish' que en España."

207 as of 2005 the ratio of English-speakers to Spanish-speakers: U.S. Census Bureau, 2005 American Community Survey, generated by the MLA Language Map Data Center, www.mla.org/map_data.

208 the highest proportion of foreign-born residents: Stepick et al., *This Land Is Our Land*, 20.

208 was fully 65 percent Hispanic/Latino: U.S. Census Bureau, "QT-P10 Hispanic or Latino by Type: 2010," generated by American FactFinder for Miami-Dade County.

208 home to nearly two times as many Spanish-speakers: U.S. Census Bureau, "QT-P16 Language Spoken at Home: 2000," generated by American FactFinder for Miami-Dade County.

208 According to the linguist and creole specialist John Holm: Holm, *An Introduction to Pidgins and Creoles*, 86.

210 Community groups such as Sant La: Metellus et al., "Risk and Protective Factors in Little Haiti and in the Haitian/Haitian-American Community in Miami Dade County."

211 With 26.3 percent of its population living below the poverty line: U.S. Census Bureau, "S0501 Selected Characteristics of the Native and Foreign-Born Populations," generated by American FactFinder for the city of Miami.

213 remittances from the diaspora make up: Forman, Lang, and Chandler, "The Role of the Haitian Diaspora in Building Haiti Back Better."

216 the city's so-called Voodoo Squad: See, for instance, Sell, "Inside Miami: A Letter."

219 Only 7 percent of the country's population: Schieffelin and Doucet, "The 'Real' Haitian Creole," 178

219 "Many educated middle-class Haitians": Ibid., 182.

220 half of Miami-Dade County's 2.5 million residents: U.S. Census Bureau, "S0501 Selected Characteristics of the Native and Foreign-Born Populations," generated by American FactFinder.

220 nearly one tenth of the Cuban population: Levine and Asís, *Cuban Miami*, 3.

220 By the end of the nineteenth century: Dixon, "An Overview of the Black Cubans Among the Mariel Entrants," quoted in García and Otheguy, "The Language Situation of Cuban Americans," 166.

222 Between 1981 and 1991: Mitchell, "U.S. Policy Toward Haitian Boat People," 73.

223 "Vouésin millò passé fanmill'!": Sylvain, *Cric? Crac!*, 16. This excerpt includes both the Haitian Creole and the Standard French versions.

223 "Neighbors better than family": Lang, *Entwisted Tongues*, 219; Lang, "A Primer of Haitian Literature in 'Kreyòl,'" 136. In *Entwisted Tongues* Lang elected to translate *coucouill'* as singular: "firefly glows for his own eyes." Here I inserted instead Lang's later, plural translation from "A Primer of Haitian Literature."

Chapter Nine: New Mexico

226 The majority of America's Latino population: Silva-Corvalán, "Spanish in the Southwest," 206.

226 Spanish had for several generations been established: Ibid., 207.

227 Though the demographics of the region changed: Lipski, *Varieties of Spanish in the United States*, 192.

227 more than 45 percent of its population: U.S. Census Bureau, "QT-P10 Hispanic or Latino by Type: 2010," generated by American FactFinder.

227 Today there are approximately 750,000: Limonic, *The Latino Population of New York City*, Table 1, 2.

228 oldest community of European-language-speakers in the United States: Lipski, *Varieties of Spanish in the United States*, 193.

228 Oñate left Zacatecas in 1598: The specifics of Oñate's expedition are taken from exhibit notes at the El Camino Real International Heritage Center (visited August 2008).

230 There were Castilian-speakers, to be sure: This and other details in this paragraph about the peculiarities of New Mexican Spanish from Cobos, *A Dictionary of New Mexico and Southern Colorado Spanish*, ix–x.

230 Some New Mexican Spanish words are radically different: New Mexican Spanish and English equivalents from Lipski, *Varieties of Spanish in the United* States, 207; Standard Spanish equivalents from *Diccionario de la Lengua Española*, 22nd ed., s.v.v. "ardilla," "murciélago," "ganso," and "colibri," and *Collins Spanish Dictionary*, 8th ed., s.v. "mazorca."

231 Cobos, in fact, suggests: Cobos, *A Dictionary of New Mexico and Southern Colorado Spanish*, xi.

231 Some, such as *bequenpaura*: Ibid., xv.

231 Moreover, ongoing hostilities: Lipski, *Varieties of Spanish in the United States*, 196.

232 as linguist John M. Lipski has pointed out: Ibid., 201.

233 Although by 1790 Germans only made up 8.6 percent: Daniels, *Coming to America*, 66.

233 In fact, the first newspaper to announce: Liberman, "English Under Siege in Pennsylvania."

233 of the fifty-eight language policies adopted before 1880: Linton, "Language Politics and Policy in the United States," 12.

234 Roger Sherman, a delegate to the Continental Congress: Baron, *Grammar and Good Taste*, 13.

234 "I am perfectly of your mind": Benjamin Franklin to Peter Collinson, May 9 1753, in *The Papers of Benjamin Franklin*, 4:483–84. Editor Leonard Labaree notes on page 477 of this volume that this particular letter "has never been printed accurately, nor can it be here, for no Franklin autograph has been found." The version cited by Labaree and here is the version included in the Hardwicke Papers at the New York Public Library.

234 The myth of this close brush with German: Baron, "The Legendary English-Only Vote of 1795."

235   In fact, early language policy generally encouraged: This observation and subsequent details from Linton, "Language Politics and Policy in the United States," 13–15.

235   In 1919, Nebraska passed a law: An Act Relating to the Teaching of Foreign Languages in the State of Nebraska, sec. 7, chap. 249 of the Session Laws of Nebraska for 1919.

235   Speaking for the majority: *Meyer v. State of Nebraska*, 262 U.S. 390 (1923).

236   "Neither the United States nor any State": SJ Res 72, 97th Cong., 1st Sess.

236   "It is the sense of the Congress that": Immigration Reform and Control Act of 1982, S 2222, 97th Cong., 2nd Sess.

236   since 1981 twenty-six states: English First, "States"; Crawford, "Language Legislation in the U.S.A."

236   Lucy Tse . . . looked at: Tse, *"Why Don't They Learn English?"* 2–5.

236n   With one quasi-exception: Tatalovich, *Nativism Reborn?*, 65–69.

237   "By encouraging people to communicate": Testimony of Senator Richard Shelby on January 9, 1995, Introduction of Bills and Joint Resolutions, 14th Cong., 1st Sess.

237   According to a 2003 Pew Hispanic Center survey: Pew Hispanic Center, "Hispanic Attitudes Toward Learning English."

240   almost 92 percent of Laredo's population: U.S. Census Bureau, 2000 Census Summary File 3, generated by the MLA Language Map Data Center, www.mla.org/map_data.

241   "As a descriptive term": Santiago, *Pardon My Spanglish*, 17.

243   But Veltman has found that the younger a person: Veltman, "Modelling the Language Shift Process of Hispanic Immigrants," 549–50.

243   A 1998 survey of eighth and ninth-grade students: Portes and Hao, "E Pluribus Unum," Table 1, 274.

243   Meanwhile, in an analysis of data: Rumbaut, Massey, and Bean, "Linguistic Life Expectancies," 455.

244   "Children whose cultural background includes Spanish": Portes and Rumbaut, *Legacies*, 140–41. See also Alba et al., "Only English by the Third Generation?"

244   The proportion of the population ages five and over: Shin and Bruno, "Language Use and English-Speaking Ability," 3.

244   According to the most recent available estimates: U.S. Census Bureau, "QT-P16 Language Spoken at Home," generated by American FactFinder.

244   In Alabama, 89 percent of voters supported an official-English measure: Nunberg, "Lingo Jingo."

244   less than 3 percent of the state's population: U.S. Census Bureau, "DP-2 Social Characteristics: 1990," generated by American FactFinder.

245   political scientist Raymond Tatalovich concluded: Tatalovich, *Nativism Reborn?*, 246.

246   these early analyses failed to account for socioeconomic differences: Portes and Hao, "E Pluribus Unum," 271.

246   only 47 percent in 2000: Greybeck, "The Effectiveness of an After-School Inter-
        vention Program," 2.

246   Median household income in the Laredo metropolitan era: U.S. Census Bureau,
        "S1901 Income in the Past 12 Months," generated by American FactFinder for Lar-
        edo, Texas, Metro Area.

246   a full quarter of the city's families: U.S. Census Bureau, "S1702 Poverty Status in
        the Past 12 Months of Families," generated by American FactFinder for Laredo,
        Texas, Metro Area.

246   45 percent of Laredoans lack a high school diploma: Greybeck, "The Effectiveness
        of an After-School Intervention Program," 2.

247   There are protections already in place: Details about legal protections for those
        with limited English proficiency from Linton, "Language Politics and Policy in the
        United States," 18–20.

248   By 1994, however, attitudes toward bilingual schooling: Ibid., 22.

248   In what they call a "meta-meta-analysis": Krashen and McField, "What Works?" 10.

249   "We should replace bilingual education": Hunt, "Gingrich: Bilingual Classes Teach
        'Ghetto' Language."

249   In a post on *Language Log*: Zimmer, "Gingrich's 'Ghetto' Talk."

Epilogue: Los Angeles

256   it has been home to speakers: Bayley, "Linguistic Diversity and English Language
        Acquisition," 269.

256   a 1975 paper: Lieberson, Dalto, and Johnston, "The Course of Mother-Tongue
        Diversity in Nations."

All URLs were accessed and active as of October 6, 2011.

Aiken-Rhett House. "African Americans." Historic Charleston Foundation. www.his toriccharleston.org/experience/arh/african_americans.html.

Alba, Richard D., John Logan, Amy Lutz, and Brian Stults. "Only English by the Third Generation? Loss and Preservation of the Mother Tongue Among the Grandchildren of Contemporary Immigrants." *Demography* 39, no. 3 (August 2002): 467–84.

Allen, William Francis, Charles Pickard Ware, and Lucy McKim Garrison. *Slave Songs of the United States*. Documenting the American South. University Library, University of North Carolina at Chapel Hill, 2000. First published 1867 by A. Simpson and Co. http://docsouth.unc.edu/church/allen/allen.html.

Andersson, Theodore, and Mildred Boyer. *Bilingual Schooling in the United States*. 2 vols. Austin, TX: Southwestern Educational Development Lab, 1970.

Andrade, Manuel J., and Leo J. Frachtenberg. *Quileute Texts*. New York: Columbia University Press, 1931.

Annual Report of the Commissioner of Indian Affairs for the Year 1868. Washington, D.C.: Government Printing Office, 1868. www.doi.gov/ost/PDFs/PDFS/T-21903.pdf.

Austin-Garrison, Martha, Bernice Casaus, Dan McLaughlin, and Clay Slate. "*Diné Bizaad Yissohígíí*: The Past, Present and Future of Navajo Literacy." In *Athabaskan Language Studies: Essays in Honor of Robert W. Young*, ed. Eloise Jelinek, Sally Midgette, Keren Rice, and Leslie Saxon, 349–90. Albuquerque: University of New Mexico Press, 1996.

Bailey, Richard W. "American English: Its Origins and History." In *Language in the U.S.A.: Themes for the Twenty-First Century*, ed. Edward Finegan and John R. Rickford, 205–29. New York: Cambridge University Press, 2004.

Baird, Keith E., and Mary A. Twining. "Names and Naming in the Sea Islands." In *The Crucible of Carolina: Essays in the Development of Gullah Language and Culture*, ed. Michael Montgomery, 23–27. Athens: University of Georgia Press, 1994.

Bakker, Peter. "Two Basque Loanwords in Micmac." *International Journal of American Linguistics* 55, no. 2 (April 1989): 258–61.

Barber, Mike. "Basket Weaver's Legacy Is Woven into Fabric of the Makah." *Seattle Post-Intelligencer*, August 21, 2002. www.seattlepi.com/news/article/Basket -weaver-s-legacy-is-woven-into-fabric-of-1094118.php.

Baron, Dennis. *Grammar and Good Taste: Reforming the American Language*. New Haven: Yale University Press, 1982.

———. "The Legendary English-Only Vote of 1795." PBS. www.pbs.org/speak/ seatosea/officialamerican/englishonly.

"Basque Language Balks Inspectors." *New York Times*, March 21, 1911.

Bayley, Robert. "Linguistic Diversity and English Language Acquisition." In *Language in the U.S.A.: Themes for the Twenty-First Century*, ed. Edward Finegan and John R. Rickford, 268–86. New York: Cambridge University Press, 2004.

Belluck, Pam. "What's the Name of That Lake? It's Hard to Say." *New York Times*, November 20, 2004. www.nytimes.com/2004/11/20/national/20lake.html.

Bilefsky, Dan. "Converging on Little Egypt, with Anger and Hope." *New York Times*, January 30, 2011. www.nytimes.com/2011/01/31/nyregion/31astoria.html.

Bohemian Hall Beer Garden. "History." www.bohemianhall.com/en/Community Bcbsa.php.

Bohrer, Becky. "Tribal Words Highlight Exit Signs." *Billings Gazette*, April 23, 2006. http://billingsgazette.com/news/state-and-regional/montana/article_e16d39bb -c199-54e0-98ea-5ddb57a8305b.html.

Bond, C. Lawrence. *Native Names of New England Towns and Villages: Translating 211 Names Derived from Native American Words*. 2nd ed. Rochester, VT: Native Names, 2000.

Bossu, Jean Bernard. *Travels in the Interior of North America, 1751–1762*. Trans. Seymour Feller. Norman: University of Oklahoma Press, 1962.

Brasseaux, Carl A. *Acadian to Cajun: Transformation of a People, 1803–1877*. Jackson: University Press of Mississippi, 1992.

———. *French, Cajun, Creole, Houma: A Primer on Francophone Louisiana*. Baton Rouge: Louisiana State University Press, 2005.

Brasseaux, Carl A., Keith P. Fontenot, and Claude F. Oubre. *Creoles of Color in the Bayou Country*. Jackson: University Press of Mississippi, 1994.

Bright, William. *Native American Placenames of the United States*. Norman: University of Oklahoma Press, 2004.

Brown, Alphonso. *A Gullah Guide to Charleston: Walking Through Black History*. Charleston, SC: History Press, 2008.

Brown, Dee. *Bury My Heart at Wounded Knee: An Indian History of the American West*. New York: Henry Holt, 2007.

Bryson, Bill. *Made in America: An Informal History of the English Language in the United States*. New York: Harper Perennial, 2001.

Burrows, Edwin G., and Mike Wallace. *Gotham: A History of New York City to 1898*. New York: Oxford University Press, 1999.

Calhoun, John C. "Speech on Slavery." U.S. Senate, *Congressional Globe*. 24th Cong., 2nd Sess., February 6, 1837, 157–59.

Claverie, Laura. "Trout Meuniere Amandine: Galatoire's Restaurant." Examiner.com, April 27, 2010. www.examiner.com/food-in-new-orleans/trout-meuniere-aman dine-galatoire-s-restaurant.

Cobos, Rubén. *A Dictionary of New Mexico and Southern Colorado Spanish*. 2nd ed. Santa Fe: Museum of New Mexico Press, 2003.

Cook, James. *The Voyages of Captain James Cook*. 2 vols. London: William Smith, 1842.

Council for the Development of French in Louisiana. "Louisiana's French History." http://codofil.org/english/lafrenchhistory.html.

Crawford, James. *Frequently Asked Questions About Official English*. Institute for Language and Education Policy, 2008. http://elladvocates.org/documents/english only/OfficialEnglishFAQ.pdf.

———. "Language Legislation in the U.S.A." Language Policy. www.languagepolicy .net/archives/langleg.htm#State.

Crystal, David. *The Stories of English*. Woodstock: Overlook Press, 2004.

Daniels, Roger. *Coming to America: A History of Immigration and Ethnicity in American Life*. 2nd ed. New York: HarperCollins, 2002.

Dillard, J. L. *A History of American English*. New York: Longman, 1992.

Dixon, Heriberto. "An Overview of the Black Cubans Among the Mariel Entrants." Conference on Immigration and the Changing Black Population in the United States, Ann Arbor, MI, May 18–21, 1983.

Domínguez, Virginia. "Social Classification in Creole Louisiana." *American Ethnologist* 4, no. 4 (November 1977): 589–602.

———. *White by Definition: Social Classification in Creole Louisiana*. New Brunswick, NJ: Rutgers University Press, 1986.

Donovan, Bill. "Census: Navajo Enrollment Tops 300,000." *Navajo Times*, July 7, 2001. http://navajotimes.com/news/2011/0711/070711census.php.

Douglass, William A. *Amerikanuak: Basques in the New World*. Reno: University of Nevada Press, 2005.

Dracon, J. I. "The Extent of Spoken Crow and Cheyenne Among Indian Students of the Crow and Northern Cheyenne Indian Reservations." Master's thesis, Montana State University, 1970.

Dubois, Sylvie, and Megan Melançon. "Creole Is, Creole Ain't: Diachronic and Synchronic Attitudes Toward Creole Identity in Southern Louisiana." *Language in Society* 29, no. 2 (June 2000): 237–58.

Egerton, Douglas R. "The Material Culture of Slave Resistance." Gilder Lehrman Institute of American History. www.gilderlehrman.org/historynow/12_2004/historian2b .php.

English First. "States." http://englishfirst.org/states.

Erikson, Patricia Pierce. *Voices of a Thousand People: The Makah Cultural and Research Center*. With Helma Ward and Kirk Wachendorf. Lincoln: University of Nebraska Press, 2002.

Estaville, Lawrence E., Jr. "The Louisiana French Language in the Nineteenth Cen-
    tury." *Southeastern Geographer* 30, no. 2 (November 1990): 107–20.
Eustat. "Evolution of the Distribution of the Population Aged 2 and Over by Socio-
    Linguistic Areas: 1981–2006." http://en.eustat.es/elementos/ele0005200/ti_Evo
    lution_of_the_distribution_of_the_population_aged_2_and_over_by_socio
    -linguistic_areas_1981-2006/tbl0005281_i.html#axzz1YOPZJ1eT.
————. "More than Half the Population Claimed to Have Some Knowledge of the
    Basque Language in 2001." July 11, 2003. www.eustat.es/elementos/ele0002200/
    ti_More_than_half_the_population_claimed_to_have_some_knowledge_of_
    the_Basque_Language_in_2001/not0002264_i.html#axzz1Xb4WMdOB.
Faltz, Leonard M. *The Navajo Verb: A Grammar for Students and Scholars*. Albuquerque:
    University of New Mexico Press, 1998.
Federal Writers' Project. *The WPA Guide to 1930s North Dakota*. Bismarck, ND: State
    Historical Society of North Dakota, 1990.
Fields, Karen. "What One Cannot Remember Mistakenly." In *History and Memory in
    African-American Culture*, ed. Geneviève Fabre and Robert O'Meally, 150–63.
    New York: Oxford University Press, 1994.
Finegan, Edward, and John R. Rickford, eds. *Language in the U.S.A.: Themes for the
    Twenty-First Century*. New York: Cambridge University Press, 2004.
Fiske, Arland O. *The Best of the Norwegian Heritage*. Minot, ND: North American Heri-
    tage Press, 1990.
Flaten, Nils. "Notes on American-Norwegian, with a Vocabulary." *Dialect Notes* 2, no.
    2 (1900): 115–26.
Flusser, Alan J. *Dressing the Man: Mastering the Art of Permanent Fashion*. New York:
    HarperCollins, 2002.
Fordham, Damon L. *True Stories of Black South Carolina*. Charleston, SC: History Press,
    2008.
Forman, Johanna Mendelson, Hardin Lang, and Ashley E. Chandler. "The Role of the
    Haitian Diaspora in Building Haiti Back Better." Center for Strategic and Interna-
    tional Studies, June 14, 2011. http://csis.org/publication/role-haitian-diaspora
    -building-haiti-back-better.
Fortier, Alcée. *Louisiana Folk-tales, in French Dialect and English Translation*. Boston:
    Houghton Mifflin, 1895.
"The 43rd President: In His Own Words." *New York Times*. December 14, 2000. www
    .nytimes.com/2000/12/14/politics/14TWOR.html.
Frachtenberg, Leo. "Abnormal Types of Speech in Quileute." *International Journal of
    American Linguistics* 1, no. 4 (December 1920): 295–99.
Fraden, Rena. *Blueprints for a Black Federal Theatre 1935–1939*. New York: Cambridge
    University Press, 1994.
Franciscan Fathers. *An Ethnologic Dictionary of the Navajo Language*. St. Michael's, AZ:
    St. Michael's Press, 1910.
Franklin, Benjamin. *The Papers of Benjamin Franklin*, vol. 4: *July 1, 1750 Through June
    30, 1752*. Ed. Leonard W. Labaree. New Haven: Yale University Press, 1961.

Frey, Rodney. *The World of the Crow Indians: As Driftwood Lodges*. Norman: University of Oklahoma Press, 1987.

García, Ofelia. "New York's Multilingualism: World Languages and Their Role in a U.S. City." In *The Multilingual Apple: Languages in New York City*, ed. Ofelia García and Joshua A. Fishman, 3–50. Berlin: Mouton De Gruyter, 1997.

García, Ofelia, and Ricardo Otheguy. "The Language Situation of Cuban Americans." In *Language Diversity: Problem or Resource? A Social and Educational Perspective on Language Minorities in the United States*, ed. Sandra McKay and Sau-ling Cynthia Wong, 165–88. Boston: Heinle and Heinle, 1988.

Goddard, Ives. "Time to Retire an Indian Place-Name Hoax." *New York Times*, September 29, 1990. www.nytimes.com/1990/09/29/opinion/l-time-to-retire-an-indian-place-name-hoax-571390.

Gonzales, Ambrose E. *The Black Border: Gullah Stories of the Carolina Coast (with a Glossary)*. Columbia, SC: State Company, 1922.

Gore, Laura Locoul. *Memories of the Old Plantation Home and a Creole Family Album*. Commentary by Norman Marmillion and Sand Marmillion. Vacherie, LA: Zoë Company, 2001.

Graczyk, Randolph. *A Grammar of Crow*. Lincoln: University of Nebraska Press, 2007.

———. "Crow." In *Concise Encyclopedia of Languages of the World*, ed. Keith Brown and Sarah Ogilvie, 267–70. Oxford: Elsevier, 2009.

Greybeck, Barbara. "The Effectiveness of an After-School Intervention Program for Improving the Reading Performance of First and Second Grade Latino Students." Texas Center Research Fellows Grant Program 2005–2006 Final Report, 2006.

Griffiths, N. E. S. *From Migrant to Acadian: A North American Border People, 1604–1755*. Montreal: McGill-Queen's University Press, 2005.

Hall, Gwendolyn Midlo. *Africans in Colonial Louisiana: The Development of Afro-Creole Culture in the Eighteenth Century*. Baton Rouge: Louisiana State University Press, 1995.

Hancock, Ian F. "A Provisional Comparison of the English-Based Atlantic Creoles." *African Language Review* 8 (1969): 7–72.

Haugen, Einar. "Language and Immigration." *Norwegian-American Studies and Records* 10 (1938): 1–43. www.naha.stolaf.edu/pubs/nas/volume10/vol10_1.htm.

———. *The Norwegian Language in America: A Study in Bilingual Behavior*. 2 vols. Philadelphia: University of Pennsylvania Press, 1953.

Harrington, John P. "The Original Strachey Vocabulary of the Virginia Indian Language, Anthropological Papers, no. 46." *Bureau of American Ethnology Bulletin* 157 (1955): 189–202.

Hess, Thom, and Vi Hilbert. *Lushootseed Dictionary*. Ed. Dawn Bates. Seattle: University of Washington Press, 1994.

Hieber, Danny. "Rising to the Challenge: Producing Navajo." Rosetta Stone, August 25, 2010. http://blog.rosettastone.com/2010/08/25/rising-to-the-challenge-producing-navajo.

Hirsch, Arnold R., and Joseph Logsdon. *Creole New Orleans: Race and Americanization*. Baton Rouge: Louisiana State University Press, 1992.

Holm, John A. *An Introduction to Pidgins and Creoles*. New York: Cambridge University Press, 2000.

Holton, Gary. "Inuit or Eskimo?" Talking Alaska, November 8, 2010. http://talking alaska.blogspot.com/2010/11/inuit-or-eskimo.html.

Houk, Rose, and Tracy J. Andrews. *Navajo of Canyon de Chelly: In Home God's Fields*. Tucson, AZ: Southwest Parks and Monuments Association, 1995.

House, Deborah. *Language Shift Among the Navajos: Identity Politics and Cultural Continuity*. Tucson: University of Arizona Press, 2002.

Hunt, Kasie. "Gingrich: Bilingual Classes Teach 'Ghetto' Language." *Washington Post*, April 1, 2007. www.washingtonpost.com/wp-dyn/content/article/2007/03/31/AR2007033100992.html.

Huntington, C. A. Letter to Commissioner of Indian Affairs. In *Annual Report of the Commissioner of Indian Affairs to the Secretary of the Interior for the Year 1874*. Washington, D.C.: Government Printing Office, 1874. www.doi.gov/ost/PDFs/PDFS/T-21909.pdf.

"Indian Entities Recognized and Eligible to Receive Services from the United States Bureau of Indian Affairs." *Federal Register* 75, no. 190 (October 1, 2010): 60810-60814. www.bia.gov/idc/groups/xofa/documents/document/idc012038.pdf.

"Indians Named Puyallup, and This Is Why!" *Chicago Daily Tribune*, December 18, 1955, D10.

Ingersoll, Thomas N. "The Slave Trade and the Ethnic Diversity of Louisiana's Slave Community." *Louisiana History: The Journal of the Louisiana Historical Association* 37, no. 2 (Spring 1996): 133–61.

Iverson, Peter. *Diné: A History of the Navajos*. Albuquerque, NM: University of New Mexico Press, 2002.

Jackson, Kenneth T. *The Encyclopedia of New York City*. New Haven: Yale University Press, 1995.

Jacobsen, William. *First Lessons in Makah*. 2nd ed. Neah Bay: Makah Language Program, Makah Cultural and Research Center, 1999.

———. "The Heterogeneity of Evidentials in Makah." In *Evidentiality: The Linguistic Coding of Epistemology*, ed. Wallace Chafe and Johanna Nichols, 3–28. Norwood, NJ: Ablex.

Jones, Charles C. *Gullah Folktales from the Georgia Coast*. Athens: University of Georgia Press, 2000.

Jones-Jackson, Patricia. *When Roots Die: Endangered Traditions on the Sea Islands*. Athens: University of Georgia Press, 1987.

Kalm, Peter. *Peter Kalm's Travels in North America: The English Version of 1770*. 2 vols. Rev. and ed. Adolph B. Benson. New York: Wison-Erickson, 1937.

Kibrik, Aleksandr E. "Archi (Caucasian—Daghestanian)." In *The Handbook of Morphology*, ed. Andrew Spencer and Arnold M. Zwicky, 455–76. Oxford: Blackwell, 2001.

Kneale, Albert H. *Indian Agent*. Caldwell, ID: Caxton Printers, 1950.

Krapp, George Philip. "The English of the Negro." *American Mercury* 2, no. 6 (June 1924): 190–95.

Krashen, Stephen, and Grace McField. "What Works? Reviewing the Latest Evidence on Bilingual Education." *Language Learner* 1, no. 2 (November-December 2005): 7–34. www.elladvocates.org/documents/RCN/Krashen-McField.pdf.

Krauss, Michael. "The Condition of Native North American Languages: The Need for Realistic Assessment and Action." *International Journal of the Sociology of Language* 132 (1998): 9–21.

Kurlansky, Mark. *The Basque History of the World*. New York: Walker, 1999.

Lafayette, Robert C. "États-Unis: Où va l'enseignement précoce?" *Le Français dans le Monde* 241 (May-June 1991): 40–41.

LaFleur, Amanda. "Faux Amis Cadiens." Louisiana State University. http://appl003 .lsu.edu/artsci/frenchweb.nsf/$content/Cajun+French+False+Cognates?Open Document.

Lane, George S. "Notes on Louisiana-French." *Language* 10, no. 4 (December 1934): 323–33.

Lane, Richard H. "Trouble in the Sweet Promised Land: Basques in Early 20th Century Northeastern Nevada." In *Anglo-American Contributions to Basque Studies: Essays in Honor of Jon Bilbao*, ed. William A. Douglass, Richard W. Etulain, and William H. Jacobsen Jr., 33–41. Reno: Desert Research Institute Publications on the Social Sciences, 1977.

———. "The Cultural Ecology of Sheep Nomadism: Northeastern Nevada 1870–1972." PhD diss., Yale University, 1974.

Lang, George. *Entwisted Tongues: Comparative Creole Literatures*. Amsterdam: Editions Rodopi, 2000.

———. "A Primer of Haitian Literature in 'Kreyòl.'" *Research in African Literatures* 35, no. 2 (Summer 2004): 128–40.

Laura Plantation. "5 Centuries of Habitation." www.lauraplantation.com/gen_w_nav .asp?cID=36&grp=6.

———. "Slave Registry." www.lauraplantation.com/gen_w_nav.asp?cID=39&grp=6.

Leap, William L. "American Indian Language Maintenance." *Annual Review of Anthropology* 10 (1981): 209–36.

Lee, Tiffany S. "Language, Identity, and Power: Navajo and Pueblo Young Adults' Perspectives and Experiences with Competing Language Ideologies." *Journal of Language, Identity, and Education* 8, no. 5 (2009): 307–20.

Lee, Tiffany S., and Daniel McLaughlin. "Reversing Navajo Language Shift, Revisited." In *Can Threatened Languages Be Saved? Reversing Language Shift Revisited: A 21st Century Perspective*, ed. Joshua A. Fishman, 23–43. Clevedon, UK: Multilingual Matters, 2001.

Levine, Robert M., and Moisés Asís. *Cuban Miami*. New Brunswick, NJ: Rutgers University Press, 2000.

Lewis, M. Paul, ed. *Ethnologue: Languages of the World*, 16th ed. Dallas, TX: SIL International. www.ethnologue.com.

Liberman, Mark. "English Under Siege in Pennsylvania." Language Log, July 25, 2006. http://itre.cis.upenn.edu/~myl/languagelog/archives/003389.html.

Lieberson, Stanley, Guy Dalto, and Mary Ellen Johnston. "The Course of Mother-Tongue Diversity in Nations." *American Journal of Sociology* 81, no. 1 (July 1975): 34–61.

Limonic, Laura. *The Latino Population of New York City, 2007*. New York: Center for Latin American, Caribbean, and Latino Studies, 2008.

Linton, April. "Language Politics and Policy in the United States: Implications for the Immigration Debate." *International Journal of the Sociology of Language* 199 (2009): 9–37.

Lipski, John M. *Varieties of Spanish in the United States*. Washington, D.C.: Georgetown University Press, 2008.

Lockard, Louise. "New Paper Words: Historical Images of Navajo Language Literacy." *American Indian Quarterly* 19, no. 1 (Winter 1995): 17–30.

"Louisiana French Try to Keep Language Alive." *Evening Star* (Washington, D.C.), April 28, 1969.

Lovoll, Odd S. "The Norwegian Press in North Dakota." *Norwegian-American Studies* 24 (1970): 78–101. www.naha.stolaf.edu/pubs/nas/volume24/vol24_3.html.

———. *Norwegians on the Prairie: Ethnicity and the Development of the Country Town*. Minneapolis: Minnesota Historical Society Press, 2006.

———. *The Promise Fulfilled: A Portrait of Norwegian-Americans Today*. Minneapolis: University of Minnesota Press, 1998.

MacArthur Foundation. "Jessie Little Doe Baird." John D. and Catherine T. MacArthur Foundation, September 28, 2010. www.macfound.org/site/c.lkLXJ8MQKrH/b.6241221/k.5A66/Jessie_Little_Doe_Baird.htm.

Mantilla, Jesús Ruiz. "Más 'speak spanish' que en España." *El Pais* (Madrid), June 10, 2008. www.elpais.com/articulo/cultura/speak/spanish/Espana/elpepucul/2008 1006elpepicul_1/Tes.

Marckwardt, Albert Henry. *American English*. 2nd ed. Rev. J. L. Dillard. London: Oxford University Press, 1980.

Matthews, G. Hubert. "Glottochronology and the Separation of the Crow and Hidatsa." *Archaeology in Montana* 20, no. 3 (1979): 113–25.

McDonough, Joyce Mary. "How to Use Young and Morgan's *The Navajo Language*." *University of Rochester Working Papers in the Language Sciences* 1, no. 2 (2000): 195–214. www.bcs.rochester.edu/cls/f2000n2/mcdonough.pdf.

McMillan, George. "An Island of Gullah Culture." *New York Times*, February 2, 1986. www.nytimes.com/1986/02/02/travel/an-island-of-gullah-culture.html?scp=3 &sq=gullah&st=cse.

Meany, Edmond S. "Origin of Washington Geographic Names." *Washington Historical Quarterly* 12, no. 3 (July 1921): 211–18.

Medicine Crow, Joseph. *From the Heart of the Crow Country: The Crow Indians' Own Stories*. New York: Orion Books, 1992.

Mencken, H. L. *The American Language: An Inquiry into the Development of English in the United States*. 2nd ed. New York: A. A. Knopf, 1921.

Metcalf, Allan. "How 'OK' Took Over the World." BBC News, February 18, 2011. www.bbc.co.uk/news/magazine-12503686.

Metellus, Gepsie, Sheba St. Hilaire, Leonie Hermantin, and Sophia Lacroix. "Risk and Protective Factors in Little Haiti and in the Haitian/Haitian-American Community in Miami Dade County." Working Paper Series, SL WPS 02. Sant La, Miami, 2004.

Meyer, Stephenie. "The Story Behind Twilight." StephenieMeyer.com. www.stephenie meyer.com/twilight.html.

Mille, Katherine Wyly, and Michael D. Montgomery. "Introduction." In Turner, *Africanisms in the Gullah Dialect*, xi–lvii.

Mills, Elizabeth Shown. "Forgotten People of America." *Ancestry Magazine* 22, no. 3 (May-June 2004). www.ancestrylibrary.com/learn/library/article.aspx?article=9214.

Mills, Gary B. *The Forgotten People: Cane River's Creoles of Color*. Baton Rouge: Louisiana State University Press, 1977.

Mitchell, Christopher. "U.S. Policy Toward Haitian Boat People, 1972–93." *Annals of the American Academy of Political and Social Science* 534 (July 1994): 69–80.

Mithun, Marianne. *The Languages of Native North America*. Cambridge: Cambridge University Press, 1999.

Mizuno, Yumiko. "*Diné bi Olta* or School of the Navajos: Educational Experiments at Rough Rock Demonstration School, 1966–1970." *Japanese Journal of American Studies* 9 (1998): 143–69.

Montana Office of Public Instruction. "Crow Reservation Timeline." March 2010. www .opi.mt.gov/pdf/IndianEd/IEFA/CrowTimeline.pdf.

Moore, William Haas. *Chiefs, Agents, and Soldiers: Conflict on the Navajo Frontier, 1868–1882*. Albuquerque: University of New Mexico Press, 1994.

Mosely, Christopher, ed. *Atlas of the World's Languages in Danger*. 3rd ed. Paris: UNESCO Publishing, 2010. http://www.unesco.org/culture/languages-atlas/.

Munger, Robert S. "Guaiacum, the Holy Wood from the New World." *Journal of the History of Medicine and Allied Sciences* 4, no. 2 (1949): 196–229.

Nadeau, Jean-Benoît, and Julie Barlow. *The Story of French*. New York: St. Martin's Press, 2006.

National Park Service. "Canyon de Chelly National Monument." www.nature.nps.gov/ geology/parks/cach/index.cfm.

———. "Canyon de Chelly National Monument: History and Culture." www.nps.gov/ cach/historyculture/index.htm.

National Public Radio. "'New Testament' Translated into Gullah." March 16, 2006. www.npr.org/templates/story/story.php?storyid=5283230.

Natsis, James J. "Legislation and Language: The Politics of Speaking French in Louisiana." *The French Review* 73, no. 2 (December 1999): 325–31.

Nelsen, Frank C. "The School Controversy Among Norwegian Immigrants." *Norwegian-American Studies* 26 (1974): 206–20. www.naha.stolaf.edu/pubs/nas/volume26/ vol26_10.htm.

Neumann, Ingrid. *Le créole de Breaux Bridge, Louisiane: Étude morphosyntaxique, textes, vocabulaire*. Hamburg: Helmut Buske, 1985.

New York Community Media Alliance. "Members." www.indypressny.org/nycma/ members/.

Nichols, Patricia Causey. "Creole Languages: Forging New Identities." In *Language in the U.S.A.: Themes for the Twenty-First Century*, ed. Edward Finegan and John R. Rickford, 133–52. New York: Cambridge University Press, 2004.

———. *Voices of Our Ancestors: Language Contact in Early South Carolina*. Columbia: University of South Carolina Press, 2009.

Nunberg, Geoffrey. "Lingo Jingo: English-Only and the New Nativism." *American Prospect*, June 30, 1997. http://prospect.org/cs/articles?article=lingo_jingo.

Opala, Joseph A. "The Gullah Language." Yale University. www.yale.edu/glc/gullah /06.htm.

Peabody Museum of Archaeology and Ethnology. "The Harvard Indian College." www .peabody.harvard.edu/node/477.

Perrottet, Tony. "Little Bighorn Reborn." *Smithsonian Magazine*, April 2005. www .smithsonianmag.com/travel/des_bighorn.html?c=y&story=fullstory.

Pew Hispanic Center. "Hispanic Attitudes Toward Learning English." June 7, 2006. http://pewhispanic.org/files/factsheets/20.pdf.

Picone, Michael. "Enclave Dialect Contraction: An External Overview of Louisiana French." *American Speech* 72, no. 2 (Summer 1997): 117–53.

Platero, Paul. "Navajo Head Start Language Study." Window Rock, AZ: Navajo Nation, Division of Diné Education, 1992.

Powell, Jay, and Vickie Jensen. *Quileute: An Introduction to the Indians of La Push*. Seattle: University of Washington Press, 1976.

Portes, Alejandro, and Lingxin Hao. "E Pluribus Unum: Bilingualism and Loss of Language in the Second Generation." *Sociology of Education* 71, no. 4 (October 1998): 269–94.

Portes, Alejandro, and Rubén G. Rumbaut. *Legacies: The Story of the Immigrant Second Generation*. Berkeley: University of California Press/Russell Sage Foundation, 2001. http://ark.cdlib.org/ark:/13030/kt629020v5.

Pratt, Richard H. "The Advantages of Mingling Indians with Whites." In *Americanizing the Indians: Writings by the "Friends of the Indian" 1880–1900*, ed. Francis Paul Prucha, 46–59. Lincoln: University of Nebraska Press, 1978. Originally published in an extract of the Official Report of the Nineteenth Annual Conference of Charities and Correction (1892).

Qitsualik, Rachel. "Are Eskimo and Inuit the Same People?" AAA Native Arts. www .aaanativearts.com/alaskan-natives/eskimo-vs-inuit.htm.

Queens Immigrant Guide: Common Threads. 2006. *Queens Tribune*. www.queenstribune .com/guides/2006_ImmigrantGuideCommonThreads/ThroughTheirEyes/ index.htm.

Queens Library. "Community and Library History." www.queenslibrary.org/index .aspx?page_nm=CL-Communityinfo&branch_id=F.

Read, Allen Walker. "The Rationale of 'Podunk.'" *American Speech* 14, no. 2 (April 1939): 99–108.

Reeves, Sally. "French Quarter Fire and Flood." FrenchQuarter.com. http://frenchquarter .com/history/elements.php.

Renker, Ann M. "The Makah Tribe: People of the Sea and Forest." University of Washington Libraries Digital Collections. http://content.lib.washington.edu/aipnw/renker.html.

Reports of the Committees of the Senate of the United States for the Second Session Thirty-Ninth Congress, 1866–67. Washington, D.C.: Government Printing Office: 1867.

Review of *Collections of the New York Historical Society,* 2nd ser., vol. 1. *North American Review* 54, no. 115 (April, 1842): 299–338.

Reyhner, Jon. "Cultural Survival vs. Forced Assimilation: The Renewed War on Diversity." *Cultural Survival Quarterly* 25, no. 2 (Summer 2001). www.culturalsurvival.org/ourpublications/csq/article/cultural-survival-vs-forced-assimilation-renewed-war-diversity.

Rhodes, Nancy C., and Ingrid Pufahl. *Foreign Language Teaching in U.S. Schools: Results of a National Survey.* Executive Summary. Washington, D.C.: Center for Applied Linguistics, 2010. www.cal.org/projects/Exec%20Summary_111009.pdf.

Roberts, Sam. "Listening to (and Saving) the World's Languages." *New York Times,* April 28, 2010. www.nytimes.com/2010/04/29/nyregion/29lost.html.

Robinson, Elwyn B. *History of North Dakota.* Lincoln: University of Nebraska Press, 1966.

Rumbaut, Rubén G. "Language, Identity, and Imagined Communities in the Post-Immigrant Generation." In *The Changing Face of Home: The Transnational Lives of the Second Generation,* ed. Peggy Levitt and Mary Waters, 43–95. New York: Russell Sage, 2002.

———. "The Making of a People." In *Hispanics and the Future of America,* ed. Marta Tienda and Faith Mitchell, 16–65. Washington, D.C.: National Academies Press, 2006.

Rumbaut, Rubén G., Douglas S. Massey, and Frank D. Bean. "Linguistic Life Expectancies: Immigrant Language Retention in Southern California." *Population and Development Review* 32, no. 3 (September 2006): 447–60.

Russell, Dick. "Environmental Racism." *Amicus Journal* 9, no. 15 (Spring 1989).

Sage, Leland L. *A History of Iowa.* Ames: Iowa State University Press, 1974.

Santiago, Bill. *Pardon My Spanglish: One Man's Guide to Speaking the Habla.* 2nd ed. Philadelphia: Quirk Books, 2008.

Sapir, Edward, and Morris Swadesh. "American Indian Grammatical Categories." In *The Collected Works of Edward Sapir,* vol. 5: *American Indian Languages,* ed. William Bright, 133–42. Berlin: Walter de Gruyter, 1989. Originally published in *Word* 2 (1946): 103–12.

Schieffelin, Bambi B., and Rachelle Charlier Doucet. "The 'Real' Haitian Creole: Ideology, Metalinguistics, and Orthographic Choice." *American Ethnologist* 21, no. 1 (February 1994): 176–200.

Sell, Mark. "Inside Miami: A Letter." *New England Review* 18, no. 1 (Winter 1997): 30–31.

Semmingsen, Ingrid. *Norway to America: A History of the Migration.* Minneapolis: University of Minnesota Press, 1978.

Shin, Hyon B., and Rosalind Bruno. "Language Use and English-Speaking Ability: 2000." U.S. Census Bureau, Washington, D.C., October 2003. www.census.gov/prod/2003pubs/c2kbr-29.pdf.

Shorto, Russell. *The Island at the Center of the World: The Epic Story of Dutch Manhattan and the Forgotten Colony That Shaped America*. New York: Doubleday, 2004.

Silva-Corvalán, Carmen. "Spanish in the Southwest." In *Language in the U.S.A.: Themes for the Twenty-First Century*, ed. Edward Finegan and John R. Rickford, 205–29. New York: Cambridge University Press, 2004.

Silver, Shirley, and Wick R. Miller. *American Indian Languages: Cultural and Social Contexts*. Tucson: University of Arizona Press, 1997.

Smith, John. *The Generall Historie of Virginia, New England, and the Summer Isles: With the Names of the Adventurers, Planters, and Governours from Their First Beginning Ano. 1584 to This Present 1624*. London: Michael Sparkes, 1624. Early English Books Online. http://gateway.proquest.com/openurl?ctx_ver=Z39.88-2003&res_id=xri:eebo&rft_id=xri:eebo:citation:99847142.

Smith, Reed. *Gullah: Bulletin of the University of South Carolina, No. 10*. Columbia: University of South Carolina Press, 1926.

Smith, William. *History of New-York: From the First Discovery to the Year MDCCXXXII*. Albany, NY: Ryer Schermerhorn, 1814.

Spolsky, Bernard. "Prospects for the Survival of the Navajo Language: A Reconsideration." *Anthropology and Education Quarterly* 33, no. 2 (June 2002): 139–62.

Standifer, James. "The Complicated Life of Porgy and Bess." *Humanities* 18, no. 6 (1997). www.neh.gov/news/humanities/1997-11/porgy.html.

Stepick, Alex, Guillermo Grenier, Max Castro, and Marvin Dunn. *This Land Is Our Land: Immigrants and Power in Miami*. Berkeley: University of California Press, 2003.

Stewart, George R. *Names on the Land: A Historical Account of Place-Naming in the United States*. New York: New York Review of Books, 2008. Originally published 1945 by Random House.

Swan, James G. *The Indians of Cape Flattery: At the Entrance to the Strait of Fuca, Washington Territory*. Washington, D.C.: Smithsonian Institution, 1870. http://books.google.com/books?vid=HARVARD32044043428598.

Sylvain, Georges. *Cric? Crac!: Fables de la Fontaine racontées par un montagnard haïtien et transcrites en vers créoles*. 2nd ed. Port-au-Prince: Chez Mme Georges Sylvain, 1929.

Tatalovich, Raymond. *Nativism Reborn? The Official English Language Movement and the American States*. Lexington: University Press of Kentucky, 1995.

Taylor, N. G., J. B. Henderson, W. T. Sherman, Wm. S. Harney, John B. Sanborn, Alfred H. Terry, S. F. Tappan, and C. C. Augur. "Report to the President by the Indian Peace Commission, January 7, 1868." In *Annual Report of the Commissioner of Indian Affairs for the Year 1868*. Washington, D.C.: Government Printing Office, 1868. www.doi.gov/ost/PDFs/PDFS/T-21903.pdf.

Thompson, Gerald. *The Army and the Navajo: The Bosque Redondo Reservation Experiment 1863–1868*. Tucson: University of Arizona Press, 1976.

Thomson, Virgil. "George Gershwin." In *A Virgil Thomson Reader*, ed. Richard Kostel-
    anetz, 149–53. New York: Routledge, 2002.

Tooker, William Wallace. *The Indian Place-names on Long Island and Islands Adjacent:
    with Their Probable Significations*. New York: G. P. Putnam's Sons, 1911.

Trask, Larry. "FAQs About Basque and the Basques." Larry Trask Archive. www.buber
    .net/Basque/Euskara/Larry/WebSite/basque.faqs.html.

Trépanier, Cécyle. "The Cajunization of French Louisiana: Forging a Regional Iden-
    tity." *Geographical Journal* 157, no. 2 (July 1991): 161–71.

Tse, Lucy. *"Why Don't They Learn English?": Separating Fact from Fallacy in the U.S.
    Language Debate*. New York: Teachers College Press, 2001.

Turner, Lorenzo Dow. *Africanisms in the Gullah Dialect*. Columbia: University of South
    Carolina Press, 2002.

Twain, Mark. *Life on the Mississippi*. New York: Harper and Brothers, 1901.

"U.S. Helps Small Tribe To Save Its Language." *New York Times*, April 9, 1978.

U.S. Census Bureau. *Census 2000 Briefs: The Hispanic Population:2000*, May, 2001.

———. "DP-1 Profile of General Population and Housing Characteristics: 2010." 2010
    Census.

———. "DP-2 Social Characteristics: 1990." 1990 Summary Tape File 3.

———. "PCT018 Ancestry (Total Categories Tallied) for People with One or More
    Ancestry Categories Reported." Census 2000 Summary File 3.

———. "QT-P10 Hispanic or Latino by Type: 2010." 2010 Census Summary File 1.

———. "QT-P16 Language Spoken at Home: 2000." Census 2000 Summary File 3.

———. "QT-P17 Ability to Speak English: 2000." Census 2000 Summary File 3.

———. "S0501 Selected Characteristics of the Native and Foreign-Born Populations."
    2005–2009 American Community Survey 5-Year Estimates.

———. "S1601 Language Spoken at Home." 2005–2009 American Community Sur-
    vey 5-Year Estimates.

———. "S1702 Poverty Status in the Past 12 Months of Families." 2005–2009 Ameri-
    can Community Survey 5-Year Estimates.

———. "S1901 Income in the Past 12 Months (In 2009 Inflation-Adjusted Dollars)."
    2005–2009 American Community Survey 5-Year Estimates.

———. "Table 6. Mother Tongue of the Foreign-Born Population: 1910 to 1940, 1960,
    and 1970." March 9, 1999. www.census.gov/population/www/documentation/
    twps0029/tab06.html.

U.S. Department of Health and Human Services. "ANA Grant Awards." www.acf.hhs
    .gov/programs/ana/grants/grant_awards.html.

———. *Trends in Indian Health, 2002–2003*. Washington, D.C.: Government Printing
    Office, 2009. www.ihs.gov/nonmedicalprograms/ihs_stats/files/Trends_02-03_
    Entire%20Book%20(508).pdf.

U.S. Department of the Interior. "$52.5 Million Recovery Project Gets Underway to Re-
    place Rough Rock Community School." September 17, 2009. http://recovery.doi
    .gov/press/2009/09/project-underway-to-replace-rough-rock-community-school/.

U.S. Department of Labor. *Annual Report of the Commissioner General of Immigration to the Secretary of Labor.* Washington, D.C.: Government Printing Office, 1921.

Valdman, Albert, and Thomas A. Klingler. "The Structure of Louisiana Creole." In *French and Creole in Louisiana*, ed. Albert Valdman, 109–44. New York: Plenum Press, 1997.

Veltman, Calvin. "Modelling the Language Shift Process of Hispanic Immigrants." *International Migration Review* 22, no. 4 (Winter 1988): 545–62.

Watts, John Graham. "Crow Language Teachers' Views of the Incorporation of the Written Form of Crow in Language Classes." Ed.D. diss., Montana State University, 2005.

Wenz, Peter S. "Just Garbage." In *Faces of Environmental Racism: Confronting Issues of Global Justice*, 2nd ed., ed. Laura Westra and Bill E. Lawson, 57–71. Oxford: Rowman and Littlefield, 2001.

Window Rock Unified School District. "About Us." www.wrschool.net/tdb/about_TDB .htm.

World Bank. *World Development Indicators 2011.* Washington, D.C.: World Bank, 2011.

Yamamoto, Akira Y., and Ofelia Zepeda. "Native American Languages." In *Language in the U.S.A.: Themes for the Twenty-First Century*, ed. Edward Finegan and John R. Rickford, 153–81. New York: Cambridge University Press, 2004.

Yardley, Jim. "Minding Our Tongues: Once Banned, French Bounces Back in Louisiana Schools." *Atlanta Constitution*, September 15, 1995: A14. Available from Lexis-NexisAcademic, www.lexisnexis.com/lnacui2api/api/version1/getDocCui?oc= 00240&hl=t&hns=t&hnsd=f&perma=true&lni=3SD9-F400-009T-X2HS&hv= t&csi=8379&hgn=t&secondRedirectIndicator=true.

Young, Robert W. *The Navajo Verb System: An Overview.* Albuquerque, NM: University of New Mexico Press, 2000.

Young, Robert W., and William Morgan Sr. *The Navajo Language: A Grammar and Colloquial Dictionary.* Albuquerque: University of New Mexico Press, 1987.

Zehr, Mary Ann. "A Culture Put to the Test." *Education Week* 26, no. 28 (March 21, 2007): 25–28. http://edweek.org/ew/articles/2007/03/21/28navajo.h26.html.

Zempel, Solveig. *In Their Own Words: Letters from Norwegian Immigrants.* Minneapolis: University of Minnesota Press, 1991.

Zimmer, Benjamin. "Gingrich's 'Ghetto' Talk." *Language Log*, April 3, 2007. http://itre .cis.upenn.edu/~myl/languagelog/archives/004364.html.

———. "MacArthur Fellowships for Two Linguists." *Language Log*, September 28, 2010. http://languagelog.ldc.upenn.edu/nll/?p=2669.

An "n" following a page number indicates material covered in a footnote. A "t" following a page number indicates material covered in a table.

A NOTE ON THE AUTHOR

Elizabeth Little is the author of *Biting the Wax Tadpole: Confessions of a Language Fanatic*. A Harvard graduate with a degree in social studies, she has studied ancient Greek, classical Chinese, standard Mandarin, French, Italian, and Spanish and at any given time she has plans to study any number of other languages. A full-time writer and occasional editor, she lives in Los Angeles with her family. Her website is www.elizabeth-little.com.